Revelation
and Revolution

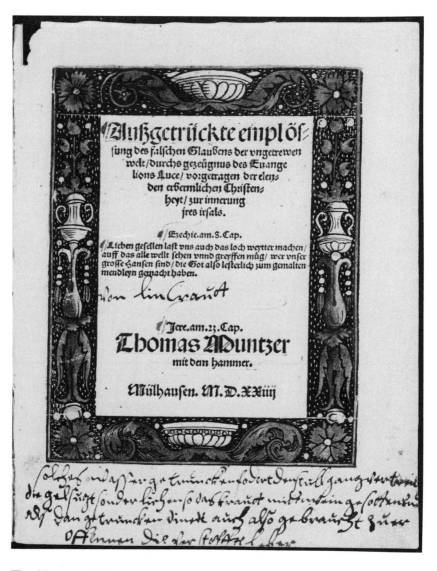

The title page of Thomas Müntzer's *Special Exposure of False Faith*. The place of publication is incorrect; the work was not printed at Mühlhausen, but surreptitiously at Nuremberg. The marginalia at the bottom was added later. (Reproduced by kind permission of the Berlin Staatsbibliothek, Sammlung Preussische Kulturbesitze.)

Revelation
and Revolution
Basic Writings of Thomas Müntzer

Translated and Edited by
Michael G. Baylor

Lehigh University Press

Bethlehem: Lehigh University Press
London and Toronto: Associated University Presses

Associated University Presses
440 Forsgate Drive
Cranbury, NJ 08512

Associated University Presses
25 Sicilian Avenue
London WC1A 2QH, England

Associated University Presses
P.O. Box 338, Port Credit
Mississauga, Ontario
Canada L5G 4L8

The paper used in this publication meets the requirements
of the American National Standard for Permanence of Paper
for Printed Library Materials Z39.48-1984.

Library of Congress Cataloging-in-Publication Data

Müntzer, Thomas, 1490 (ca.)–1525.
   [Selections. English. 1993]
   Revelation and revolution : basic writings of Thomas Müntzer/
translated and edited by Michael G. Baylor.
     p.   cm.
   Includes bibliographical references and index.
   ISBN 0-934223-16-5 (alk. paper)
   1. Theology—Early works to 1800.   2. Reformation—Early works to
1800.   3. Müntzer, Thomas, 1490 (ca.)–1525—Correspondence.
4. Anabaptists—Germany—Correspondence.   I. Baylor, Michael G.,
1942– . II. Title.
BX4946.M8A25   1993
284′.3—dc20
                                    91-58965
                                      CIP

PRINTED IN THE UNITED STATES OF AMERICA

For Carol

Contents

Preface

This book makes available to general readers and English-speaking students of European history the essential writings of one of the most difficult and controversial—yet one of the most creative and original—thinkers of early sixteenth-century Germany. Thomas Müntzer (born before 1491–1525) was a key figure of the early Reformation in Germany. He was one of Martin Luther's first and most insightful critics from within the ranks of the evangelical reformers; he is widely regarded as among the most important founders of a distinctive "Radical Reformation"; and he was an influential leader of the great German Peasants' War that shook the political and social structure of the Holy Roman Empire. His writings permit us, for perhaps the first time in European history, to know intimately and in detail the mind of a religious revolutionary.

Despite the 1989 publication of Peter Matheson's *Collected Works of Thomas Müntzer*, it seems worthwhile to make available to English-language readers an alternative edition of Müntzer's writings. Müntzer's German is notoriously difficult; translating it can only affirm that every translation is an interpretation. At many specific points Matheson and I interpret quite differently what Müntzer wrote. It is an advantage to the English reader to have access to another version of the basic writings.

My sense of the need that an English edition of Müntzer's writings should fill is different from Matheson's. His edition of Müntzer's complete works is testimony to his diligence and his great respect for Müntzer, but the attempt was premature. Matheson excluded the longer liturgical writings, and, within the past few years, several new texts by Müntzer have been discovered. The 1968 Franz edition of Müntzer's writings, on which Matheson largely relied, was deeply flawed. A new three-volume critical edition is still in preparation. Reformation specialists will continue to read Müntzer in the original; students and general readers need something less than a collection of all the known documents by, to, and about him. From the total corpus of Müntzer's works, I have selected those writings which seem the most important, especially the series of religious and political tracts and a large selection of his letters. Only a small part of his liturgical works, whose appeal is primarily to a German audience, is included. Except for the letters, which are grouped together, the writings are presented in chronological order so that the reader can follow the development of Müntzer's thought during the crucial period 1521–25.

The introductory essay places Müntzer's writings in the larger context of his career, especially with regard to his stay at Allstedt where he wrote most of these works, and discusses their interrelationship. Any attempt to interpret Müntzer's activities as religious reformer and revolutionary will be controversial. The Introduction will have served its purpose if it opens rather than closes discussion, and, above all, if it stimulates readers to examine Müntzer's writings for themselves. Since the Introduction focuses on the texts, a brief Chronology of the most important events in Müntzer's life is appended as a biographical supplement. The Bibliography is not comprehensive; it focuses instead on the recent literature, although a few important older studies are included, and on materials in English. A large number of publications appeared at the time of the celebration of the 500th anniversary of Müntzer's birth in 1989 (although the exact year of his birth is not known); it is primarily this newer literature which the Bibliography brings together.

Readers who find it difficult to come to terms with Müntzer in the original deserve to be informed about the textual basis of the translations, the major deviations from the form and literal sense of the German, and the conventions adopted here in presenting his works in English. Because of the unreliability of the Franz edition, wherever possible I have used other sources for the translations. The Franz edition has been used only for *The Prague Protest*, the letters, and the documents pertaining to the final days of Müntzer's life. For Müntzer's three short tracts of 1523—*Open Letter to the Brothers at Stolberg*, *Protest or Offering*, and *On Contrived Faith*—as well as the short liturgical work—*Order and Account of the German Service at Allstedt*—I have relied on the facsimile reprints edited by Siegfried Bräuer and Wolfgang Ullmann. For the prefaces to the *German Evangelical Mass* I also used the facsimile edition edited by Siegfried Bräuer. The staff of the Staatsbibliothek in West Berlin kindly allowed me to photocopy the original exemplar of the *Special Exposure of False Faith* in the collection of the Cultural Possessions of the Prussian State. Max Steinmetz's edition *Die Fürstenpredigt* contains facsimile reprints of all three of the longer tracts 1524; I have used it for both the *Sermon to the Princes* and the *Highly Provoked Defense*.

As a result of his study of the Vulgate, Müntzer was sensitive to the problem of how literal or free to make translations of centuries-old sources in a foreign language. His interest in the "living spirit" of a text rather than its "dead letter" suggests his point of view. In the preface to his *German Evangelical Mass* he acknowledged that he translated "more according to the sense than according to the words." I too have taken a number of liberties with the format and the literal meaning of Müntzer's writings; the reader should be warned of these concessions to the modern ear. In many cases I have added paragraph divisions where Müntzer moves forward without benefit of a longer pause. Even more frequently I have broken up Müntzer's long, complex sentences. Other forms of punctuation—dashes, semi-colons, quotation marks, etc.—have been freely introduced. Müntzer made use of parentheses to set off certain remarks, and, where these are found, they are his. The material that I have interpolated into the texts has been placed in brackets. Often, this was done to clarify pronoun references and the meaning of special terms or to effect a smoother transition between sentences when it seemed necessary to section Müntzer's thought. Sometimes interpolated material has been added to clarify the meaning of difficult or ambiguous constructions or simply to make the translation more readable. There are a few other ways in which the literal form of the originals has been changed. Müntzer commonly used familiar second-person verb and pronoun forms, but I have rejected the English equivalents as archaic. His repetitive and sometimes confusing use of connective words (*da*, *deshalb*, *aber*, etc.) has occasionally been altered or omitted. The names of people and places and the few titles of the literary works he mentioned have been modernized.

The treatment of Müntzer's references to Scripture merits a special word. A basic feature of his thought was that authentic faith is not dependent on scriptural revelation. Nevertheless, he prized Scripture for the evidence it provided about God's dealings with the elect, and Müntzer's writings are filled with direct and indirect references to the Bible. The margins of some of his earlier works and the texts of all his writings are crowded with supporting or clarifying citations—to the point that they tend to become intrusive and obscure Müntzer's line of thought for most modern readers. Since the Vulgate Bible that he used lacked modern verse divisions, his references are also quite general, e.g., to a whole chapter or a whole psalm. No attempt has been made here to identify every citation of, or allusion to, Scripture. Marginal references have been omitted. In cases in which Müntzer referred to Scripture directly in the body of his text, these references are cited according to modern biblical nomenclature. Attempts to identify specific verses to which Müntzer may have wished to draw attention have been enclosed in brackets. In some cases these verse identifications are obvious, in others they are not. It should be remembered as well that Müntzer repeatedly insisted that the meaning of a particular scriptural passage or verse could only be understood in its larger context. There is a danger in ascribing to him a greater specificity of reference than he intended.

Despite taking some liberties with the form and literal meaning of Müntzer's works, I have also tried to make translations that are faithful to the originals. Since the German texts are often ambiguous and cryptic, I feel that the reader would be better served with translations that err on the side of slavish and nonidiomatic literalness than by ones that impose a plausible but contrived meaning. No doubt Müntzer would wonder, as I often have, whether the "spirit"—the message—has managed to cross the frontiers of time and language.

Some of the translations have been published previously in modified form. More elaborately annotated versions of *The Prague Protest* and *Open Letter to the Brothers at Stolberg* appeared, respectively, in *Sixteenth Century Journal* and *Mennonite Quarterly Review*. By contrast, the versions of *The Prague Protest*, *Sermon to the Princes*, and *Highly Provoked Defense* which appear in my reader *The Radical Reformation* (Cambridge University Press, 1991) differ only slightly from those presented here.

Several individuals share the credit for whatever merits the edition has, without incurring blame for its defects. Professor Hans-Christoph Rublack generously invited me to participate in a seminar on Müntzer that we taught together at the University of Tübingen during the summer semester 1984; he did much to help me come to grips with Müntzer's thought and to see his career in its larger social context. Dieter Jellinghaus kindly and patiently worked through first-draft translations of most of Müntzer's writings with me, and I benefited greatly from his insights and the many discussions we had. Professor Heiko Oberman encouraged the project and provided the venue of his Oberseminar at Tübingen for an initial presentation of my views about Müntzer. Dr. Bob Scribner of Cambridge University offered numerous specific suggestions and saved me from several errors. Professor Joe Dowling, head of the Lehigh University history department, arranged reductions in my teaching load so that I could have time to work on the manuscript. My parents, Elisabeth and Murray Baylor, offered support and many suggestions for more readable translations. Most of all, I would like to acknowledge the help of my wife, Carol Egerton Baylor, who is more aware than anyone of the difficulties the book has presented, and who did all that she could to lighten or share them. A dedication is meager recompense. Finally, I would like to express my gratitude to the National Endowment for the Humanities, whose Division of Research Programs in 1988–89 provided a generous grant that helped fund the final stages of the project.

Introduction

The literary legacy of Thomas Müntzer is diverse. It includes, in addition to his correspondence and a miscellany of notes and drafts, several liturgical works and, most importantly, a series of religio-political writings. These pamphlet-length expositions of his religious and political ideas, written between 1521 and late 1524, contain our best evidence of Müntzer's positions on the burning religious and social questions of his day, and they are in a form in which he wished to communicate these positions to a wider reading public. The tracts consist of *The Prague Protest* (1521, also commonly termed *The Prague Manifesto*), which exists in several manuscript versions but was not published, and six printed pamphlets which Müntzer produced in 1523–24. Three of these pamphlets were written in the latter half of 1523: an *Open Letter to the Brothers at Stolberg*, Müntzer's first published work, dated 18 July and printed in the late summer or fall, and two spiritually oriented works written at the end of 1523 and published early in 1524, the *Protest or Offering* and *On Contrived Faith*. The three works of 1523, composed at a time when Müntzer was also engaged in his liturgical writings, are sometimes viewed as earlier "theological" works.[1] Little more than six months separates them from the first of Müntzer's three major "political" works of 1524.[2] His *Sermon to the Princes* (or *An Exposition of the Second Chapter of Daniel*) was preached to the princes of Saxony on 13 July and published shortly thereafter. Later in 1524 Müntzer also wrote two polemics directed against Luther's conception of faith and its socio-political implications: *A Special Exposure of False Faith*, Müntzer's longest tract, and his final *Highly Provoked Defense*, a vindication of his teachings against the charges made by Luther in his *Letter to the Princes of Saxony Concerning the Rebellious Spirit*.[3] Both of the final tracts were printed at Nuremberg in late October and early December 1524.

Müntzer's liturgical materials say much less than the religio-political tracts about the ecclesiastical and social conflicts of the age and about Müntzer's unique religious ideas. Although his liturgy was innovative—the first attempt during the Reformation to develop an evangelical service—it was also conservative, essentially a vernacular translation of the traditional Roman Catholic liturgy. Müntzer was aware that he would be accused of being a liturgical reactionary. His reply sought to explain how his liturgy was related to his larger reform program, but it also conceded the substance of the accusation. Müntzer's surviving letters shed more explicit light than the liturgical works on his distinctive religious and political views, particularly as expressed in the context of specific events in his stormy career. The letters written after late 1524, when the *Defense* was finished, constitute our only direct evidence about his motives and intentions during the Peasants' War. They are equally valuable as testimony to the intensity of his engagement in the popular cause. Despite the usefulness of the letters in tracing the evolution of Müntzer's thought, it is doubtful that any conclusions about final major changes in his thinking can be drawn on the basis of these letters. The correspondence as a whole, addressed both to individuals and to specific groups, is less reliable as a guide to the substance of his thought than the documents that he composed for a wider audience and sought to publish.

Müntzer's *The Prague Protest* is the first reasonably full, detailed presentation of his ideas. In it the basic principles of his thought first become visible. Our information about the ideas he held before coming to Prague is fragmentary and consists mostly of the reports of others. The Prague work thus constitutes the essential benchmark document for interpreting the subsequent development of Müntzer's mind and career. Accounts of his further intellectual evolution and the ideas motivating his political activism in Allstedt and Mühlhausen and later during the German Peasants' War must pass the test of consistency with the Prague work.

As the opening of *The Prague Protest* makes clear, Müntzer was drawn to Prague by its reputation as the center of the Hussite movement, which had rocked the Holy Roman Empire in the early fifteenth century. Undoubtedly he hoped, through the proclamation of his message there, to rekindle the cause of radical religious and social change. But so little is known about Müntzer's early biography that it is difficult to say how and why he reached the decision to travel to Prague for this purpose.

Recent research on the earlier stages of Müntzer's life has stressed two basic points. First, his education, reading, and personal contacts exposed him to the ideas of a variety of intellectual traditions and currents.[4] These ideas he drew together in his own distinctive synthesis. Second, the early influences, especially Renaissance humanism and Wittenberg evangelicalism, were modified as a result of his experiences as a preacher at the church of St. Catherine in the important Saxon textile and mining center of Zwickau.[5] Müntzer held this position during the second phase of his stay in Zwickau, from October 1520 until April 1521, just prior to his departure for Bohemia.

Born in the town of Stolberg in the Harz Mountains before 1491, Müntzer was the son of a propertied burgher—perhaps, as the name suggests, a coiner or mint master.[6] The family evidently valued education and had sufficient wealth for Müntzer to acquire one. Müntzer probably studied at the University at Leipzig (1506), certainly at Frankfurt-on-the-Oder (1512), and undoubtedly elsewhere, eventually obtaining the master of arts degree, as well as the *Baccalaureus biblicus*, the lowest advanced degree in theology.[7] In 1514 he received a prebend as a chantry priest in Brunswick, but he may not have been newly ordained at this date, as most biographers assume.[8] Between 1514 and 1516, in addition to his Brunswick benefice, he also stayed for a period at Frose near Aschersleben where he was a teacher and a chaplain at a convent of canonesses. During the winter semester 1517–18, when Luther wrote his *Ninety-five Theses*, Müntzer was at Wittenberg. Here he came into contact with Luther, but he may have been more impressed by Andreas Karlstadt, Luther's colleague on the theology faculty. In addition to being exposed to the revival of Augustinian theology that was sweeping the university, Müntzer was more decisively influenced by two other intellectual currents at work in Wittenberg, Renaissance humanism and German mysticism, both of which may have been familiar to him before his arrival at Wittenberg. The universities at Leipzig and Frankfurt-on-the-Oder were early centers of German humanism; while in Brunswick, Müntzer had contact with reform-minded merchants whose piety was rooted in the tradition of the Brethren of the Common Life and included themes drawn from medieval mysticism. At Wittenberg, Müntzer attended lectures on St. Jerome's letters by the humanist Johannes Aesticampianus, who had recently moved to Wittenberg from Leipzig. Between January and April 1519, Müntzer lived in the parsonage at Orlamünde, where he read the sermons of Johann Tauler, a fourteenth-century Dominican mystic. The Orlamünde benefice was held by the Wittenberg theologian Andreas Karlstadt, and he may have sent Müntzer there, to live with his vicar and Müntzer's countryman, Konrad Glitsch. In short, while Müntzer was partly influenced by developments at Wittenberg and came to identify himself for a time with the evangelical reform movement centered there, he never saw himself as a follower of Luther's theology in any strict sense.[9]

During a brief period as a substitute preacher in Jüterbog (April 1519), Müntzer espoused the cause of evangelical reform, sharply criticized the church hierarchy, and came into conflict with the local Franciscans. Then, after a period of study while acting as a confessor at a nunnery at Beuditz, in early May 1520, he came to Zwickau, initially as a substitute preacher for the humanist Johannes Sylvius Egranus at the church of St. Mary. He resumed his battle with the Franciscans.

An important shift in Müntzer's thinking occurred after October 1520, when he transferred from St. Mary's to St. Catherine's church in Zwickau. Here he came into contact with a circle of devout laymen who lacked theological training but knew Scripture well, who were interested in dreams and visions as potential sources of divine revelation, and who practiced prophesy. Nicholas Storch, a master clothier, was an influential figure in this circle, some of whom were later called the "Zwickau prophets." In contact with this circle, Müntzer's humanistic concerns, including his views about the function of learning and scholarship, were altered; conflict with Egranus ensued.

It is impossible to determine precisely the extent of Storch's influence on Müntzer, who praised him from the pulpit—or of Müntzer's influence on Storch. But, when Müntzer left Zwickau in April 1521 after a series of violent episodes, it was with a transformed sense of self and his reforming mission. He signed the receipt for the final payment of his stipend as "Thomas Müntzer, who fights for truth in the world." Further, as *The Prague Protest* indicates, after Zwickau, Müntzer saw himself as a prophet, called by God to preach a message about authentic faith as the attainment of divine illumination through suffering and tribulation. The prophetic message of this tract also predicted an imminent apocalyptic upheaval that would destroy the existing, corrupt church and replace it with a purified church of the elect, to whom God would grant power over the world. This message was, for Müntzer, a universal one, directed to non-Christians as well as Christians; *The Prague Protest* stressed the utter inadequacy of previous efforts to explain and defend the true Christian faith to nonbelievers. Müntzer decided to go to Bohemia to launch this mission while he was still in Zwickau, which lay close to the Bohemian border.

Some at Prague saw him as a representative of the Wittenberg cause.[10] He may have discussed religious issues with leaders of the various groupings within the Bohemian church. But above all he preached—in his native language to the sizable German community at Prague, in Latin to the university audience and the educated, and in Czech, with the help of translators, for the majority of the city's inhabitants. In late 1521, Müntzer's message to the Bohemians assumed written form. *The Prague Protest* survives in four versions, testimony to the diverse groups in the social spectrum with whom Müntzer attempted to gain sympathy and influence. In the most likely order of composition,[11] they are: a Latin version using a traditional theological vocabulary, moderately critical in tone, and evidently designed to appeal to Prague's reform-minded and educated elites; two German versions, a shorter one, dated 1 November 1521, about half as long as the Latin version and also temperate in tone, and an extended German version, dated 25 November, nearly three times as long as the shorter one and much more polemically pitched; and a partial Czech translation of the longer German version. It is the longer

German version, the most detailed and radical of the statements, which has been selected for translation here.[12]

A striking feature of the work is its combination of an intensely mystical conception of faith—grounded in the experience of suffering and culminating in direct revelations—and a caustic assault on the clergy, seen as the propagators of an erroneous "dead word" or literalistic theology and as the beneficiaries of a corrupt and unjust society that their theology reinforced. Already, by 1521, Müntzer had linked the personal and the social dimensions of his thought. There is in *The Prague Protest* no explicit call for rebellion—in fact, no mention at all of secular or temporal authority—and only vague suggestions of a positive program. But there is enough to establish that Müntzer's later socio-political radicalism was not an inconsistent development, contradicting the message of his early theology. The Prague writing reveals that its author saw the issue of personal salvation as profoundly linked to the religious and moral life of society as a whole.

What Müntzer was protesting in Prague was what he perceived as a condition of utter corruption within "Christendom" (*Christenheit*, i.e., existing society as a whole). This vision of social rot pervades all his works; its most prominent feature in *The Prague Protest* concerns corruption among the clergy. The reader confronts a sustained, sweeping, and sometimes crude anticlerical diatribe. The clergy in general he described as "diarrhea-makers" (*lapscheyssern*) and "whore-mongers" (*hurentsuchtig*). They possess a "whore's brazenness" (*hurischen stirn*) and are "money-hungry rogues" (*geltdorstigen buben*). The rationale for the strong language began, but did not end, with his view of the clergy's conception of the Christian faith.

The contrast that Müntzer drew in *The Prague Protest* between scriptural revelation and the experience of personal revelations is the key to what he saw as distinctive in his own theology, which he regarded as a practical instruction in the art of developing an "experienced faith." The point of the contrast between book and experience was not that Scripture is false—although it is evidence of Müntzer's originality that he raised this possibility. He valued the Bible, when rightly used, and saw its evidence as one criterion for testing the authenticity of personal revelations. What Müntzer opposed was the view that divine revelation is confined to Scripture, and—what followed from this—that one is dependent on Scripture as the sole authority in matters of faith. If Luther, in the name of "Scripture alone" (*sola scriptura*), challenged traditional assumptions about the teaching authority of the Roman church, Müntzer's demand for an "experienced faith" thus cut more radically through traditional positions on the issue of religious authority.

Müntzer described the psychological process that leads to experiences of revelation in language that owed much to medieval mysticism and that gave *The Prague Protest* an opaque, cipherlike quality. In attacking the clergy for having an inexperienced faith, for example, he asked, "Since they are not sprinkled with the spirit of the fear of God on the third day, how can they be cleansed on the seventh?" Such mystical terminology gives the impression that Müntzer had a systematized conception of the process that leads to direct revelations. But it may be a mistake to attempt to discover an elaborate system. Müntzer was not advocating an esoteric theology intended for use in meditation by a literate, cloistered elite. In his view, "all true parsons must have revelations so that they are certain of their cause." The task of the parson, the shepherd, "is simply that the sheep should all be led to revelations." The commoners too, that is, "should all have revelations."

Müntzer's "experienced faith"—what he also called "learning what God is through experience"—was not described in detail in the Prague work; this would come later. But the process leading to divine illumination begins with a dark night of the soul, an emotional or affective *via negativa*. Müntzer termed the onset of this negative phase "the fear of God," one of the most recurrent phrases in his writings. This stage of suffering and anguish—the "beneficial tribulations" and "useful abyss" in which the elect are "submerged and drowned"—is one through which the elect "become conformed to Christ" through their suffering. The experience of the fear of God is also a process of purgation, an "emptying" of the mind, a "cleansing" of the soul, and an "opening" of the reason, through which worldly and material ("creaturely") attachments and fears are expunged. Then the "living voice of God" can speak directly to the heart. Precisely what is said on such occasions remained unspecified; Müntzer offered only such generalities as "God writes the true holy Scripture with his living finger" in the hearts of people. But Müntzer clearly believed that the arrival of the holy spirit transformed the recipient— "the word of God penetrates the heart, brain, skin, hair, bones, limbs, marrow, fluids, force and power," and "he who has once received the holy spirit as he should, can no longer be damned." As this last remark suggests and as the whole tone of *The Prague Protest* demonstrates, an experienced faith is one that is certain of salvation. Through the experience of revelations, one becomes "sure that one is chosen for eternal life," i.e., a member of the elect.

The acid anticlericalism of the piece finds its structural opposite in the assertion, "But I do not doubt the people." No small part of Müntzer's attack on the clergy stemmed from the fact that they were a ruling elite within the church, one that he regarded as inherently power hungry, greedy and rapacious—"a plague on people"—seeking to exploit economically· and to dominate politically those in their charge. The common people, "a poor, poor, pitiable mass," are the victims of this rapacity, and Münzter claimed that they "get no justice either from God or from man."

But beyond the overthrow of the clerical ruling elite within the church, what other changes were needed and how were they to be brought about? What, in short, was Müntzer's program and strategy in Prague? The work is nebulous and incomplete concerning these important questions—nothing like a "manifesto," as the work is commonly described. The only firm suggestion of a positive program is found in his account of the decline of the apostolic church, which he said took place because the laity neglected to exercise their right to elect their clergy. The implication is that he was committed to some form of congregationalism, a democratic localism, as the appropriate form of ecclesiastical government.[13] His failure to treat secular authority in the work may have been a result of his conviction that the basic distinction between secular and spiritual government was itself a manifestation of the corruption of Christian society. Or the omission may have been merely tactical—a desire to avoid direct conflict with the authorities in Prague. If the latter were true, the tactic failed. Müntzer was placed under house arrest, and shortly after the completion of his *The Prague Protest*, the rulers forced him to leave the city.

There is a similar indeterminacy in the work's strategic ideas. The final passages of the longer German version express an internationalist hope that the restoration of the apostolic church will begin "in your land"—i.e., Bohemia—"and afterward everywhere." But Müntzer appears to have assumed that the proclamation of his message—especially when coupled with apocalyptic predictions and warnings of an imminent Turkish invasion to be followed by the reign of Antichrist—would be sufficient to galvanize the elect to action. Müntzer's strategy in Prague was little more than the apocalyptic component of his thought, his sense of himself as an eschatological prophet.

At the end of 1521 or early in 1522, Müntzer left Prague, undoubtedly aware that much rethinking needed to be done on the problem of how the sweeping reformation that he sought was to be brought about. Despite subsequent developments in his thinking that took place on programmatic and strategic issues, *The Prague Protest* reveals that the essential framework of his religio-political vision was formed by 1521. The intimate relationship that Müntzer posited between the personal dimension of salvation through an experienced faith and the public dimension of a sweeping transformation of society, remained the constant touchstone in his thought.

After *The Prague Protest*, the remainder of Müntzer's tracts were written, or begun, while he was a preacher at St. John's church in the small Saxon market town of Allstedt, a position he held from late March 1523 until 8 August 1524. Since his liturgical works were also composed at this time, the sixteen months that Müntzer spent in Allstedt were extraordinarily creative. The period was also productive from a strategic and organizational standpoint. After the failure of his Prague mission, he returned to the parish work that had previously occupied him in Zwickau. The slower work of building up a community of committed believers replaced dramatic public proclamations.

At Allstedt, a community of about 2,500 people, including those in outlying villages, Müntzer attempted to construct what Carl Hinrichs called a "counter-Wittenberg,"[14] a model of a reformed church diametrically opposed to that being developed in Wittenberg by Luther and his associates. The Wittenberg model was university-based. The gospel was to be brought to the laity by ordained ministers, who preached the gospel as they had been taught by professional theologians. Professors of theology remained the authoritative interpreters of Scripture. The laity received the faith by hearing the correctly preached word (*fides ex auditu*, as Luther put it). Also, in the Wittenberg model, changes in existing ecclesiastical arrangements, including public worship, should be made only with the consent of established temporal authorities. In Allstedt, Müntzer attempted something very different, the formation of a religious community in which the holy spirit would be awakened in the minds of laity directly. The community as a whole, or at least the elect within it, would become the recepient of divine revelations, and the community would decide which of these revelations were authentic and which were spurious. Lay commoners, in Müntzer's view, should also be taught the skills of literacy, rather than being dependent on a learned elite. Under the guidance and advice of their pastor and using Scripture as a testimonial guide, the community would decide how it would be governed, both temporally and spiritually, and how it would worship. In short, there were egalitarian or democratic as well as participatory qualities in the Allstedt model which were lacking in that of Wittenberg.

With respect to how this model of evangelical reform could be brought about, given existing political conditions, Müntzer pursued a twofold strategy in Allstedt, one public and legal, the other secret and illegal. On the one hand, he sought to improve the spiritual life of the parish as a whole through liturgical reform, preaching, and teaching, and by offering admonition, consolation, and encouragement. This he did openly, although he never felt constrained to effect changes only with the approval of temporal authorities. In fact, he encouraged passive resistance against persecuting secular governments. But he also sought not to challenge or provoke rulers publicly; he even entertained the hope that some princes might be won to his cause. Secondly, however, he also sought to develop a secret organization within the community, a "league" or "covenant" of God's elect (*Bund der Auserwählten*)—a sworn association of those who felt themselves to be among the elect—dedicated to more active purposes. The League of the Elect was prepared to engage in illegal actions for the sake of the gospel. It is unclear to what extent Müntzer also saw the league at this time as providing the mass of the commoners, when adequately developed, with the leadership they needed in order to purify and transform society.

This dual strategy corresponded to a central element of Müntzer's theology, his notion of the elect.[15] Already, in the Prague work, he had identified the elect with the broad mass of the laity, the common people. But he also recognized that this simple equation was little more than a potentiality. Many of the commoners were spiritually "coarse"— undeveloped, lazy, and negligent. The common people, too, were damaged by the pervasive decay in society. There were among them, however, members of the elect in a more specific and realized sense, those who had attained authentic faith, those who were aware of their election and were serious, zealous, and active. It was these whom Müntzer sought for league membership. The dual strategy was given its plausibility because of Müntzer's view that some secular rulers might also be among the elect, willing to support and defend a restructuring of Christian society.

In mid-July 1524, Müntzer made a bid to wrest control of the emerging Reformation movement from Wittenberg, hoping to replace it with All-stedt in the favor of Saxony's rulers. The hope was mistaken. The attempt to gain a territorial base that might be a fulcrum for the transformation of the empire failed. But the equivocating posture of the Saxon princes when it came to religious change suggests that Müntzer's public and legal strategy was not out of touch with reality.

The political position of Allstedt had a bearing on developments. After 1485, Saxony was a divided state, a condition that reflected the prevailing assumption of German princes that their states were pieces of family property, partible among offspring like any other portion of the patrimony. The town of Allstedt was subject to the rule of Ernestine or electoral Saxony, whose ruler was Frederick the Wise, Luther's princely protector. Although Frederick remained an adherent of the traditional Roman faith, he was a self-professed neutral in the religious controversies that divided the empire. Closely associated with Frederick's electoral government were his brother, Duke John, and his son, the crown prince John Frederick, who held court at Weimar; it was they who ruled the region of electoral Saxony in which Allstedt lay. Duke John, by the early 1520s, was willing to accept the displacement of Roman Catholicism, but was unsure of the proper shape of a new church order. As a secular ruler, he, like Frederick, felt incompetent to judge. The crown prince, John Frederick, was of a clearer mind and favored the reforming cause of Luther.

What made the situation at Allstedt especially complex was that it was an Ernestine enclave embedded in the midst of Albertine or ducal Saxony, whose territories were ruled by a cousin of Frederick and John, Duke George, a prince who remained firmly committed to Rome. Furthermore, close to Allstedt lay the lands of lesser nobles, such as Count Ernst of Mansfeld, also a devout Roman Catholic, who became Müntzer's first princely opponent and later his archenemy among secular rulers. Allstedt, then, was an outpost of a principality that cautiously tolerated the emergent Reformation, but one located amid the territories of princes who vigorously opposed the evangelical movement.

Patronage rights for the church of St. John were held by the elector, but Müntzer was appointed by the town council of Allstedt and installed without the elector's formal approval. The provisional nature of his position, the indecisiveness of his princely rulers, the jealous rivalry of Wittenberg, and the proximity of Roman Catholic opponents all played a part in the development of Müntzer's strategy after the spring of 1523.

Almost as soon as he arrived, Müntzer had an impact—and not just on Allstedt. At Easter, he inaugurated his reform of the liturgy. He preached powerful sermons that addressed social and political issues. He soon gained a certain influence on the local electoral officials, the *Schösser* Hans Zeiss, who collected taxes and policed the town from the electoral castle above Allstedt, and Nicholaus Rukker, the *Schultheiss* or electoral representative on the town council. Sometime after 29 July 1523, Müntzer openly married Ottilie von Gersen, a woman of noble family who had fled a convent and who gave birth to a son at Easter 1524. By the summer of 1523, "foreigners," nonresidents from the surrounding region, had begun flocking to Müntzer's innovative Allstedt services, sometimes to the displeasure of their rulers. When Count Ernst of Mansfeld attempted to prohibit his subjects from visiting Allstedt, Müntzer's conflict with secular authorities began.

Contrary to the common view of Thomas Müntzer as a bloodthirsty fanatic, the first of his Allstedt writings was an injunction not to take up arms or engage in violence. In it he urged friends and associates— perhaps including relatives—in his hometown of Stolberg to avoid rebellion. This work is his *Open Letter to the Brothers at Stolberg*, dated 13 July 1523 and printed in the late summer or early fall in Eilenburg by Nikolaus Widemar.[16] The letter was the first writing since his unpublished *The Prague Protest* that Müntzer intended for a wide circle of lay readers.

The events in Stolberg that occasioned Müntzer's letter remain unclear.[17] After leaving Stolberg, Müntzer must have remained in contact with friends and relatives who continued to live there. Before coming to Allstedt, in the fall of 1522, he returned to Stolberg and preached there. By the summer of 1523, the evangelical movement had entered Stolberg and, as at many other places, had begun a process of differentiation into moderate and radical camps. The radicals favored the immediate introduction of sweeping changes, using violence if necessary to deal with governmental opposition. The moderates opposed this course of action, insisting on the need to proceed only with the approval of the established rulers. It is uncertain to what extent this division cut across class lines, with representatives of the propertied and educated joining members of the lower classes in the radical party. We do know that after the collapse of the Peasants' War in 1525, nine leaders of the popular rebellion were executed in Stolberg. They may have been among those to whom Müntzer directed his letter.

It is noteworthy that, while warning against rebellion, the letter did not in principle disavow violence as a legitimate way of bringing about needed changes. What Müntzer cautioned against was not an illegal or unjustified rebellion but an "inappropriate" (*unfüglich*) one. Convinced that the times were not yet ripe for insurrection, Müntzer urged his associates to prepare themselves inwardly. But the inner, personal development he sought to promote was directly related to an impending political transformation that he foresaw.

The letter is, first of all, a written instruction about the meaning of this inner or personal improvement, which Müntzer characterized as the need to develop "poverty of the spirit." But it also reveals Müntzer's intense concern for the Christianization of social and political life. The printed version of the letter does not include the pregnant phrase that the Lord "will throw the tyrants to the ground," which is contained in a draft of the letter,[18] but it clearly views the process of personal enlightenment as both a preparation for political action and a prerequisite for a genuinely Christian government. Only when the elect have armed themselves with divine revelations and have come to power "will the world be confirmed as the assembly place of the elect, so that the world will obtain a Christian governance that no sack of gunpowder"—i.e., tyrannical secular ruler—"will be able to overthrow." It is uncertain whether in 1523 Müntzer was in contact with a secret organization in Stolberg, but there is little doubt that the "cause" that he warned his associates against discussing when they had been drinking included more than purely personal piety.

Both the *Protest or Offering* and *On Contrived Faith* were written at about the same time—late November and December 1523—and published for distribution at New Year 1524, a year about which popular prophesies had made ominous and momentous predictions. The two works were the outcome of Ernst of Mansfeld's prohibitions and of an attempt by the electoral government and by Luther and others associated with Wittenberg to investigate what Müntzer was teaching at Allstedt. In early November, the elector's court traveled to Nuremberg to attend the imperial diet there. The retinue stopped at Allstedt on the way, partly to allow theologians to examine Müntzer's orthodoxy and the character of his Allstedt reformation. The impetus for the investigation evidently came from Luther.[19] The Wittenberg reformation was represented in these talks by Johann Lang, a colleague of Luther who traveled to Allstedt from Erfurt, and by George Spalatin, the elector's secretary and court preacher who was also Luther's confidant at the electoral court. A record of their conversations with Müntzer, which went on for two days, has not survived, but undoubtedly Lang and Spalatin questioned him about his theological views, his liturgical reforms, and his controversy with Count Ernst of Mansfeld. They also apparently broached the possibility of a private hearing between Müntzer and Luther or a disputation at the University of Wittenberg. Spalatin submitted eleven questions on the origins and nature of faith which were to be answered by Müntzer and his Allstedt associate, Simon Haferitz.[20]

Müntzer's *Protest or Offering*, the longer of the two works of late 1523, was written as an exposition of his theology that he prepared in connection with the discussions with Lang. Internal evidence suggests that a version of it may have been presented orally. The briefer *On Contrived Faith*, printed shortly afterward, may have derived from the questions put to him by Spalatin concerning faith. The work does not take the form of a point-by-point reply, but its sections cover the issues raised by Spalatin's questions. The printed version included as an appendix a letter from Müntzer to Zeiss dated 2 December 1523, in which he denied being a Joachimite millenarian.

The investigative circumstances of their composition influenced the content of both works. Their focus is on theological issues, especially the source and character of true faith, the language of the discussion is fairly conventional, and there is an abundance of scriptural reference. For these reasons the writings are valuable as straightforward presentations of Müntzer's views on theological issues, couched in traditional terms and without emphasis on such controversial issues as personal, extrascriptural revelations. There is also a notable absence of Müntzer's ideas on political and social questions, something that the investigators did not explicitly inquire about and about which Müntzer did not volunteer his views. Other features of the *Protest or Offering*, especially, reveal its origin as a defense in theological investigations. Müntzer sharply repudiated the practice of creating schisms by hereticizing those who differ doctrinally.

An odd feature of the work is its four endings, a series of responses to what Müntzer felt was mounting pressure from Wittenberg for private doctrinal discussions or a university disputation with Luther. Instead Müntzer requested, if he were to be found in error, a fraternal and public reproach rather than a private hearing. He offered to expand on anything he had asserted that presented problems, and finally he proposed a hearing or disputation before a universal forum, one that would include representatives of all religions.

If they were a defensive reaction to Wittenberg-initiated investigations, both works were also molded by Müntzer's pastoral work in Allstedt. They are especially concerned with what the common people should be taught if they were to arrive at true faith. Müntzer speaks of himself here, for perhaps the only time, as among those learned in theology with an obligation to set forth the truth for the uninformed laity. The pastoral concern is evident in Müntzer's awareness that he was now engaged in a two-front theological war: both Wittenberg and Rome were the antagonists. Müntzer summarized the false views of salvation that he found in the camps of his enemies as "contrived faith" and "glittering works." Rome was misleading the people by insisting that righteousness is rooted in works that are pleasing to God and impressive to others, but are in fact trivial externalities. Wittenberg was seducing the people with an easily attained, but essentially contrived or counterfeit, faith: a painless acceptance of Christ as a redeemer, a literalistic belief in Scripture and its promises, and the notion that the Christian faith is readily compatible with worldly pleasures. Luther is not mentioned by name in the works, but it is clear that his is the theology of "contrived faith." Müntzer sought to combat these views of salvation with an account in both works of his own conception of faith, one that stressed its enormous difficulty, the need to undergo suffering and tribulation and, in this way, become at one with Christ and prepared to receive the living word.

Müntzer's pastoral concerns are also evident in two other features of the works. They both deal with sanctification, stressing the irreconcilability of the Christian life with worldly comfort and pleasure. The *Protest or Offering* especially sought to point out how the Roman faith had engendered superstition among the people, a belief in the efficacy of holy signs and rituals. The invocation of the saints is attacked as illustrative of such superstition. It is in this context too that Müntzer rejected infant baptism as a mere "external sign," a piece of "ritualistic monkey business" that has turned the whole community of Christians into infants in their faith. He described the practice of infant baptism as the source of a conception of faith that has corrupted Christian society. The denunciation of this corruption encompassed Luther's theology, which Müntzer attacked not only for accepting infant baptism, but also for assuming that certain ideas should be withheld from the laity as too difficult or demanding. He also criticized Luther's university-based theology, calling it the faith of "untested scribes" who presume to charge money for their teaching, preach only a "honey-sweet Christ" that fails to challenge worldly pleasure, and "snarl like dogs when contradicted."

On Contrived Faith was composed as a kind of sequel to the *Protest or Offering* and apparently with the longer work at hand. It is in part a précis of the *Protest*—particularly in its treatment of the hardship that real faith involves—but it also covers new ground in its use of scriptural example and remarks on the function of Scripture. The shorter work was the more popular of the two and was printed three times during 1524.[21]

These two short works were read in Zurich by some of those dissatisifed with Zwingli's reformation. On 5 September 1524, Conrad Grebel and his associates wrote to Müntzer expressing reservations with what they had heard about his liturgical reforms and about his willingness to use violence, but praising him as a "sincere and true proclaimer of the gospel" and signing themselves "seven new young Müntzers against Luther."

Although it did not meet with the wholehearted approval of the Zurich radicals, an important part of Müntzer's reforming work in Allstedt was the development of a new vernacular liturgy to replace the traditional Latin Mass and other ceremonies, including a reorganization of the liturgical calendar. Already, in *The Prague Protest*, Müntzer had complained of how little attention had been given to a proper liturgy, and his liturgical reforms began soon after he arrived in Allstedt. Their success gave Müntzer's Allstedt reformation an important advantage over that of Wittenberg and transformed the city into an independent center of the evangelical movement. Müntzer produced the first comprehensive liturgy in the German language at a time when Luther was still reluctant to abandon Latin. Liturgical reform clearly meant a great deal to Müntzer, who was aware that a liturgy shapes as well as reflects religious beliefs and that a liturgy is a social phenomenon shared by the community as a whole. After fleeing Allstedt and settling at Mühlhausen, he wrote to Allstedt requesting that the copies of his liturgies be forwarded to him. The liturgical materials as a whole comprise about one third of the total corpus of Müntzer's writings.

Müntzer's two major liturgical works are beyond the scope of this edition; they were his *German Church Office* (*Deutsches Kirchenamt*) and *German Evangelical Mass* (*Deutsche-evangelische Messe*).[22] Both were arranged like missals and were intended for use by literate parishoners. The expense and difficulty of printing these works, particularly the preparation of woodcuts used for the music, meant a delay of several months between Müntzer's composition and their publication. The *German Church Office* came first. It was printed at Eilenburg by Nikolaus Widemar in the spring of 1524, but was probably composed four to six months earlier, in late 1523. The *German Evangelical Mass* was printed at Allstedt in early August 1524, assisted by a subvention from the town council. The time necessary to prepare the woodcuts for the *Mass* implies a composition period ending at least three or four months prior to publication.

In addition to the two major liturgical works, Müntzer also wrote a shorter *Order and Account of the German Service at Allstedt*, which he composed late in 1523 or early in 1524, between the completion of the *Church Office* and the *Mass*. It is this shorter work, printed three times by Nikolaus Widemar of Eilenburg in 1524—together with the prefatory materials to the *German Evangelical Mass*—that have been included here as illustrative of Müntzer's liturgical ideas.

The *Order and Account* allowed Müntzer to summarize for his readers the changes he had made in the Mass, to report on the completion of a liturgy for the sacraments and sacramentals, and to present a justification for his reforms, including their biblical basis. By the time he published his *Mass*, the liturgical experiments were being criticized not only as deviations from the Roman liturgy, but also, by other reformers, as retaining too much of papal ceremony. Hence the prefatory material for the *Mass* consisted of two separate statements, Müntzer's response to each camp of critics.

The opening section of the *Order and Account* makes plain that Müntzer saw the function of his liturgy as the "elevation and edification" of the whole community.[23] This implied several things for him. First of all, it meant a vernacular liturgy, capable of being understood by all, so that there would be nothing secret or private, accessible only to the priest. Secondly, he wanted liturgical passages of Scripture to be understood in their larger context. Müntzer insisted that the whole psalm, or the whole chapter of an epistle or gospel, be recited, rather than the traditional excerpt. Thirdly, linking these and also continuing a theme from earlier writings, the spiritual improvement of the community meant an attack on all forms of superstition or magic, whether that which was associated with the priest as an "enchanter," with holy signs or objects, or with an imagined incantatory power possessed by Latin words. The proper preparation for communion, according to Müntzer, was developing the knowledge that God is not a thousand miles away but within the individual. The community's elevation also meant its development as an active liturgical participant. Müntzer advanced the view that it is the assembled congregation, not the minister, that effects the consecration. He also argued that it is the faith of the many pious people that a congregation surely contains that guarantees Christ's presence in the sacrament.

It is unfortunate that the description of the sacramental liturgy that concludes the *Order and Account* is not more detailed. These ritual accompaniments of basic transitions in the course of human life potentially reveal much about how life itself is conceived. Müntzer's comments are disappointingly brief. He naturally devoted considerable attention to baptism, criticizing—but not explicitly forbidding—infant baptism. Of marriage we learn little beyond Müntzer's disapproval of levity at marriage celebrations.

The first preface to the *German Evangelical Mass* included a brief statement of the changes Müntzer made in the liturgical calender, changes that he developed at much greater length in his *German Church Office*. The medieval liturgical year, coordinated with the cycle of agricultural life, was bipartite. In the first half of the year, when the days were lengthening, the liturgy centered on the three great feast periods in the Lord's Year (*Herrenjahr*): the Incarnation, the Easter reenactment of Christ's Passion, Death, and Resurrection, and the period from the Ascension to Corpus Christi Sunday. In the second half of the year the traditional liturgy focused on a variety of solemn feasts for various saints. Müntzer proposed instead a liturgical year that set aside feasts of the saints, even those of the Virgin, and that was divided into five "offices," spread over the year. These offices were oriented exclusively on Christ and the holy spirit. In addition, over the course of the year he sought to expound liturgically the whole Bible, the Old Testament as well as the New. Thus the liturgical calendar became a means for redirecting the religious life of the community away from beliefs that Müntzer regarded as superstitious and toward what he saw as the true understanding of God's word.

The second preface to the *Mass* contained Müntzer's defense against the charge by fellow reformers that his liturgy was too conservative. Müntzer's reply to this criticism stressed his pastoral intentions. He argued that his first priority was to struggle against superstition by translating the liturgy with which people were familiar into the vernacular. This would also enable the weak in the congregation to accept the changes, effecting—as he put it in the *Order and Account*—a "gradual and gentle breaking" with "superstitious ceremonies and rituals." In addition Müntzer argued his case on the grounds of localism: traditionally there has been much regional variety in liturgical usage, and it is the local pastor who is best capable of judging the specific needs of his congregation.

Müntzer saw his liturgical reforms, then, as provisional and experimental, subject to future revision or local adaptation, and he attempted to defend them on these grounds. But finally, perhaps feeling that criticisms from Wittenberg were primarily jealous carping, Müntzer's defense turned into an anticlerical attack on the "pampered parsons" and "lazy rogues" who were removed from the needs of the humble commoners and who wanted only to "preach a sermon on Sunday and be like Junkers the rest of the week."

During the first half of 1524, Müntzer's Allstedt reformation was dramatically radicalized as the second component of his strategy—the path of illegality given organizational form in the League of the Elect—assumed a larger role in events. The League may have been constituted at Allstedt as early as the summer of 1523.[24] Its formal inauguration took place in the town's dry moat; about thirty people met and swore an oath to stand by the gospel, to refuse dues to nuns and monks, and to drive these same from the region. The members also agreed to fraternal and egalitarian relations among one another. The organization included messengers who were to establish and maintain contact with similar groups elsewhere. Five lay leaders were chosen; Müntzer was acknowledged as the spiritual director.

The League's first object of attack was a chapel at nearby Mallerbach, the property of a cloister of Cistercian nuns at Naundorf, to whom Allstedters also owed dues. The chapel had a reputation for miraculous cures effected by an image of the Virgin. From the pulpit, Müntzer attacked the Mallerbach chapel as an evil den, a source of rank superstition. On 24 March 1524, members of the League—including Müntzer, who according to his confession was present on the occasion—burned down the chapel.

The Naundorf nuns understandably complained to the elector, who urged his local agent, Hans Zeiss, and city officials to bring the culprits to justice. Initially Zeiss, as well as Nicholaus Rukker and the town council as a whole, supported Müntzer and the League, adopting delaying tactics that amounted to passive resistance. They reported that the guilty parties could not be identified and that to arrest the innocent was to risk rebellion.[25] As electoral pressure for action increased—partly due to the growing hostility of nearby Catholic lords—Müntzer grew more outspoken in his defense of the arson and in his criticism of the elector. In June, the Allstedters prepared to cross the line between passive and active resistance. A new defense ordinance was introduced in the town, organizing the citizenry into military units for the protection of the community; these units could be mustered at the sounding of an alarm bell. Müntzer's wife, Ottilie von Gersen, took charge of the organization and training of the women. When Zeiss and Rukker, caught in the conflict between the elector and Müntzer, tried to placate higher authorities by initiating arrests, Müntzer raised the alarm on 13 June. The military units appeared, and the efforts of the officials were cut short. Shortly afterward Zeiss decided it best to release an Allstedt councilman, Ciliax Knauth, whom he had detained.

In addition to the mounting displeasure of the princes, Müntzer had to deal with the growing hostility of Wittenberg. Although Luther did not participate directly in the efforts to bring the Mallerbach culprits to justice, he must have known through Zeiss's reports, as transmitted to him by Spalatin, a good deal of what was taking place at Allstedt.[26] Zeiss wrote to the elector recommending that Müntzer be given a hearing before a public assembly, including the "learned" (i.e., Wittenberg theologians). If his teaching was declared to be false, Zeiss suggested, he could be expelled; to proceed against him otherwise was to risk insurrection. In the end, it was Müntzer's escalating difficulties with both the Saxon princes and with Wittenberg—an escalation triggered, but not fundamentally caused, by the affair of the Mallerbach chapel—that led to the composition of his three final writings.

Müntzer's *Sermon to the Princes* (or, as the printed version was entitled, *An Exposition of the Second Chapter of Daniel*), was preached at the castle church in Allstedt on the morning of 13 July 1524 to an audience that included Duke John, Crown Prince John Frederick, and several of their officials and attendants. The initiative for the sermon apparently came from Müntzer,[27] who was aware of mounting opposition to him. He hoped to forestall further investigation and possible punishment by appealing directly to the rulers. The Saxon princes were on a journey between the ducal court at Weimar and Mansfeld, the residence of Duke George. They had stopped at the electoral castle at Allstedt during the night of 1–2 July on their way to Mansfeld, when the idea for such a sermon may have presented itself to Müntzer, and again on 12–13 July on the return trip. Perhaps through Zeiss, and perhaps only on the evening of 12 July, when the princes and their entourage arrived at Allstedt, Müntzer requested an opportunity to preach to them during their stay there. The following morning he was allowed to do so.

The sermon provoked no immediate response from the princes. Probably Müntzer received from Duke John and his chancellor, Gregor Brück, permisssion to print the sermon at the time it was delivered.[28] Within a week the sermon was published in Allstedt, so we may assume that the printed version, although certainly longer than the oral presentation, reproduced the substance of the sermon without major revision. The wish to publish was perhaps designed to put additional pressure on the territorial rulers to declare themselves for Müntzer. If so, the ploy failed. True to the Saxon princes' tendency to avoid hard choices whenever possible, no decision was made immediately. It is also likely that Müntzer wanted to publish the sermon because he had spent much time developing its contents, and he wanted its message to have a wider audience.

The text that Müntzer chose for his sermon was highly appropriate to his situation and purpose. Daniel 2 tells the story of a prophet at a princely court who is challenged to prove the authenticity of his prophetic gifts by interpreting a dream whose details he has not been told. Unlike the prince's seers, savants, and scribes, Daniel succeeds; he is rewarded by being elevated to office, so that the prince's rule might be pleasing to God. The text allowed Müntzer the opportunity to explore his notion of direct, personal revelations that are contained in dreams and visions, to lambaste Luther and others at Wittenberg as false scribes, and to develop a vision of history with powerful implications about the proper role of temporal government during the dangerous Last Days. Scripture functions in the sermon, as elsewhere in Müntzer's writing, as testimony about how God deals with the elect and as a body of wisdom whose teachings are directly and immediately applicable to the existing situation.

Müntzer's notion that dreams and visions can contain divine revelations, especially warnings about the future, was basic to his theology. But Müntzer was also cautious about such experiences. He sought to clarify a middle ground between Luther's rejection of extrascriptural revelation and a superstitious credulity about the meaning of dreams. Much of the sermon's discussion of dreams and visions was an examination of the criteria for distinguishing between authentic and spurious revelations, among which Müntzer included mystical visions that are self-induced through monastic asceticism.

Central to the sermon's social concerns is a theme that appears in virtually everything he wrote: the corruption that has befallen Christendom. Here it is described not only in the same terms that he used in *The Prague Protest*—the decay of true faith, the rule of godless parsons, and the merging of the elect and evildoers. A note directly pertaining to temporal government is sounded for the princes. Godless lay rulers are also blamed for the corruption. The Emperor Augustus, the presumed founder of the Holy Roman Empire, is described as a power-hungry "scumbag" (*Drecksack*). In addition, the corruption of contemporary Christendom is given historical depth by locating it within a larger interpretation of world history. There was nothing original about regarding the five parts of the statue in King Nebuchadnezzar's dream as symbols for five successive world empires. More innovative was Müntzer's view of the Holy Roman Empire as the abysmally corrupt successor of Rome's iron empire of coercion, with the iron of temporal rule now mixed with the clay of clerical power. Surely startling to the princes was the way in which Müntzer symbolized this feudal cooperation of lay and clerical authorities: as a huge pile of snakes and eels copulating with one another. The "temporal lords" are the eels and the "evil clergy" are the snakes, among whom Müntzer clearly intended to include Luther and those allied with him.

The sermon also asserted that "the work of ending the fifth empire of the world is in full swing," and that "the spirit of God now reveals to many pious people that a momentous, invincible, future reformation is very necessary." The call was for a radical transformation of society in the face of an apocalyptic upheaval. The princes were urged to join, indeed to exercise their power as rulers, in bringing about this change. Müntzer presented himself as the "new Daniel" who would counsel them. If other princes tried to oppose them, Müntzer asserted, the subjects of these princes would rise up to overthrow them. The final section of the sermon cited Christ's most merciless injunctions about how to deal with the wicked; it informed the princes that the godless have no right to life when they hinder the elect.

The political theory elaborated in the sermon has been widely misinterpreted. Müntzer did not make an opportunistic bid for princely favor and, only after failing, turn to the lower classes for support.[29] Nor did he articulate a new theory of legitimacy concerning temporal government. In fact, the sermon presented the elaboration of a conception of politics that he had already asserted in the fall of 1523.[30] In Müntzer's view, the Pauline insistence on obedience to temporal authority found in Romans 13:1–2, a passage that Luther had used to argue that active resistance against divinely ordained authority is never justified, was conditional on verses 3–4, that the sword is given to rulers to punish the wicked and to protect the pious. If the princes fail to do this, Müntzer held, the people have a right to resist unjust government—to overthrow rulers who are "godless tyrants" and to replace them with a genuinely Christian governance. In this way, Müntzer developed a scriptural foundation for a theory of revolution. The implicit presupposition to the argument, however inchoate, was a theory of popular sovereignty. The sermon, in fact, presented the princes with an ultimatum: either they defend the gospel and make common cause with their subjects in the transformation of society, or their power would be taken from them and exercised by the commoners.

Müntzer's last two tracts, *Special Exposure of False Faith* and *Highly Provoked Defense*, are similar in concept and composition. Together they represent a sustained attack on Luther—Müntzer's final settlement with the theology of Wittenberg. After the collapse of the strategy of legality that he had publicly pursued at Allstedt, they were also an open declaration of his revolutionary identity and intentions. The *Sermon to the Princes* is filled with tension and mounting eschatological excitement. The *Special Exposure* and the *Defense* are more fulminating and polemical, with sudden shifts in the argument—not the product of a temperate mood. Yet it is striking how many of the central ideas of both writings, the concepts beneath the agitated surface, were notions he had expressed as early as *The Prague Protest*.

In terms of length, the *Special Exposure of False Faith* is Müntzer's magnum opus, a work on which he expended much effort. The work exists in two versions, one brief and mild in tone, the other—that presented here—far more detailed and radical. The two versions reflect the dual strategy that Müntzer pursued at Allstedt; the precise relationship between the two is difficult to determine.

Although there was no official repudiation of his *Sermon to the Princes*, the same lack of response was not true of another sermon Müntzer delivered at Allstedt eleven days later, on 24 July 1524.[31] Müntzer publicly called for an opening of the League to general membership. Undoubtedly he sought to fuse it with the new military organization of the community and to extend its membership beyond Allstedt. On the single day of 24 July, about 500 members were sworn in, including many miners from nearby Mansfeld. Müntzer may have felt this step was now necessary because of two developments. Refugees from persecution elsewhere, such as those from Sangerhausen, were entering Allstedt in search of protection. Also, Allstedt began receiving reports of military depredations by Catholic nobles against reforming communities, such as Friedrich von Witzleben's attack on Schönewerda. By the end of July 1524, Müntzer felt things were coming to a head. He wrote Zeiss an instruction (letter #59), which he knew would be passed on to the Saxon princes, about how princes should meet future rebellion in a godly way.

When ducal officials learned of Müntzer's League sermon, with its call for a political association of Christians outside princely control, they quickly summoned Müntzer and the secular officials of Allstedt (Zeiss, Rukker, members of the town council) to appear at Weimar for a hearing. In Müntzer's case, this examination took place on 1 August 1524. At the hearing, and in accordance with the agreement not to publish anything without permission, Müntzer submitted to ducal officials one version of a work expounding Luke 1, his *Witness of the First Chapter of the Gospel of Luke*. This work, written in the latter half of July, between the *Sermon to the Princes* and the Weimar hearing, was fully in accord with the strategy of legality that Müntzer had publicly advocated, even in the *Sermon to the Princes*. The second version, *A Special Exposure of False Faith*, was an elaboration of the first, completed later. But it is also possible that much of the content of the *Special Exposure* was worked out at the same time as the *Witness*, which may have been abbreviated in the hope of meeting the requirements of the Weimar censor.[32]

Why was the path of legality set forth in the *Witness* abandoned and the revolutionary strategy, previously pursued in secret, now openly proclaimed in the *Special Exposure*? The change was due to the outcome of the Weimar hearing and its repercussions at Allstedt.[33] Müntzer got off lightly at Weimar. He was accused of inciting princely subjects to disobedience, but then he was only informed that the duke would consult with the elector about the future disposition of his case.[34] The Allstedt officials were not dealt with so leniently. Ducal officials forbade them having a printer at Allstedt and told them to cease contact with nonresidents—i.e., to stop turning Allstedt into a center of agitation and a refuge for those persecuted elsewhere—and to end their resistance to electoral efforts to arrest and punish the Mallerbach criminals. When they returned to Allstedt, Zeiss, Rukker, and the city councilors called Müntzer to the castle and informed him on 3 August of these decisions. While they told him they would help him gain a public disputation on his theology and the restoration of the press, they also told him that the League would have to be dissolved and those guilty of arson at Mallerbach would be arrested. Müntzer now faced the alternatives of meekly submitting to the will of the electoral government or of risking the future of the League by open insurrection. He opted for a third choice. During the night of 7–8 August, he climbed over the town wall and left Allstedt, accompanied by a goldsmith from Nordhausen.

A week later, in mid-August Müntzer arrived at the free imperial city of Mühlhausen, his next base of operations. With about 7,500 inhabitants, Mühlhausen was much larger than Allstedt, and a radical reform movement, centered around the preaching of an ex-monk, Heinrich Pfeiffer, was already developing in the city. Müntzer joined Pfeiffer's cause, but their initial efforts to bring about political transformation failed. Following a week of disturbances from 19 to 26 September, during which Müntzer and Pfeiffer assisted in the drafting of a radical program, "The Eleven Mühlhausen Articles," the two preachers were expelled from the city.

At this point, Müntzer's desire to publish his *Special Exposure of False Faith* led him to the religious radical and bookseller, Hans Hut, who had the contacts needed to get a revolutionary writing into print.[35] Müntzer traveled to Bibra, near Meiningen, to visit Hut at his home and delivered the manuscript of the *Special Exposure* to him there. The work's title page states that it was printed in Mühlhausen, but this was either an attempt to deceive authorities or a indication of Müntzer's recent experience. The work was in fact printed in Nuremberg in late October 1524, secretly printed by an apprentice to the printer Hans Hergot, who was out of the city. Hergot's trip may explain the delay in publication; Hut and Hergot's apprentice may have had to wait for an opportune moment to do the printing.[36] But publication came to light in any event. On 29

October, the Nuremberg city council handed the work over to the preacher Dominicus Schleupner, an ally of Luther, for a judgment. They arrested Hergot's apprentice and ordered that future writings be submitted to the city government for prepublication censorship. Hut was also arrested, but released when he agreed to pay the printing costs. Of an original edition of five hundred copies, four hundred were confiscated and destroyed. A hundred had already been sent to Augsburg.

The "false faith" that the work sought to expose was Luther's. Much of the criticism had already been set forth earlier in the short works of late 1523. In the *Special Exposure of False Faith*, the focus was sharpened by concentrating on the issue of religious authority—the authority of the written text of Scripture and of university theologians as its interpreters. Personal religious experience, not a book, was for Müntzer what faith was about. He argued that it was inadequate to defend the authority of Scripture merely by asserting that it has been so accepted "by tradition, that is by many people." Like many other biblical texts, Luke 1 served Müntzer as a way of using Scripture itself to argue against the sole authority of Scripture. The story of the Annunciation was one of simple, unlettered people who found true faith other than through Scripture and who experienced direct revelations. For Müntzer, simply to believe in the supreme authority of the literal text led to a faith that denied revelations in personal experience, hence one "stolen" from Scripture.

The opening of the work presented Müntzer's rejection of a closed examination by university theologians, whom Müntzer charged with being presumptuous scribes who sought "to give the witness of Jesus's spirit a higher education." The *Special Exposure* assailed the authority of professional theologians and Luther's central assumption that "scribes should read the beautiful books and the peasants should listen to them, for faith comes through hearing." Müntzer was not antiintellectual in the sense of being opposed to learning.[37] Indeed, his criticism of the mandarin theologians was their failure to educate the commoners and their propagation of a faith that reinforced the pervasive illiteracy of the commoners.

Despite the polemical character of the work, it was also positive in tone. The work is especially important as Müntzer's fullest account of the psychological process through which authentic faith might be attained. The emphasis, as elsewhere in his writings, is upon the difficulty of faith, which must be attained in tribulation and suffering. The argument begins dialectically, with the assertion that "every truth contains its diametrical opposite." Hence real faith begins with a discovery of one's unbelief and a recognition of the apparent impossibility of faith. This recognition is experienced with amazement and takes the form of "fear of God." Fear impells the soul to empty itself of worldly values and attachments. The negative process of purification reaches its culmination in a condition of "release" or "tranquility" (*Gelassenheit*), a state of disassociation from worldly concerns, in which the soul is prepared for the reception of divine revelations. These Müntzer described using the terminology of late medieval mysticism, as the "breakthrough" of the divine spirit in the "abyss" of the soul. Müntzer associated this breakthrough with the release of transrational forces within the human spirit; the result, he asserted, is a "deification" of man.

Analagous to the apparent impossibility of personal faith—the enormous difficulty the elect have in recognizing that they are the elect—was another problem. It seemed impossible that the existing structures of political and social life could be transformed in the same sweeping way as the human spirit. Yet, Müntzer insisted, faith means believing that they could be. The *Special Exposure* contains one of Müntzer's most detailed discussions of how he conceived a future revolution.

With the failure of the princes to accept the ultimatum of the *Sermon to the Princes*, Müntzer was now ready to dispense with them. He lashed out at princes who are afraid to do what is right because they fear the response of other princes, and he termed existing rulers "nothing but hangmen and knackers" (*Büttel*, i.e., dealers in corpses and carrion). Part of the "false faith" of Luther and the university theologians is "to preach shamelessly that the poor man should let himself be sheared and clipped by tyrants." Godless lay rulers, as well as clerical authorities, must be overthrown—and the two "hang onto each other like toads" in pursuing a life of power and pleasure by the labor of others.

Like the *Sermon to the Princes*, the *Special Exposure of False Faith* is filled with apocalpytic foreboding. The conflict between God and Mammon seemed to be building to a climax. Fear of God should replace fear of human authority because both masters cannot be served. Soon God must shorten the days of suffering for his elect, the commoners. In short, the eschatological "harvest time" has arrived, when the wheat and the chaff, the elect and the godless, will be separated—even though "the chaff everywhere now screams that it is not yet harvest time."

The revolutionary transformation was thus to be an apocalyptic one, as might be expected in an age when speculation about the future inevitably turned to eschatology. Equally important, the social upheaval would consist of a transformation by "inversion" or "reversal." Using the carnival motif of "the world turned upside down," Müntzer described the revolution as a divinely staged drama or play (*Spiel*), in whose performance the mighty would be knocked from their thrones and the humble would be raised up. What gave the inversion its logic was Müntzer's belief—already expressed in *The Prague Protest*—that the elect were to be found among the lay commoners. Just as now the elect are debased and the godless swollen with pride, in the future "the mighty ones must give way to the small and be ruined by the small. Oh, if the poor rejected peasants knew this, it would be most useful to them." Müntzer saw the political and social transformation as the public counterpart of the personal transformation through divine revelations that was the message of his spiritual psychology.[38] The process by which unbelief is transmuted into authentic faith and earthly life is transformed into heavenly, had its social counterpart in Müntzer's theory of revolution. His teaching about this apocalyptic unheaval, he wrote, ". . . seems to countless people to be utter fanaticism. They can only judge it impossible that such a play could be presented and performed, knocking the godless from their thrones and raising up the lowly and the coarse." Müntzer depicted his own function in bringing about this social transformation as that of a preacher and prophet, a new John the Baptist or Elijah, working to generate the "correct momentum" (*den rechten schwanck*) in society for the approaching upheaval.

In August 1524, Luther's *Letter to the Princes of Saxony Concerning the Rebellious Spirit* was published, a denunciation of any attempt to associate the cause of the gospel—as Luther understood it—with civil disorder or political radicalism. The work argued that no ruler had the right to interfere with the proclamation of the gospel; but, as soon as preaching incited insurrection, secular rulers had the right and duty to meet force with force. Luther made it clear how he viewed Müntzer, "the Satan of Allstedt," with respect to this issue. Müntzer, in Luther's view, was a diabolically possessed fanatic, full of babble about the holy spirit and revelations in visions, but incapable of producing miracles to prove himself. Above all, his preaching bore no other fruit than that of inciting the rabble to violence.

Müntzer's *Highly Provoked Defense* was his response to Luther's attack. It was a defense that assumed the offensive, a rich invective against Luther's character, his role in the Reformation, and his theology, especially its socio-political message. Never before had Luther been held up to such public excoriation by a fellow reformer. The work is also informative for its presentation of Müntzer's interpretation of the events that led to the collapse of his strategy of legality in Allstedt and for the openness of its advocacy of revolution.

The exact time when the *Defense* was written is difficult to determine. Since Müntzer fails to mention his first stay in Mühlhausen in the work, the manuscript may have been substantially complete by the time he fled Allstedt on 7–8 August, an event that is discussed at the close of the tract.[39] But subsequent revisions must have also been made, probably as late as September, for the work also refers to Luther's visitation trip to Orlamünde on 24 August and the sharp conflict that occurred there between Luther and members of Karlstadt's congregation. Probably the manuscript was substantially completed before 19 September, the start of the unrest at Mühlhausen that led to Müntzer's explusion on 27 September. The pace of events between 19 and 27 September, none of which are mentioned in the work, would hardly have allowed time for Müntzer to continue revisions.

The work was printed at Nuremberg in mid-December 1524. Müntzer traveled to Nuremberg that fall, perhaps bringing the manuscript with him. Publication was facilitated through the efforts of Hans Denck, a Nuremberg teacher and fellow religious radical, who had contacts among Nuremberg's publishers.[40] The printer Hieronymus Hölzel undertook publication. However, like the *Special Exposure* before it, the *Defense* was discovered by Nuremberg authorities, who arrested Hölzel on 17 December. Müntzer's manuscript and the printed copies were confiscated, and nearly the whole edition was destroyed. Only a few copies of the original have survived.

The opening of the work parodies Luther's salutation to the princes in his *Letter to the Princes of Saxony* by denying them all the titles that Luther had used in addressing them and by announcing that the author of the *Defense* recognizes only Christ as his prince. The titles that Müntzer ascribed to Luther throughout the work were designed to provoke public ridicule. The scornful epithets had begun already in the *Sermon to the Princes*—where Luther was referred to as "Brother Fattened Swine" and "Brother Soft-life"—but in the *Defense* they heap up in abundance ("the spiritless, soft-living flesh at Wittenberg," "Doctor Liar," "Doctor Mockery," "the pope of Wittenberg," etc.). Above all Luther was depicted as jealous of Müntzer's popular success in Allstedt and as willing to engage in any malicious scheme to silence him.

Underlying the personal animosity is the criticism of Luther's theology. In the *Special Exposure of False Faith*, the central point of attack had been Luther's literalistic belief in the sole authority of Scripture. In the *Highly Provoked Defense* Müntzer denounced Luther's famous distinction between law and gospel, arguing that the way Luther divided the two had catastrophic consequences for spiritual and social life. Luther's doctrine of justification by faith and grace alone meant that people no longer saw that the law was essential to the inward preparation for faith. Müntzer's own position on justification was synergistic—to the extent that the divine and human are separable in his thought—and he berated Luther's Augustinian denial of the freedom of the will as making God responsible for sin and as an insult to human nature.

Especially significant, however, was the link that Müntzer saw between Luther's theory of justification and his social views. In a reference both to Genesis 8 and Luther's black Augustinian habit, Müntzer described him as a "black raven," who "in order to get the carcass, picks out the eyes of the swine's head." In other words, Luther's teaching about law and gospel has blinded the rulers to their true obligations and whetted their greedy ambitions—ambitions that Luther shared. Luther was accused of advocating a reformation that serves the interests of the nobility and the princes and of seeking to inveigle them into favors and honors by presenting them with "Bohemian gifts" of church property. At the same time, Luther's doctrine that subjects must be obedient to princes, whom God has ordained to rule over them, meant that people cannot justly resist being exploited by lords and princes; and that their exploitation embraces all creation: "The fish in the water, the birds in the air, the animals of the earth must all be theirs." In short, Müntzer saw Luther's distinction between law and gospel as meaning law and obedience for the subjects and freedom for the princes to exercise their rapacity.

Interwoven into the diatribe against Luther are a series of remarks indicating how Müntzer now conceived the cause of revolution. The Last Days were at hand; the changes to be brought about would no longer be pursued through the instrumentality of a secret league; instead, now was the time to raise the commoners as a whole. There are indications in the *Highly Provoked Defense* that Müntzer was aware of mounting popular unrest, an approaching mass insurrection. "The lords themselves are responsible for making the poor people their enemy," he wrote. "They do not want to remove the cause of insurrection, so how, in the long run, can things improve? . . . I warn you that the peasants may soon strike out."

But Müntzer had grave doubts about whether the commoners were sufficiently prepared psychologically for revolution. Contrary to the wanton destructiveness that Luther attributed to him, Müntzer did not favor the chaos of mob riot. Revolutionary violence should be properly motivated and directed toward right goals. The *Highly Provoked Defense*, like the *Special Exposure* before it, openly treated the problem of the people's inadequate preparation. In the *Special Exposure*, Müntzer lamented the dangers of an illiterate commoner, traditionally respectful of authority, immature in spiritual development, and filled with disorderly desires. In the *Defense*, he pointed out also the illusory nature of a revolution defined by anticlericalism, and he cautioned the commoners against thinking that all is well because they no longer obey the clergy.

Despite Müntzer's reservations about the inward readiness of the commoners for the kind of transformation he wanted, the *Highly Provoked Defense* makes clear his commitment to the popular cause. To find the ground between Luther's insistence that revolution is never justified and Luther's characterization of him as only interested in violence, Müntzer asserted, "Whoever wants to have a clear judgment here must not love insurrection, but equally he must not oppose a justified rebellion. He must hold to a very reasonable middle way. Otherwise he will either hate my teaching too much or love it too much, according to his own convenience. I never want this to happen." The work, with its vitriolic descriptions of injustice and exploitation, leaves no doubt that Müntzer saw existing conditions as justifying revolution. Luther has asserted, said Müntzer, that "I must be rebellious. So be it."

After Müntzer's capture in the aftermath of the disastrous defeat of the commoners' army at the battle of Frankenhausen (15 May 1525), two sacks of his letters and personal papers were seized. One was discovered when he was captured and was used to identify him; the other, he later told his interrogators, was to be found with his wife at Mühlhausen. The material in these sacks included correspondence from and to Müntzer, notes, drafts, book lists, and other miscellaneous papers. Several considerations governed the selection of the letters chosen for this edition. Letters to him have been excluded since the aim is to present the basic writings of Müntzer. Those chosen for inclusion are the letters that cast the most light on his major writings and on the final stages of his career, the letters that Müntzer wrote after the summer of 1523, when his conflict with Count Ernst of Mansfeld brought him to the attention of electoral authorities and when he wrote directly to both Count Ernst and Frederick the Wise.

These letters from the final year and a half of Müntzer's life are valuable from several standpoints. His formal writings are our best source for establishing the larger contours of Müntzer's thought—his theology of personal tribulation and revelation, with its socio-political values and implications—but the letters contribute to an understanding of what this theology meant in the context of specific relationships. In addition to their importance for tracing the evolution of Müntzer's thought, the letters shed much light on his actual political practice, particularly his role as an organizer of, and participant in, the Peasants' War. Several of the letters he wrote during his stay in Allstedt, or shortly thereafter, pertain to the dual strategy he pursued until the late summer of 1524. His efforts to win over political authorities and to maintain the legality of his reform program, his insistence on the right to engage in passive resistance, and his sympathy for those willing and prepared to engage in illegal activities are all illustrated in these letters. Finally, there are the letters Müntzer wrote in the last climactic months of his life, when he was fully engaged in the Peasants' War. The letters of April and May 1525, written from his new base in Mühlhausen or from peasant military encampments, reveal much about his efforts and concerns as a leader in the commoners' revolution.

Müntzer's correspondence, particularly many of the earlier letters, but also several of those written in Allstedt (see letters #47, #49, #53, #55, and #61), reveal an aspect of his personality which is not well conveyed in the generally hard tones of his formal writings: a solicitous concern to provide spiritual counsel and personal instruction. The burden of this advice is a theme that figures centrally in his formal writings—the need for suffering and tribulation in the arduous process of attaining authentic faith. In the personal, concrete context of the letters, the result is to illuminate sharply the asceticism that underlay much of Müntzer's thought. The emotional "night" of suffering which Müntzer described to the unknown George (#61) is the product of an effort to free the soul, not just from excessive worldly greed or ambition, but from all material or "creaturely" attachments. Müntzer sought to distinguish his understanding of "spiritual poverty" from the ascetic practices of monastic life, which he detested, but in the last analysis he advocated what Max Weber described as "worldly, active asceticism."[41] Both monastic asceticism and Müntzer's were metaphysically based upon a Platonic (and Augustinian) opposition of matter and spirit that denied positive value to the realm of the material, the sensual, and the creaturely. The personal cross that Müntzer called for, although encompassing much more, was rooted in the repression of fleshly desires. Müntzer's sense of the sharp conflict between the material and the spiritual, and his distaste for anything material, also underlay his notion of what counted as superstition and his support for iconoclasm (#67a).

This personal asceticism, with its body/spirit ontological dualism, also influenced the way in which Müntzer developed the dualistic political strategy that he pursued in Allstedt. Most of his letters to the Allstedt official Hans Zeiss (#46, #57, #58, and #59) are ambiguous. Müntzer hoped to influence Zeiss, but he was aware that in the last analysis, Zeiss was an agent of the electoral government. The final letter (#59) was more forthright. In it, Müntzer advocated the fusion of the two components of his strategy, calling for the public creation of a mass-based league, in which godly princes should be willing to enroll. It is noteworthy, however, that chiefly for ascetic reasons, Müntzer disavowed any intention of removing dues that league members might owe even to tyrants, and he insisted that "no one should put his trust in the league," which was, after all, an earthly and human contrivance.

Other letters deal with the relation of Müntzer's Allstedt reforms to external political authorities and other communities of Christians. The letters he wrote to persecuted sympathizers in Sangerhausen (#53 and #55) called for a readiness to sacrifice "body, property, house and plot, wife and children, father and mother, in fact the whole world" for the sake of

God's will. It was only when it came to their spiritual life, especially maintaining the purity of their consciences, that Müntzer counseled the persecuted to resist secular authority, which had no right to rule over the soul.

The same ideas, differently applied, inform many of the letters he wrote to princely and civic authorities in an effort to win sympathy and support for his program, or to admonish and rebuke those whom he saw as violators of their proper political function (#44, #45, #50, #52, #54, #65, and #67a). For Müntzer, like Machiavelli, the political obverse of love was not hate but fear. Just as spiritual enlightenment requires the soul to be purged of "creaturely" loves and attachments, so it must also overcome all earthly and worldly fears, and develop a "pure fear of God alone."[42] Good government does not hinder this ascetic process. Any government that does, for Müntzer, was by definition "tyrannical" and deserved to be overthrown. His letter to Count Ernst of Mansfeld in September 1523 (#44) threatened him with popular revolt—"the old raiment will tear"—unless he ceased prohibiting his subjects from developing spiritual poverty and fear of God.

Müntzer's revolutionary impulse was in conflict only superficially with this mystical asceticism and its injunction to endure and profit from suffering. Tribulation that purges the soul of worldly attachments and fears could also be a preparation for selfless action. He offered encouragement to the persecuted at Sangerhausen by telling them that "more than thirty groups and organizations of the elect" had been formed and that "in every territory the play is about to begin." Müntzer was of course aware that there is a contradiction between seeking reformation by legal means, with its acceptance of passive resistance, and advocating revolution. His public renunciation of the strategy of legality is indicated at the end of his Allstedt stay in his letter to Zeiss about the mass-based league and in an otherwise repectful letter to Frederick the Wise (#64), in which he informed his prince directly that he now rejected passive resistance, which only did tyrants a favor.

After fleeing Allstedt, the final ten months of Müntzer's life ran a complex, even hectic course. His first stay in Mühlhausen was brief, slightly more than a month, and ended in his expulsion at the end of September 1524. Then, after visiting Nuremberg to get his *Highly Provoked Defense* published, he engaged himself increasingly in the momentous political and military upheaval of the Peasants' War. He traveled to southwestern Germany and Switzerland, where mass rebellion was already underway. There he met with evangelical leaders sympathetic to the popular cause, preached to the insurgents, and gave them political advice. Early in 1525, he returned to the more familiar ground of Saxony and Thuringia. By late February 1525, he had again established himself at Mühlhausen, this time

more successfully, and it remained his final base of operations. In Mühlhausen, Müntzer again worked with Heinrich Pfeiffer. Under their leadership the old city council was overthrown and a new "Eternal Council"
installed to rule the city (17 March). At Mühlhausen Müntzer and Pfeiffer
also created a new league organization, the "Eternal League," whose
membership drew heavily on the lower orders of the city's population.

The letters that Müntzer wrote in April and May 1525, at the height of
the Peasants' War, forcefully convey the depth of his commitment to the
popular cause. They also reveal the circumscribed position of leadership
that he exercised in the revolution. He was, in the first instance, neither a
military commander nor a political leader. He did not have a seat on the
new "Eternal Council" at Mühlhausen. The holders of command positions in the commoners' military formations (*Haufen*, or bands) were
chosen by the rank and file and filled by laymen. Müntzer was, above all,
a charismatic spiritual guide and adviser to the insurgents—an ideologist
and propagandist attempting to incite participation, to strengthen the
military courage and political resolve of the participants, and to ensure
that decisions taken served the larger, properly defined purposes of the
revolution. Only in the latter capacity did he have some influence over
campaign decisions or political demands and programs. There is little
doubt, for example, that Müntzer influenced the conditions that the band
laid down for accepting a member of the nobility into its ranks (#79).

Müntzer's letter of 26 April to former followers and league members at
Allstedt (#75, also known as the "Manifesto to the Mansfeld Miners") is
perhaps his most ardent appeal for immediate and resolute action. "At
them, at them, at them, while the fire is hot!" he wrote. "Do not let your
swords get cold, do not let your arms go lame! Strike—cling, clang—on
the anvils of Nimrod. Cast their thrones to the ground!" And he attempted to instill courage by insisting that, "even if there are only three
of you" who seek the honor of God alone, "you need not fear a hundred
thousand." This letter, like other last letters, is suffused with the conviction that the rebellion is an apocalyptic conflict which will separate the
people of God, the elect commoners, from godless, wicked rulers. But
these letters contain little evidence of "millenarianism" or "chiliasm" in
the strict sense. During the Peasants' War, Müntzer was not consumed
with fantasies of a thousand-year reign of peace and perfection to be realized after the Second Coming.

There is an equal need for caution before charging Müntzer with "uto-
pianism," in the sense of advocating a naïve, unrealistic program of social
change, or of being out of touch with the pragmatic interests of those engaged in the rebellion. The letters show little interest in setting forth
specific socio-economic grievances or in drawing the plans for a future
society. But perhaps Müntzer felt the former were best left to those

concerned, and the latter were something to be formulated by the elect as a whole after the conflict had reached a successful conclusion. What the letters demonstrate, however, and what does not conform to the image of a utopian dreamer, is Müntzer's concern to overcome the specific problems of the revolution. How could aid be given to those from Schmalkalden in trouble at Eisenach (#81)? What could be done about the arrest of a leader and the confiscation of sorely needed funds (#84)? How could the people of Erfurt be persuaded to join the cause (#91)? He was aware of the enormous difficulties confronting an insurrection of the commoners, and he insisted that these difficulties be confronted, not wished away (#81). Given his position as spiritual leader, he naturally saw the major problem as a lack of proper mental preparation, which made it difficult to mobilize people or get them to see the larger goals.

It is also noteworthy that, despite his reputation as a bloodthirsty fanatic, Müntzer never sought to use his position of influence to promote a general liquidation of the "godless." Nothing of the kind took place in Mühlhausen or during the military campaigns in which Müntzer participated. At Frankenhausen, three captives were executed for specific reasons. Müntzer pronounced their death sentence, but he did so in the name of the assembly, which had decided their fate. There was of course considerable random violence against noble and ecclesiastical property during the military campaigns—what Engels described as the "robust vandalism" of the Peasants' War[43]—and Müntzer probably approved at least that which was directed against symbolic ecclesiastical targets (#75). In any case, his influence over such actions was minimal.

At the final battle of Frankenhausen, Müntzer is commonly seen as a man out of touch with reality, suffering from delusions of grandeur and power. The diagnosis is retrospective. When the battle began and the commoners faced the artillery barrage and cavalry charge of those whose profession was war, they panicked, broke, and ran. The result was the kind of bloodbath Müntzer is accused of favoring. More than 5,000 commoners were slaughtered, against losses of only six in the princely army. Before the battle, the insurgents did not see their spiritual leader as mentally incapacitated. Emmisaries from the princes offered the commoners clemency if they would hand Müntzer over; they refused. Nor do two of Müntzer's final letters written as a free man (#88 and #89) support such a diagnosis. Later described as efforts to "convert" the counts of Mansfeld—the brothers Ernst and Albrecht—the letters were, in fact, ringing ultimatums. The religious sympathies of the brothers differed, and Müntzer questioned the faith of both in challenging them to prove, if they could, that they were Christians and not tyrants who deserved to be overthrown. The letters were written in the name of the community of the common people, where Müntzer placed political and ecclesiastical sovereignty. If he was deceived about what would happen in battle, this was not a mental breakdown, but simply a result of his moralistic belief that God "puts more worth on his people than on you tyrants."

The three documents pertaining to the final days of Müntzer's life are of uneven reliability.[44] There is, first, his Confession, an interrogation report of statements extracted from him in the torture chamber of Count Ernst of Mansfeld's castle at Heldrungen. Müntzer's responses to the questions put to him are divided into those he made without the application of torture and those made with it. It is unclear into which category one fragment of further testimony belongs. Although what he said was clearly guided by the interests of the interrogators—coercing him into confessing to blasphemy and sedition, and into naming his co-conspirators—there is nothing in the confession that is demonstrably false and much that is confirmed by other sources. The confession therefore sheds valuable light on Müntzer's activities and beliefs, not only during the Peasants' War, but earlier in his career as well.

The interpretation of the last two documents, a retraction and a final letter to the council and community of Mühlhausen, depends partly on how one gauges the impact of torture on Müntzer's spirit. Some have held that torture broke him and that the retraction is pitiful evidence of the collapse of his commitment to a vision and purpose that had defined the trajectory of his life. Others have suggested that he may have remained unrepentant, that the final words are worthless as evidence of anything other than what he was coerced to say before his inevitable execution.

But the retraction and the letter differ in certain respects. The final letter—Müntzer's "political testament"[45]—may in fact have been written on 15 May, before his interrogation and torture, but later published with the date altered to 17 May.[46] The retraction of 17 May, although purportedly made freely by Müntzer, in order to reconcile himself before his death to the one true church, reads very much like a statement composed for him by his captors. In it, he confessed to having corrupted his listeners by preaching seditiously against the authorities ordained by God and by participating in a wanton and diabolical rebellion. He begged forgiveness for what he had done and urged obedience to divinely established authority. He also confessed to having preached many delusions and errors about the sacrament of communion—surely a subject of much greater importance to his Roman Catholic captors than it was to him. Only the final pleas have the ring of authenticity—that his wife and child be allowed to have his personal property and that the people of Mühlhausen be allowed to receive his final letter.

This last letter accepts the defeat of the revolution as the will of God, but makes no apology for having advocated or participated in it. There is no mention of the insurrection as the work of the devil, or of the obligation to obey divinely ordained authorities. The defeat is ascribed repeatedly to the commoners having pursued private, selfish interests—i.e., to the lack of interior preparation for political action, which had concerned Müntzer from the outset. The pleas to avoid further bloodshed and to petition the victors for mercy were a natural response to the evident failure of the revolt and to the futility of further resistance. The only passage in the letter in which there is mention of the revolution as "seditious" comes in connection with the obviously true point that the majority of the people of Mühlhausen were not active participants in the revolt; perhaps the passage was designed to buttress the city's appeal for mercy.

The letter also expresses a desire that the people draw a positive lesson from the military defeat. Müntzer called their attention to the need to distinguish, in what God does, between external appearance and true, interior essence; and he cited John 7:24, the only scriptural reference in the letter.[47] His followers, familiar with his principle that any passage of Scripture should be read in context, would have read the whole chapter for relevant instruction. There, assuming that they accepted the symbolic identification of Jesus and Müntzer, his readers may have found an admission that he had read the signs of the times incorrectly (verses 6 and 8), but also an assertion that the essential message that he had taught was true (16 and 28) and an awareness that in the future there would be much controversy about him and his teachings (12–13, 15, and 43).

Ten days after the retraction, on 27 May 1525, Müntzer and his associate Heinrich Pfeiffer were beheaded outside the walls of Mühlhausen. The princes punished Mühlhausen as a center of the revolution by imposing fines that damaged its economy and by depriving it of its political independence as a free imperial city. After his execution Müntzer's head was impaled and posted at the city's gate. It was still on display years later, a warning to the common people from those who found in what he taught only blasphemy and treason.

Chronology

before 1491	Müntzer's birth at Stolberg in the Harz Mountains; virtually nothing is known about his parents.
before 1506	Possible move of family to Quedlinburg and attendance at Latin school there.
October 1506	Likely matriculation at the University of Leipzig as "Thomas Müntzer from Quedlinburg."
October 1512	Matriculation at the University of Frankfurt-on-the-Oder.
before August 1513	Assistant teacher at Aschersleben and Halle. Organizer of a "league" against archbishop Ernst of Magdeburg (d. 3 August 1513).
6 May 1514	Received benefice as chantry priest at St. Michael's church in Brunswick; contact with reform-minded merchants.
after 25 July 1515	Chaplain at canonesses' convent at Frose near Aschersleben; private tutor to pupils from Brunswick.
October 1517–19	Stay at the University of Wittenberg.
1519	
11 January	Stay at Leipzig.
January–April	Stay at Orlamünde; read sermons of mystic Johann Tauler (d. 1361).
24–26 April	Preacher at St. Nicholas's church, Jüterbog, substituting for Franz Günther; conflict with Franciscans.
before 12 December	Confessor at Cistercian convent at Beuditz near Weissenfels.
1520	
May	Preacher at St. Mary's church, Zwickau, substituting for humanist Johannes Sylvius Egranus; conflict with Franciscans.
October	Transfer to St. Catherine's church, Zwickau; contact with circle of devout laity led by Nicholas Storch; conflict with Egranus.

47

1521

16 April	Departure from Zwickau following disturbances.
after 16 April	Stay at Žatec during first trip to Bohemia.
before 16 June	Death of Müntzer's mother.
16 June	Return from Bohemia; stay in the Vogtland near Elsterberg.
late June	Preparations for a second trip to Bohemia.
July–November	Stay at Prague; preaching in various churches; placed under house arrest.
1 November	*The Prague Protest* (shorter German version).
25 November	*The Prague Protest* (longer German version).
end 1521–early 1522	Return from Prague; stay in Thuringia, perhaps as teacher at St. Peter's Cloister at Erfurt.

1522

before 22 February	Resignation of chantry benefice at Brunswick.
February–March	Stay at Wittenberg or environs; conversations in Wittenberg with Philipp Melanchthon and Johannes Bugenhagen.
April	Return to Stolberg; several sermons preached there.
July–September	Stay at Nordhausen; conflict with Lawrence Süsse (?).
December (?)	Stay in Weimar; conversations with court preacher Wolfgang Stein and Jakob Strauss.
21 December	Invitation from Andreas Karlstadt to visit him at Wittenberg.
from December	Preacher and confessor at Cistercian convent at Glaucha near Halle.

1523

March	Appointed preacher at St. John's church, Allstedt, without investiture by the elector of Saxony.
about Easter	Liturgical reform initiated at Allstedt.
July	First published work, *Open Letter to the Brothers at Stolberg*, printed at Eilenburg.
after 29 July	Marriage to former nun, Ottilie von Gersen.
September	Initial conflict with Count Ernst of Mansfeld.
summer or fall	Founding of first Allstedt "League of the Elect" with thirty members.
November	Wittenberg investigation into Müntzer's teaching at Allstedt.

before 31 December	*On Contrived Faith* and *Protest or Offering* written; printed at Eilenburg early in 1524.
1524	
24 March	Destruction of the Mallerbach chapel belonging to convent of Cistercian nuns at Naundorf.
spring	*German Church Office* and *Order and Justification of the German Service at Allstedt* printed at Eilenburg.
Easter	Birth of Müntzer's son.
13–14 June	Emergency defense measures instituted at Allstedt following the arrest of a councilman, Ciliax Knauth.
9 July	Elector Frederick the Wise and Duke George of Saxony consider preventing Müntzer from publishing.
13 July	*Sermon to the Princes* preached at Allstedt castle before Duke John and others; printed shortly after at Allstedt as *An Exposition of the Second Chapter of Daniel*.
24 July	Sermon calling for the formation of a league of the people; the original Allstedt league of thirty members extended to form a new league for the defense of the gospel with more than 500 members; they assemble with arms.
31 July–1 August	Hearing of Müntzer and Allstedt officials before the ducal court at Weimar; *Witness of the First Chapter of the Gospel of Luke* presented for prepublication censorship.
early August	*German Evangelical Mass* printed at Allstedt.
6 August	Duke John considers expelling Müntzer from Saxony.
7–8 August	Flight from Allstedt.
mid-August	Arrival at Mühlhausen; preaching and reform work with the former monk, Heinrich Pfeiffer.
22–23 September	The Eleven Mühlhausen Articles, influenced by Müntzer and Pfeiffer, written during a week of disturbances.
27 September	Expulsion from Mühlhausen; start of trip to southwest Germany.
October	Meeting at Bibra with Hans Hut, who arranged the printing of the *Special Exposure of False Faith* at Nuremberg.

October or November	Stay at Nuremberg without a public appearance.
2 November	Nuremberg authorities confiscate most of the printed copies of the *Special Exposure of False Faith*.
November–December	Meeting with Johannes Oecolampadius and Ulrich Hugwald at Basel.
mid-December	Nuremberg authorities confiscate printed copies of the *Highly Provoked Defense*.
<u>1525</u>	
December–February	Stay at Griessen and nearby places in Hegau and Klettgau; preaching to insurgent peasants and giving political advice.
before 22 February	Return to Thuringia; arrested briefly at Fulda, then released.
after 22 February	Second stay in Mühlhausen. Preacher at St. Mary's church.
9 March	Mühlhausen militia mustered amid disturbances.
16–17 March	Mühlhausen city council deposed and replaced by a new "Eternal Council."
late March–April	Formation of the Eternal League of God at Mühlhausen—supporters of Müntzer.
after 26 April	Efforts to win over for the insurrection the inhabitants of Salza, Eichsfeld, Allstedt, Frankenhausen, Eisenach, Sondershausen, Ehrich, Walkenried, and Erfurt.
27 April	Formation of the Mühlhausen–Thuringian band.
30 April–6 May	On campaign with the Mühlhausen band in the Eichsfeld.
11 May	Mühlhausen contingent led by Müntzer marches to assist peasant army at Frankenhausen.
12 May	Arrival at peasant encampment at Frankenhausen.
15 May	Battle of Frankenhausen; peasants defeated and Müntzer captured; writes last letter to people of Mühlhausen.
16 May	Delivery of prisoner to Count Ernst of Mansfeld; interrogation and torture at Heldrungen castle.
25 May	Surrender of Mühlhausen; Müntzer brought to Görmar, near Mühlhausen.
27 May	Execution outside walls of Mühlhausen.

Revelation
and Revolution

1

The Prague Protest

A Protest about the Condition of the Bohemians

I, Thomas Müntzer, born in Stolberg and residing in Prague, the city of the precious and holy fighter Jan Hus,[1] think that the loud and moving trumpets [that once sounded in this city] were filled with the new praise of the holy spirit. With my whole heart, I will testify about my faith and lamentingly complain about present conditions to the whole church of the elect and to the whole world, wherever this document may be received. Christ and all of the elect who have known me from my youth on confirm such a project.

I pledge on my highest honor that I have applied my most concentrated and highest diligence in order that I might have or obtain a higher knowledge than other people of the foundations on which the holy and invincible Christian faith is based. The truth makes me so bold as to say that no pitch-smeared parson[2] and surely no pseudospiritual mònk can say anything about the foundation of the faith in even its smallest point. In addition many people have complained with me that they too, burdened by the unbearable and evident deception of the clergy, were never consoled, and that they have had to direct their desires and works carefully in the faith themselves and to elevate themselves spiritually. The clergy have never been able to discover, nor will they ever, the beneficial tribulations and useful abyss that the providential spirit meets as it empties itself.[3] The spirit of the fear of God has never possessed the clergy, but the elect firmly cling to this spirit as their only goal. The elect are submerged and drowned in an outpouring of this spirit (which the world cannot tolerate). In brief, each person must receive the holy spirit in a sevenfold way,[4] otherwise he neither hears nor understands the living God.

Freely and boldly I declare that I have never heard a single donkey-cunt doctor of theology, in the smallest of his divisions and points, even whisper, to say nothing of speaking loudly, about the order (established in God and all his creatures).[5] The most prominent among the Christians (I mean the hell-based parsons) have never had even a whiff of the whole or undivided perfection,[6] which is a uniform measure superior to all parts, 1 Corinthians 13[:10], Luke 6[:40], Ephesians 4[:3], Acts 2[:27],

15[:18?] and 17[:24–26]. Again and again, I hear nothing from the doctors of theology but the mere words of Scripture, which they have knavishly stolen from the Bible like malicious thieves and cruel murderers. They will be damned for this theft by God himself, who spoke thusly through Jeremiah 23[:18], "Behold, I have said to the prophets: I never once spoke to those who steal my words, each from his neighbor, for they deceive my people, and they usurp my words and make them putrid in their stinking lips and whoring throats. For they deny that my spirit speaks to people." So they display their monasticism with flattering, high mockery. And they say that the holy spirit gives them an invincible witness that they are children of God, Romans 8[:16], Psalm 192.[7]

It is certainly not surprising that these damned people, the clergy, in their impudence are opposed to my teachings. For Jeremiah (in the aforementioned chapter 23 [Jer. 23:18]) says of their person, "Who has stood in the counsel of the Lord? Who has perceived and heard the speech of God? Who has marked it, or who can say that he has heard God speaking?" At the present time, God will pour forth his invincible wrath over such arrogant people, hardened like blocks of oak, callous to all good, Titus 1[:7], in that they deny the basic salvation of faith. For, otherwise, they would repudiate their lives and defend the elect like an iron wall from the harm of the blasphemers, as Ezekiel says (in chapter 3, etc.). But, as they are, nothing else comes out of their hearts, brains, and snouts than derision about such revelations. Who among all people can still say that these parsons are true servants of God, bearing witness to the divine word? And that they are fearless preachers of divine grace? They have been smeared by the Nimrodian papacy[8] with the oil of the sinner, Psalm 141[:5], which flows from the head down to the feet and befouls and poisons the whole Christian church. That is to say, the parsons come from the devil, who has corrupted the foundation of their heart, as it is written in Psalm 5[:10], for they are entirely without the possession of the holy spirit. Therefore, they have been ordained by the consecration of the devil, their rightful father, who with them cannot hear the true living word of God—John [8:38–44], Isaiah 24[:18], and Hosea 4[:6?]. Zechariah 11[:17] also says that such people are scarecrows in green bean fields.[9]

And in sum, this much can be said: the parsons are damned people, John 3[:18], who have already been long condemned. And indeed they are not the least, but the most highly placed damned rogues, who have been everywhere in the world from the very beginning, set as a plague on poor people, who as a result are truly coarse. These poor people receive absolutely no justice from either God or men, as Paul adequately showed in Galatians [4:22ff.], where he describes two kinds of people.

Therefore, as long as heaven and earth stand, these villainous and

treacherous parsons are of no use to the church in even the slightest matter. For they deny the voice of the bridegroom, which is a truly certain
sign that they are a pack of devils. How could they then be God's servants, bearers of his word, which they shamelessly deny with their
whore's brazenness? For all true parsons must have revelations, so that
they are certain of their cause, 1 Corinthians 14[:30]. But the parsons,
with their stubborn hearts, say that this is impossible. Because they are
convinced of this—after they presume to have devoured the whole of
Scripture—they shall be struck down with the words of St. Paul, 2 Corinthians 3[:3], as with thunder and lightning, for there Paul makes the distinction between the elect and the damned.

The gospel and the whole of Scripture are closed to some people—
Isaiah 29[:11] and 22[:22] on the key of David, Revelation 3[:7] on the
locked book. Ezekiel unlocked past events.[10] Christ says in Luke 11[:52]
that the parsons will steal the key to this book that is locked. They lock
up Scripture and say that God must not speak to people in his own person. But where the seed falls on good ground [Mt. 13:5]—that is, in
hearts that are full of the fear of God—this is then the paper and parch-
ment on which God does not write with ink, but rather writes the true
holy Scripture with his living finger, about which the external Bible truly
testifies. And there is no more certain testimony, as the Bible verifies,
than the living speech of God, when the father speaks to the son in the
hearts of people. All of the elected people can read this Scripture, for
they increase their talent.[11] But the damned will surely let God's living
voice pass. Their heart is harder than any flint, and it repels the chisel of
the master [God] for eternity. Therefore our dear Lord calls them stone,
on which the seed falls and fails to bring forth fruit [Mt. 13:5], although
they accept the dead word with joy, great joy, and praise.

Upon my soul, only scholars and priests and monks accept the truth
from books with hearty flattery and pomp. But when God wants to write
in their heart, there is no people under the sun who are a greater enemy
of the living word of God than they. They also suffer no tribulation of
faith in the spirit of the fear of God, so they are on their way into the
fiery lake,[12] where the false prophets will be tormented with the Antichrist for ever and ever, amen. Moreover, they do not want to be disturbed by the spirit of the fear of God. So they mock the tribulation of
faith for eternity. They are precisely the people about whom Jeremiah
8[:8–9] speaks, for they have no experience of holy Scripture that they
have sensed and that they can apply in their exposition. They have no
other manner of writing than that of hypocrites, who throw away the
truthful word and all the same need it. So they will never hear it in an
eternity of eternities. For God speaks only in the suffering of creatures, a
suffering that the hearts of the unbelievers do not have because they be-

come more and more hardened. Unbelievers can and will not empty themselves. They have a slippery foundation and loathe their owner [God]. Therefore, in a time of tribulation, they collapse. They retreat from the word that became flesh. In no way does the unbeliever want to become conformed to Christ through suffering; rather he seeks conformity only with honey-sweet thoughts.

Therefore, it is these damned parsons who take away the true key [to divine truth] and say that such a way [as direct revelations] is fantastic and fool-headed, and that it is most impossible. These are the ones already condemned, with skin and hair, to eternal damnation. Why should I not damn them as well, John 3[:18]? Since they are not sprinkled with the spirit of the fear of God on the third day, how can they be cleansed on the seventh day, Numbers 19[:19]? So they have already been cast into the abyss of the pit [hell].

But I do not doubt the [common] people.[13] Oh, you righteous, poor, pitiful little band! How thirsty you still are for the word of God! For now are the days when none, or only a few, know what they should hold or which side they should join. They would gladly do what is best, and yet they do not know what this is. For they do not know how to conform to or comply with the testimony that the holy spirit speaks in their hearts. They are so greatly disturbed by the spirit of the fear of God that in them the prophecy of Jeremiah [4:4] has indeed become true, "The children have prayed for bread and there was no one there to break it for them." Oh, oh, no one broke it for them! There have been many money-hungry rogues who have thrown to the poor, poor, poor little people the inexperienced papal text of the Bible, as one usually throws bread to dogs. But they have not broken it with the knowledge of the holy spirit. That is, they have not opened their reason, so that they might recognize the holy spirit in themselves. For the parsons, even if they were all gathered together in one pile, do not have the power to make a single individual sufficiently sure that he has been chosen for eternal life. What more can I say?

Parsons are lords, who only devour, swill, and steal, day and night seeking to contrive how they can feed themselves and get many fiefs, Ezekiel 34[:2,8,10]. They are not like Christ, our beloved Lord, who compares himself to a hen that makes her chicks warm.[14] Nor do they give milk to the disconsolate, forsaken people from the fountain of the inexhaustible admonitions of God. For they have not tested their faith. They are like a stork that gobbles up frogs in the fields and ponds, and then afterwards spits them out, just as raw, to its young in the nest. So, too, are the profit-seeking and interest-boosting parsons who gobble whole the dead words of Scripture and then spit out the letter and their inexperienced faith (which is not worth a louse) to the righteous, poor, poor people. The result of what they do is that no one is certain of his soul's salvation. For these servants of Beelzebub bring to market only a fragment of holy Scripture. Indeed, no one knows if he is worthy of God's love or hate. This poison comes out of the abyss, for each and every whoremongering priest has the devil as his most deceitful and villainous prince, as the Revelation of John [Rev. 13:4–8] proclaims.

The parsons scatter the sheep of God so widely through this evil that no one looks to the church any more. For no one there separates good people from the impudent band that is unknown [to God]. There is also no knowledge of the diseased and the healthy—that is, no one pays attention to the fact that the church is rotten to its floor and foundations with damned people. For the sheep do not know that they should hear the living voice of God. That is, they should all have revelations, Joel 2[:28–29] and David in Psalm 87[:7]. The office of the true shepherd is simply that the sheep should all be led to revelations and revived by the living voice of God, for a master should teach the knowledge of God, Matthew 23[:10,26]. This has not happened for a long time, and, as a result, the elect and the damned are just the same in many respects, and the elect have been almost swallowed up by the damned. Therefore, nearly the whole world also thinks that it is not necessary that Christ himself must preach his own gospel to the elect.

I affirm and swear by the living God: he who has not heard the righteous, living word of God out of the mouth of God, [and can discern] what is Bible and what is Babel, is nothing but a dead thing. However, the word of God penetrates the heart, brain, skin, hair, bones, limbs, marrow, juice, force, and power. It is able to stride in a different way from that about which our foolish, scrotum-like doctors of theology prattle. Otherwise, one can neither be saved nor found. The elect must clash with the damned, and the power of the damned must yield before that of the elect. Otherwise you cannot hear what God is. Whoever has once received the holy spirit as he should, can no longer be damned, Isaiah 55[:3] and 60[:15,21], John 6 [Rev. 6:44–45]. Oh ho, woe, woe to those preachers who proclaim the way of Baal! For they have uttered the words in their snouts, but their hearts are more than a thousand times a thousand miles away from the word.

Thus, people live without true shepherds. The experience of faith is never preached to them. The Jewish, heretical parsons[15] may well say that such a strong thing is not necessary for salvation. They say that one can indeed flee the wrath of God with good works, with precious virtues. However, the people do not learn from all this what God is in experience, what true faith is, what strong virtue is, and what good works are after conversion to God. Therefore it would not be surprising if God were to destroy us all, the elect with the damned, in a much more severe deluge than that of former times, and crumble us to dust and rubble in body and life. And it would also be no surprise if he were to damn all the people who have suffered these cursed seductions. For is our faith indeed not oriented more to the face of Lucifer and Satan than to that of God? And the devil is coarser than wood and stone.

In my view it is not without reason that all other peoples call our faith monkey business. For it is evident and cannot be denied that unbelievers have demanded a serious accounting from us. And we have returned an answer from a chicken coop—with immense pride we have spattered great books full, saying, "We have written this and that in our laws; for if Christ said this, Paul has written that; the prophets have foretold this and that; holy mother church (a madam in a whorehouse) has proclaimed this and that." Indeed, the Nero-like, "holy," most wooden pope and chamber pot at the brothel of Rome has commanded this and that great thing, defending them with the ban of excommunication. And in the opinion of the little straw doctors of theology, for the sake of the conscience this ban is not to be despised.

My good reader, let the words [of the Bible] simply be different or arranged differently. Then our theologians could not defend the Christian faith with their inexperienced Bible, no matter how great the twaddle they talk. Oh, alas, alas, woe, woe, woe to the hell-fiery and Asmodaeical[16] parsons who publicly seduce the people.

Yet no one wants to see or hear it when such reasons for our faith, and similar ones, are presented to unbelievers. Do you not think that non-Christians, too, have a brain in their heads? They may indeed think to themselves, What kind of assurance of faith is this which comes from books? Perhaps [the authors of Scripture] have lied in what they have written? How can one know whether it is true? Without a doubt Turks and Jews would gladly hear our invincible basis for believing, and many of the elect would also like the same thing. But the devil's parsons wrinkle up their noses and damn them forthwith. And yet the parsons cannot judge correctly, since they deny that a person can have revelations. They speak with the mere words of Scripture, "He who believes and is baptized will be saved" [Mk. 16:16]. Such a firmly grounded account, and no other, they give to our opponents. It cannot be otherwise, nor do I perceive it differently, than that the parsons who thus seek to expound the faith so badly to our enemies are completely mad and foolishly inane. One should call such rascals to account, and those who offer such a lame excuse should be shoved into the abyss of hell. Is not this [defense of the faith] much more insane than insanity itself? Who can complain about it and bemoan it enough? Do we lack blood in our body and life that affairs proceed in such a mad and stupid way?

Does one not feel at least a small spark that virtually seeks to expand into tinder?[17] Indeed, one feels it and I feel it too. I have very bitterly pitied the fact that the Christian church has become so badly crushed that God could only do it more damage if he wanted to annihilate it altogether. But God would not want to do this except for the diarrhea-makers [the clergy], for they have taught the people to pray to Baal. They are so highly "worthy" that one may say in the midst of them what Daniel says [Dan. 9:5,10], that they have not practiced the judgments of God.

I have read here and there in the histories of the ancient fathers of the church. And there I find that, after the death of the pupils of the apostles, the untarnished, virgin church soon became a whore at the hands of seducing parsons. For parsons have always wanted to have a ruling position in the church. Hegesippus and Eusebius[18] and others testify to all this. [The downfall of the church came about] because the people neglected to exercise their right to elect their priests. And it has not been possible to hold a true council since the onset of such negligence.[19] Be this as it may, it is still the work of the devil, for matters are only treated in councils and synods as they would be in a child's game. Things dealt with are the ringing of bells, chalices, hoods, lamps, and [ecclesiastical titles like] procurators and sextons. But no one has once—no, not once!—opened his snout concerning the true, living word of God. Nor has any thought been given to the proper liturgy.

Such errors had to occur so that the works of all people, the elect and the damned, would be fully manifest.[20] In our time God wants to separate the wheat from the chaff [Mt. 13:26], so that one can grasp, as though it were bright midday, who it is that has seduced the church for such a long time. All the villainy, even in the highest places, must come to light. Oh ho, how ripe are the rotten apples! Oh ho, how mushy the elect have become! The time of the harvest is at hand! Thus God himself has appointed me for his harvest. I have made my sickle sharp, for my thoughts are zealous for the truth and my lips, skin, hands, hair, soul, body, and my life all damn the unbelievers.

In order that I may do this properly, I have come into your country, my most beloved Bohemians. I desire from you only that which your diligence should demand—you should study the living word of God out of God's own mouth. Through this you will see, hear, and grasp how the whole world has been seduced by deaf parsons. Help me, for the sake of Christ's blood, to fight against such high enemies of the faith. In the spirit of Elias, I want to ruin them in your eyes. For the new apostolic church will arise first in your land, and afterward, everywhere. I want to be prepared, if in church people question me in the pulpit, to do enough to satisfy each and every one. If I cannot demonstrate such a skillful mastery of the truth, then may I be a child of both temporal and eternal death. I have no greater pledge. Whoever despises such warnings as these is

2
Open Letter to the Brothers at Stolberg

A Frank, Open Letter to His Dear Brothers at Stolberg to Avoid Inappropriate Rebellion

I wish you, dear brothers, firstly, salvation with the spirit of Jesus. It is staggeringly foolish that many of the elect friends of God[1] think that God must hasten to remedy Christendom and speedily come to help them, while, nevertheless, no one longs for or stresses becoming poor in spirit through suffering and perseverence, Matthew 5[:3], Luke 6[:20]. Whoever has not put the poverty of his spirit to the test is not worthy of being ruled by God. He is not worthy of undergoing tribulations by the devil or the slightest creature. Thus, everything has to go well for him, according to his interests as he perceives them. But should he be reduced to genuine, naked poverty of the spirit, then (according to human opinion) God must also have abandoned him. And the person who is truly poor in spirit must divest himself of any solace in "creaturely" goods.[2] But as long as the elect do not exert themselves to heed God's actions, it is not possible for God to do anything about it. It suits the divine, fatherly goodness to allow the tyrants to rage more and more,[3] 1 Samuel 8[:7–18]. Through this [oppression] the countenances of his elect will be filled with shame and vice, so that they seek the name, fame, and honor of God alone, Psalm 83[:17–19]. For the reward and the prize of the lazy among the elect[4] is exactly the same as the portion of the damned, Luke 12[:45]. The true kingdom of God begins with genuine pleasure when the elect first see what God lets them discover in themselves, through his action, in the experience of the spirit. People who have not experienced the bitter opposite of faith do not know this, for they have not believed against belief, or hoped against hope, or hated against the love of God,[5] 1 Corinthians 2[:5]. Therefore they do not know what is harmful or advantageous to Christendom, for they are not spiritually tested. They cannot believe that God himself instructs the person with a diligent, active goodness and that he tells him everything that is necessary for him. Therefore, the whole world lacks the core of blessedness, which is the faith that we are not to expect so much [temporal]

61

good from God as that he wants to be our teacher, Matthew 23[:8–10], James 3[:15–17].

Oh, this enormous, greatly hardened lack of faith, which wants to assist itself with the dead letter [of Scripture] and denies the [living] finger [of God], which writes in the heart, 2 Corinthians 3[:2ff]. What do foolish people know about what causes them to be Christians rather than pagans, or why the Koran is not as true as the Gospel? They cannot refute the contrary [view] from the order [of things], which the *Raka*,[6] that is, evil-doers, deny. Therefore, it is highly important that we let God rule and that we truly know that our faith does not deceive us, because we have suffered the action of the living word and we know the difference between what God does and what creatures do. But this is not pleasing to the world.

There [in knowledge of God] we don the jewels of the king [Ps. 93:1]. There is strength when we perceive the power of God penetrating us. We will be girded just like Peter, John 21[:18], Luke 12[:35]. Only then will the whole world be confirmed as the assembly place of the elect, so that the world obtains a Christian governance that no sack of gunpowder[7] will be able to overthrow. But as long as our zeal fails to grow, fails to in-crease with the spirit of truth, our souls will not be ready to become a throne of God. Rather, he who sits on the throne of pestilence [the devil] shall rule him who will not let God rule him. Therefore, the truth will not free such a person but instead his impudent boldness, which he must finally reject [when he has suffered] harm and shame.

Thus, each [of the elect] who is certain of his cause must perceive the waves within the streams [Ps. 93:3] which fall upon our spirit. A clever sailor can and must not avoid the waves; instead he must breast them in masterly fashion. All lack of faith and sin show the elect the importance of [divine] judgment, Psalm 119. For the elect perceive daily that God does not judge according to human judgment. Rather, what the world de-spises, God elevates; what to the world is foolishness is wisdom in God's eyes, etc. Therefore, no person whose faith is untested can rule, for a ruler must have the living judgment of God, Wisdom 6[:1–11], John 7[:24]. God's testimonies must be absolutely credible to those who pronounce judgment, so that the house of God, the human soul, is not stained. Our cause must be sustained by the highest knowledge in God of God, so that it endures forevermore.[8]

I wanted, dear brothers, to have the Ninety-third Psalm printed for you. For I hear that you are most boastful, do not study, and are negligent. I also hear that when you have been drinking, you talk a lot about our cause, but when you are sober, you are as fearful as sissies. Therefore, dearest brothers, remedy your lives. Guard yourselves against revelry,

Luke 21[:34], 1 Peter 5[:8]. Flee pleasures and their lovers, 2 Timothy 3[:5]. Conduct yourselves more bravely than you have, and write me about how far you have increased your talent [Lk. 19:12–27]. I commend you to God and send greetings to all who desire to do God's will according to the testimony of this instruction.

Allstedt, 18 July, in the year of our Lord 1523, Thomas Müntzer.

3

Protest or Offering

The Protest or Offering of Thomas Müntzer from Stolberg in the Harz Mountains, curate at Allstedt, concerning his teachings and derived from true Christian faith and baptism. 1524

Listen world! I preach to you the crucified Jesus Christ for the new year, and you and me with him. If what I say pleases you, accept it. If not, reject it.[1]

FIRST

I, Thomas Müntzer from Stolberg in the Harz, a servant of the living son of God, through the immutable will and steadfast mercy of God the father, offer and wish all of you elect friends of God in the holy spirit, the pure and righteous fear of the Lord and the peace to which the world is an enemy. After the omniscient and attentive father has transformed you into pure wheat and assigned you to the fruitful and productive land, you have come to the point—may it pitiably be lamented to God—where no great difference can be perceived between yourselves and the tares. For godless sons of concealed, deceitful evil gleam and twinkle far, far over you from front-and rear.[2] And because the painted masks of the red blooming roses and the cornflowers and also the prickly thistles [gleam and twinkle] so high [above you], your miserable and piteous sobbing has been transformed into a displeasing specter and a highly scorned mockery, and has been nearly obliterated. Such fervent sobbing and longing for God's eternal will is without a doubt the only undeceiving footstep for apostolic and true Christendom to follow, for it is living water that springs out of the hard cliffs [see Jn. 4:10, 14 and Ps. 77:17ff.], as the source and origin of the [faith of the] elect.[3] No other way can and should be found to help miserable, poor, pitiable, needy, coarse, and fallen Christendom, except that the attention of the elect be drawn to this sobbing and longing through keen desire, work and unsparing diligence.

64

SECOND

Otherwise [i.e., without this guide] the Christian church is more mad and nonsensical than the raging foolishness which is found among all the other peoples of the earth. This foolishness within Christendom, as is evident— indeed, as is palpable—is much more unclean and proud in our times than in the beginning [of the church] since now all the cunning tricks of every honey-sweet villainy have fully unfolded. And sometimes these tricks bedeck themselves with a contrived faith, and sometimes they preciously disguise themselves with glistening works, so that all creatures are also always caught up in them, just as a rascal is thrown into hell. So much is endured at the hands of the godless!

THIRD

The damage which has been done to the uncomprehending world must be rigorously acknowledged in all its sources. Otherwise it is not possible for the understanding father to lay aside his gracious rod of chastisement. For the heartfelt truth must liberate all the people elected by God from those who have brought about such irreparable damage to common Christendom. Therefore, it is a displeasing abomination to sit in the holy place of God and to let God's children live without discipline and free as cattle. The only consolation of the miserable church [i.e. Christ] expects that the elect should and must become conformed to him and heed God's action with manifold suffering and correction.

FOURTH

In the first place, we must consider carefully how we Christians have become such a thoroughly impenitent people that we have made our precious Christian faith into such a frivolous and unprofitable thing. In truth, we are boastful, ready to write, indeed even ready to write great booksfull, full of spatterings,[4] saying, "I believe, I believe!" Nevertheless we go around every day with vain bickering and cares about temporal affairs. And from day to day we become still more greedy for profits. And we say, "I believe, I hold that the whole Christian faith is true and my hope in God is firm and strong," etc.

My dear fellow! You do not know to what you are saying yes and no. You have not let God root out your thorns and thistles in the slightest way. You do not believe this? Then certainly your [alleged] faith about higher things is fabricated, for you are untrue and wavering about smaller matters. How can the greatest things be entrusted to you?

FIFTH

Know yourself, daughter of Zion,[5] how you were many years ago at the time of the apostles and their pupils. These [true Christians] took care with watchful rigor that the enemy, the adversary of all pious people, was not able to mix tares with the wheat. Therefore, only mature people, after lengthy instruction, were accepted as students [or prospective members] of the church. And because of the instruction they received, they were called catechumens. Then there was not the kind of superstition that relies more on the [external] signs of holiness than on its interior essence. Oh, what can I say! [God][6] never once expressed in a single thought or demonstrated in any of the books of the teachers of the church, from the beginning of their writings, what true baptism is. I bid all the literalistic scholars to show me where it stands in holy Scripture that a single infant was baptized by Christ and his apostles, or to show me where the written proof is that our children are to be baptized as they are now. Indeed, though you brag much about infant baptism, you fail to see that neither Mary, the mother of God, nor the disciples of Christ were baptized with water. If our salvation depended on infant baptism, then we should also accept a honey-sweet Christ;[7] and being so ignorant, it would be better to let ourselves be sprinkled with good Malvasian wine[8] than with water.

SIXTH

The right baptism is not understood. Therefore the entry into Christendom has become a ritualistic monkey business. From this foundation in sand, the scribes have enormously deceived our miserable, sad mother, dear Christendom. Thus, in patchwork fashion, the scribes have said, John 3[:5], "Who has not been baptized in water and the holy spirit will not enter the kingdom of God." These words are the absolute truth, but alone they conceal from poor Christendom the unanimous, entire [gospel] of the evangelist John. For the knowledge of God [suggested by one passage of Scripture] must be verified through a strict comparison of all the words that stand clearly written in both testaments, 1 Corinthians 2[:6–12]. Indeed, our scribes have not really opened their eyes. They have thought that the seventh chapter [of John] is unrelated to the third. [In the seventh chapter, Christ,] the source of truth, says [Jn. 7:37f.], "If anyone thirsts, let him come unto me and drink. For he who believes in me, as Scripture says, the stream will flow from his body, the living water." He said this about the holy spirit, whom the faithful were to receive in the future. You see, dear companions, the evangelist interprets himself and speaks about the waters as the prophets do. For the waters are the movement of our spirit in the divine spirit, as John himself explains, through Isaiah, in the first chapter [see Jn. 1:23 and Is. 40:3].

But, in the second chapter, [see Jn. 2:9] these waters of ours become wine. Our spirits are moved to accept suffering happily. And in the third chapter, [Jn. 3:23] John baptizes where there is much water, much movement of the spirit, until one can hear and grasp the voice of [Christ,] the bridegroom. And in the fourth chapter [Jn. 4:10], the waters spring from the ground of the fountain of life. In the fifth chapter, John agrees exactly with all the prophets concerning the movement of the water. In the sixth chapter [Jn. 6:19], after all the waves, the true son of God is seen walking on the waters. Expanding on this interpretation, the seventh chapter corresponds with the third, and the third with all the others.[9] Nicodemus [see Jn. 7:50 and 3:1] was moved through signs to come to Christ. Therefore, Christ referred him to the water [Jn. 3:5], as he did the other scribes as well. The sign of Jonah [see Lk. 11:29 and Mt. 12:39] also has no other meaning, even if the scribes get angry about this.

SEVENTH

Consider well now whether you want to penetrate to the heart of the matter, where the foundation of the church in mud and sand wobbles and shakes. Here in [the ceremony of baptism] is the source [of the evil] that has sprung up so very seductively before all of the elect, along with all the other pagan ceremonies or rituals of the whole abomination in the holy place. Since infants are made Christians and the status of catechumens has been given up, Christians have become children, even though Paul forbade this, because then true understanding vanishes from the church. The right baptism has been veiled with the accursed, hypocritical institution of the godfather,[10] which is much praised with great pomp, and is clung to the way a dog hangs onto a sausage. Ah, here is the soup that Cerberus cannot eat up.[11] And then came the immoral woman with her red dress,[12] the bloodshedder, the Roman church, and it was in disagreement with all the other churches. And this Roman church was of the opinion that its ceremonies and rituals, patched together out of paganism, were the best, and that all others were displeasing abominations. Oh, what can I say about it in my pain? All of Asia [Minor][13] was put under the ban and given over to the devil, as people of the flesh are accustomed to do and for childish reasons—in this case, because the fathers of [Asia Minor] began Easter on the fourteenth day of April. The Roman church dealt with all peoples in this same way, and so they have most lamentably laid waste the whole world, all on account of their meaningless trivialities. And they have made the rest of the world an apostate from our communion. Oh, what a miserable thing it is that the lands won through the precious blood of the apostles have been given over to the devil because of insignificant rituals! Therefore God blinded us more than other nations and made us err gravely. We have knowledge only of ceremonies and ecclesiastical rituals; and this all comes from a misunderstood baptism.

EIGHTH

Among us [Germans] the Christian faith has nearly collapsed due to the Romans and other sects. On the basis of the Bible, the Roman church in the beginning presented all sects to us as hateful, so that without any basis a complete distaste for these sects also became natural to us. In addition, our own cause also became so unintelligible to us, through hateful squabbles, that we have not had a single thought about the origin of faith in the heart. I say without reservation, not to abuse us but out of pity for us, that no doctor of the church has allowed this [real source of faith] to be glimpsed even slightly. Therefore the good father let his precious field go to seed with many tares, indeed great tree stumps. If our forefathers had read Isaiah 5[:1ff.], they would at least have gotten a whiff of faith's origins.

This much is certain. If mighty God lets errors or heresy arise within the host of the elect, he proves that people do not grow in faith or that they have a cunning, deceitful faith. Why then do [prelates] seek to condemn heretics, when they themselves have not been forged in the faith? The son of God says [Jn. 16:7f.] that, when he sends the holy spirit, he will surely punish the world on account of its unbelief. Since the world does not want to recognize its unbelief in itself, it must find it in other apparent unbelievers, whether they are so willingly or not. For, just as they, in our highly opinionated eyes, are erring people, so are we in the eyes of God. Because we let ourselves think that we are healthy in our faith and that we need no doctor, God always smites us with one wound after another. In such blindness and insensitivity we wander, still not wanting to believe anyone who says that we are blind, blind.

NINTH

If our eyes are to be opened, dearest brothers, we must first recognize our blindness, which we manifest especially in a contrived faith and afterward in glittering works. So we must not do what the scribes did, John 9[:29], where Christ's miracle of healing the blind man revealed their proud ignorance. For the scribes said, "We know that God spoke with Moses,"[14] just as now, you dear brothers, your scribes also do when they say, "We know that the Scriptures are right." It is true, they are right—

but in order to kill you and not to give you life. For the Scriptures have not been left on earth to vivify you. Rather, they have been written for us ignorant men so we may see that the holy faith of the mustard seed [see Mt. 17:20 and Lk. 17:6] is very hard for everyone, on account of powerful and unavoidable fear, just as if there were no Scripture. Should I accept the Scriptures because the church has accepted them outwardly and knows nothing further about faith's origins? What would I be doing? If I were to look around at the whole sphere of the earth, considering all its peoples, then I would see that heathens also believe that their gods are pious saints, vassals of the supreme God. Further, the Turks boast of their Mohammed as much as we do about our Christ. In addition the Jews, outwardly considered, have a more stable foundation for their faith than other ignorant, rash peoples. They quarrel with one another about Scripture (and it is a useful quarrel), while we alone squabble about honors and temporal goods. The Jews have their heritage, following a constant tradition for four thousand years, while we set up a new bylaw every day—which we then observe only for reasons of money or honors, until we get what we think is coming to us. For everyone recites our law, *Expiravit*, that thin tune.[15] The Jews help their brothers, we take from ours. And no one is as dear to us as we are to ourselves. Look, you most dearly beloved brothers, I tell you in friendly truth (although it is a bitter herb to our untrained hearts), we Christians have totally and completely devoured the filthy leaven of the whole world, devoured it so completely that it stinks out of our throats in a hateful and unsightly way.

TENTH

First of all, let us examine closely the "reasonable" heathen faith. Then we will find that they profess that there is an unchanging God, and that all pious people who do something special for the benefit of the world become companions of God, just as we, in our own way, believe regarding our saints. So that we tender plants[16] do not have to suffer, we call on the saints in our troubles, and yet in doing this we do not want to be called heathens but Christians. In the last analysis, however, it is evident that this attitude must yet cost many an honest person his neck before we have truly realized our malice.

ELEVENTH

Furthermore, if I also consider carefully the Turks, I find in the Koran, which Mohammed wrote, that Jesus of Nazareth was the son of a pure virgin; but (Mohammed said further) it does not have to be true that Jesus was nailed to a cross. The reason he advanced is this: the powerful, single God is much too kind to permit such a thing to come about through evil people. Therefore, Mohammed said, the true God handed over an evildoer in Jesus's place, and he was crucified; and the ignorant people were so deceived that they did not perceive the omnipotent power of God.

Look, you miserable false brother, does not the whole [Christian] world have exactly the same fantastic, sensual spirit, only in a more cosmetic way, although it still wants to ornament itself most properly with holy Scripture? And although it greatly boasts about the faith of the prophets and the apostles? But was not life extremely hard for them? So, should our faith then cost us no more than being wanton and satiated? Ah, dear sirs, stop! Throw the makeup boxes to the devil; do not paint yourselves like Jezebel, who is accustomed to murdering Naboth [see 1 Kg. 21:1–4, and 2 Kg. 9:30]. She has not yet been completely eaten by the dogs [1 Kg. 21:23, and 2 Kg. 9:36f.]. Rather, she lives and, ah! has a hard life punishing the servants of God.

TWELFTH

First of all, dear Christians, we should tweak our own noses and see if we are also like the heathens. The heathens pray to Venus, Juno, etc. so that they might have fine children. And in order that childbirth might be painless they have other divinities as well. In the same way, we call upon the mother of God [for children] in honor of her conception. And [for birthpain], we then call upon St. Margaret, although it is against the express text of the Bible [Gen. 3:16], "Thou shalt bear thy children in pain." And we never think of begetting our children in the fear of God. Do you not see that our whole life rages with open idolatry against the justice of the divine will? Still, we do not want to see this and cannot see it. This blindness produces a faith in God which is spread by untrue scribes and which today, more than at the beginning of our faith—may it be lamented to God—becomes increasingly nonsensical. As a result of this same blindness, we have also become proud, like our opponents, and we quickly want to throw to the dogs anyone who does not agree with us in everything. That such things occur is an enormous presumption. Because many people do not recognize the action of God, they think that one can easily come to the Christian faith, if only one thinks about what Christ said. No, my good man, you must suffer and feel how God himself roots out tares, thistles, and thorns for you from your fruitful land—that is, from your heart. Otherwise nothing good grows there, but only the raging devil disguised as light and beautiful little cornflowers, etc.

Even if you have devoured the whole Bible, it will not help you; you must suffer the sharp plowshare [see Ps. 129:3]. If you have no faith, then

God himself will give you one and will himself teach you this same faith. If this is to happen, you dear scribe, then, in the first place, the book of Scripture would also have to be locked to you.[17] Then, contrary to reason, no creature can open it for you, even if you break your head open trying. God must gird your loins. Indeed, you must let God, through his action, throw off the whole raiment in which you are dressed by everything creaturely. And you must not do as the clever ones do, citing one quotation here and another there, without a careful comparison of the whole spirit of the Scriptures. Otherwise we have thoroughly confused the gate [i.e., the correct entry to faith,] with the window [see Jn. 10:1]. Even if we get hold of a phrase from Scripture, it is much too abbreviated for us if we do not grasp the other texts next to it. Take, for example, when one says that Christ alone accomplished everything. This is much, much too abbreviated. If you do not grasp the head [Christ] together with the members, how can you then follow in his footsteps? [Reclining] on a good insulating fur or on a silk cushion, I assume.

THIRTEENTH

The papists have given indulgences forgiving pain and guilt. And should we now straightaway build on such a foundation? This would be as if an old house were whitewashed and we said that it was a new house. We would be doing just this if we preached a honey-sweet Christ, one fully pleasing to our murderous nature.[18] Yes, if our nature does not need to suffer and if it is given everything freely, what would we be proposing? Would we not be doing exactly as the Turks? Mohammed denied the historicity of the suffering of Christ, our savior. And we want to disavow this suffering in a clandestine, thievish way, so that we do not need to suffer. And thus we let the wheat and the thorns entangle and splendidly ornament each other. Oh no, my brothers, this is not the right way to life; it contradicts clear texts of Scripture—Matthew 7[:14], 1 Peter 2[:21], 1 John 2[:3ff.], and John 14[:15f.]—for it is easy for us to accept. In short, the narrow way must be followed, in which all knowledge is gained, not from external appearances, but from the most dearly beloved will of God in his living word and is experienced in every kind of tribulation of faith, as Christ himself says (in the abovementioned seventh chapter of Matthew [Mt. 7:14]). Then the person first becomes aware that his house— that is, he himself—is built on immovable stone.

St. Peter, and we with him, did not understand such a firmly based building. Even though his foundation was based on the rock [see Mt. 16:18, Lk. 22:56ff.], he still had to fall, for he was not secured everywhere. And his faith was not diminished through such falls, rather it was greatly increased. Since he recognized his impudence,[19] after the fall he was secure—and not before. But we must examine this in light of the truth that the apostles and all the prophets could not maintain an enduring relationship with the word of God until all the tares and the impudence of a contrived faith had been uprooted. And those of us learned in Scripture still want to fancy that it is sufficient if we have the Scriptures, and that we do not need to perceive the power of God. It clearly states in Romans 1[:16] that the gospel is a power of God for those to whom it is not concealed. Since I must know whether God has spoken this and not the devil, I must be able to distinguish the actions of both in the foundation of the soul. Otherwise I let myself be easily convinced by crazy talk, as the untested scribes do to themselves and to others, Matthew 7[:29]. Their speech lacks the power of God for they speak with a shameless brazenness, saying that they have no other faith or spirit than that which they have stolen from Scripture. But they do not call it "stolen," rather "believed." The light of natural reason is so conceited that it believes one can come to faith so easily.

FOURTEENTH

If it is only preached that faith must make us justified and not works, the goal is missed by far.[20] This is presumptuous talk. For in such talk nature is not shown how a person comes to faith through God's action, which he must await above and beyond all things. Otherwise faith is not worth a trifle and is false down to its foundations with respect to our effective contribution. Instead one must say how it feels to be poor in spirit, and confirm this feeling through the spiritual poverty of our forefathers from and in the Bible. For, in every passage of Scripture, God declares his omnipotent power, which has been effective in all his elect. Thus, the complete context of every word of Scripture must be grasped in its entirety, so that the cunning theft of the literal text is avoided.

FIFTEENTH

I have let this, my explanation and offering, come to you now, my most dearly beloved brothers, in a printed and publicly distributed discourse because I know for a fact (forgive me for God's sake) that at present you will not come to either faith or rightly produced works. Those who manage the gospel praise faith to the highest. The commonsense view of human nature wants to imagine this: "Ah, if nothing more is necessary for salvation than faith, oh how easily you will attain it!" Natural reason says further, "Yes, without a doubt you will attain it since you have been born to Christian parents, you have never despaired a single time, and you will be steadfast. Yes, yes, I am a good Christian." Ah, but can I be saved so easily? Shame, shame on the parsons! Ah, the cursed ones, how they have let faith become so hard for me, etc.

So the people then think they will be saved by crazy talk, and from start to finish they read or hear nothing about what one writes concerning faith or works. And they want to be nicely evangelical with many boastful words. This is a powerful, coarse, and foolish error. If this error could only be grasped! Many people still favor allowing this error free reign, and they let it cloak their disgrace.

SIXTEENTH

Some honest people, who do not allow their consciences to be satisfied with such easy chatter, are now opposed to this error; they recognize it is true that the way to heaven must indeed be a narrow way and that it cannot be found in carnal pleasure. But they fall off the narrow path into a thorny hedge—that is, into heathen ceremonies or rituals, into many fasts and prayers, etc. Yet they think that they have found the right way. Oh ho, those who let themselves be content with this heathen way and who do not allow for any uncertainty, or long for something outside themselves, are not to be helped. They become arrogant devils, and they are most certainly damned. But those who work their way through both contrived faith and outward works, as the coarsest sinners also do with their misdeeds, see that the word which is connected to right faith is not a hundred thousand miles from them. Indeed, they see how it springs from the abyss of the heart.[21] They perceive how it descends from the living God. They are well aware that to receive this word one must be sober, freed from all desires, and one must await such a word and assent from God with the greatest effort. Then a person does not believe because he has heard it from other people. It is the same to him whether the whole world accepts it or rejects it, as 1 John 4[:5-6] fervently testifies. But his inner eye[22] waits a long, long time for the Lord and for his hands—that is, for the divine action. And so he finally receives enlightenment about the whole activity of the spirit. Thus, one must wait upon the irrevocable mercy of God.

SEVENTEENTH

It is zealous expectation of the word which initially makes a Christian. This same expectation must suffer the word at first, and in this suffering there can be no consolation in [the hope of] eternal forgiveness of our deeds. In suffering, the person thinks that he utterly lacks faith. Yes, according to his own judgment, he finds no faith. He feels or finds only a paltry desire for the right faith. And this desire is so weak that he scarcely perceives it and does even this only with difficulty. Nevertheless this desire must finally burst forth, saying, "Ah, what a miserable man I am! What stirs in my heart? My conscience consumes all my vitality and strength and all that I am. Oh, what should I do now? I have gone mad without receiving any consolation from God or any creature. There in suffering God torments me with my conscience, with unbelief, despair, and with blasphemy. Externally I am attacked by sickness, poverty, misery, and every need, by evil people, etc. And this punishment pierces me internally much more than externally. But oh, how gladly I would like to rightly believe, if only everything were suitable for it, if only I knew the right way! Yes, I would even run to the end of the world!"

At this point, the pious scribes appear, when such saddened people (who are really the very best) come to them. And the sad one says, "Dear honorable, attentive, highly learned one," and much such drivel. Then the sad one says, "Ah, I, a poor man, have gone crazy. I scarcely believe in either God or in any creatures. I am in such misery that I scarcely know whether or not I would rather be dead than alive. Give me good advice, for God's sake, for I greatly fear I have been taken by the devil."

Then the learned ones, who find it enormously difficult to open their traps, for among them a word costs many a pretty penny, say, "Ah ha, dear man, if you do not want to believe, you can go to the devil."

Then the poor creature answers, "Oh, most learned doctor, I would gladly like to believe, but unbelief suppresses all my desire. What in the world should I do about it?"

But then the learned one speaks, "Yes, dear companion, you must not concern yourself about such exalted things. Simply believe and thrust these thoughts away from you. They are mere fantasy. Go to the people and be happy. In this way you will forget these cares."

See, dear brothers, such consolation and no other has ruled the church. This same consolation has made Christian rigor into an abomination.

EIGHTEENTH

If an upright Christian continues to fear that such acid, bitter thoughts and anxious needs might make him senseless and foolish, then his nature is infinitely mistrustful of God. Is not the first form of unbelief when you do not want to trust your gracious and benevolent creator to protect your mind? There [in the fear of insanity] one can see our unbelief most clearly. If we learned ones want to pursue such a cause as faith, we must learn to use our heads more. Thus the negligent learned ones say, "Yes, if such exalted teachings were brought before the people, they would become mad and nonsensical." In addition they say, "Christ says that one should not throw pearls before swine. What would such an exalted, most spiritual teaching mean to poor coarse people? It is fitting for learned men alone to know such things."

Oh no, oh no, dear Lord. St. Peter tells you who the fattened pigs are [2 Pet. 2:22]. They are all the untrue, false learned ones, regardless of whatever sect they adher to, who hold that gorging and swilling are good, who satisfy all their desires in comfort, and who bare their fangs like dogs when one says a contrary word to them.

NINETEENTH

Christ called these same fattened pigs "false prophets" [Mt. 7:15] because they remove timbers neither from their own eye nor from that of others [see Mt. 7:3–5]. They make the narrow way broad. The sweet they call bitter and the light darkness, Isaiah chapter 5[:20]. They are the clever ones—in their own eyes. I bid them, for God's sake, to get rid of their arrogance. And may they preach with great trepidation what they have not attempted themselves. And may they believe that among the neophytes[23] God has many, many people through whom he will spread his name. For all who do this [i.e., rid themselves of arrogance] will appear to the world, as did Christ, like frail earthworms. They do not treat Christ as the Gadarenes did [see Mt. 8:34, Mk. 5:17], who bid the Lord to depart from their land, even though he came there only to offer his word to the needy; they did this because they wanted to obtain this word without harming their carnal desires. This is impossible.

Therefore, dear brothers, when we are treated well and with good intentions, we should not act like horned apes or big horseflies and make a big thing out of it. Rather, we should think about what Solomon said [Prov. 27:6], "The wounds of a lover are better than the kiss of a deceiver." The prophet [Jeremiah 23:16ff.] also says, "You dear people who call yourselves holy and good deceive yourselves." When a truly clever man is punished, he improves his ways. A fool or dolt pays no attention to the word of wisdom. One can only tell him what he wants to hear. May the merciful God protect you from this, dear brothers, for eternity. Amen.

TWENTIETH

In this offering and explanation I have summarized the damage done to the church and what has befallen us through an uncomprehended baptism and a contrived faith. If I have erred in these teachings I want to be reproached in a friendly way, before a community, and without evil intention, not examined in a corner without sufficient witnesses.[24] Rather, let it be done in the light of day. Through this undertaking I want to give the teaching of evangelical preachers a better form and not displease our backward, slow Roman brothers. Judge me before the whole world and not in a corner. For my teaching I pledge my body and life, without any cunning human defense and for the sake of Jesus Christ, the true son of God. May he defend you for all eternity. Amen.

TWENTY-FIRST

For important reasons I have had to let my offering go forth in print; the footmat must be at the foot of the cross, so that the teaching of Christ suffers no damage through me. Whoever has difficulties with this writing should write me in a friendly way, and I will reply to him at greater length, so that no one judges the other unfairly. May the tender son of God, Jesus Christ, who makes us his brothers, help us in this. Amen.

TWENTY-SECOND

I want to prove the basis of my faith, and it would please me if you who have never been tested did not turn up your noses in mockery when I am examined with my opponents before the representatives of all religions. If it pleases you, then my poor body is most certainly offered for your disposal.[25] But do not rush in here with a hasty judgment, for the sake of the mercy of God. Amen.

4

On Contrived Faith

On Contrived Faith, taking as its point of departure the recent "Protest" by Thomas Müntzer, curate at Allstedt. 1524.

Against the Contrived Faith of Christendom.

FIRST

The Christian faith is a security; one relies on the words and promises of Christ. Now, if someone is to grasp these words with a righteous, uncontrived heart, his ears must be cleansed to hear [Mt. 13:13 and 16] from the sound of cares and desires. For just as no field can produce a bountiful [harvest of] wheat without the plowshare, equally, no one can say that he is a Christian unless previously, through his cross, he has been made receptive to expect God's action and word. In expectant waiting the elect friend of God suffers the word. He is not one of the contrived listeners. Rather, he is an assiduous pupil of his master [Christ], whom he always looks at with unstinting diligence, so that he is able to become equal to him, corresponding to his measure in every respect.

SECOND

What a person hears or sees that points him to Christ, he accepts as a wonderous testimony, one with which he hunts, kills, and crushes his unbelief. To this extent he sees the whole of holy Scripture as a two-edged sword. For everything in Scripture should always choke us more than vivify us. An untested person who wants to boast greatly about [believing in] God's word achieves nothing but grasping empty air. Accordingly, God has tested all of his elect greatly from the very beginning. And especially he did not spare his own son, so that the son would be the right goal of our salvation and show us the single narrow way [to salvation]. The pleasure-seeking scribes cannot find this way in an eternity. Therefore, an elected friend of God cannot easily come to faith. People who boast about [their faith] are enormously cunning and have a completely contrived faith—unless they can give an explanation of their faith's origins,[1]

77

as was done by all who are in the Bible. [Otherwise] it is not possible even to call such crazy and opinionated people "reasonable heathens," to say nothing of calling them Christians. Such people are like those who transform themselves into angels of light [see 2 Cor. 11:14] and against whom we should guard ourselves as against the devil.

THIRD

God let Abraham be miserable and abandoned so that he would not trust in any creature, but in God alone. Thus he was tormented with the promises of God. [This abandonment] began before the promises, when Abraham was punished by being forced to wander in a foreign land with a distant consolation.[2] He found [this consolation] to be inadequate according to the light of natural reason, as St. Stephen pointed out to the tender and sensitive scribes in the Acts of the Apostles of God [see Acts 7:1ff.]. People who are damned always want to hide within themselves, and at the same time comprehend the utterly forsaken Christ [of Golgotha]. The tenth and eleventh chapters of Genesis provide the context for the twelfth chapter, for [Gen. 12] brings everything together: how Abraham, after great lamentations and affliction, was worthy of seeing the day of Christ. For, from the beginning, God has had no other way [of saving people]. If the light of natural reason had to be so rigorously extinguished in Abraham, what must take place in us?

FOURTH

Moses, who announced through the law the recognition of the false light of natural reason,[3] did not want to believe the living promise of God. For his unbelief had to be most clearly recognized beforehand, if he was going to abandon himself to God in an uncontrived way, so that he would know for certain that the devil had not played a nasty trick on him.[4] But Moses may well have regarded God as a devil, as long as he failed to perceive the deceitfulness of creatures and the simplicity of God, according to the order that is fixed in God and in all creatures. Even if the whole world accepts something as coming from God, it cannot quiet [a person who is] poor in spirit, unless he evaluates it after a [period of] sadness.

FIFTH

Each pious, upright, and elected person should have a brief overview of [the message of] the Bible, without the prejudice of special pleading. And he will discover that all the fathers, the patriarchs, the prophets, and especially the apostles came to faith with great difficulty. None of them wanted to attain it instantly, like our insane, pleasure-seeking swine,[5] who are horrified by the wind of a storm, the roaring waves, and the whole ocean of wisdom. For their consciences know indeed that they will finally be destroyed in such a storm. Therefore, with all their promises, they are just like a foolish man who builds on sand. And so all that they construct collapses, etc. [see Mt. 7:26f.].

SIXTH

The apostles of God heard the bearer of the gospel himself. And Christ said to Peter [Mt. 16:17] that neither flesh nor blood had revealed it to him, but rather God himself. Nevertheless, the apostles were not able to cling to a single promise without being shamed and disgracefully failing, so that their unbelief was powerfully tested. The lot of them did not want to believe that he was resurrected—that the one [they saw] was [Christ]. They thought it was a specter or a deception [Lk. 24:37]. And we un- tested people think so much of ourselves that we want to assist ourselves with a contrived faith and with a contrived mercy of God. And we seize upon some natural promise or covenant[6] and want to storm heaven with it. Oh no, dearest Christians! Let us use the holy Bible for the purpose for which it was created: to kill (as was said above [in section two]) and not to vivify, as does the living word to which an empty soul listens. Let us not take a piece [of Scripture] from here and another piece from there. Rather, with an emptiness of the spirit and not the flesh,[7] let us grasp this [paradox] that awaits us in every place in Scripture: namely, that [Scrip- ture both] consoles and terrifies. Where a cunning faith has not been ex- posed to its foundations, the external words [of Scripture] are always accepted, but, in a storm, the fool manipulates them. Therefore, the peo- ple must be brought to [a condition of] the greatest ignorance and be- wilderment if they are to be freed from their contrived faith and correctly instructed about the true faith.

SEVENTH

The word of God is not put into the mouth of a righteous preacher with saccharine words and hypocrisy. Rather, it is put there with a fervent and truly rigorous zeal, in order to uproot the contrived Christians and to break, scatter, and utterly destroy their whole evil faith, which they have obtained through mere hearsay or have stolen from people's books like tricky thieves.

EIGHTH

As long as poor, suffering, pitiable, and lamentable Christendom does not recognize its defilement, it cannot be helped. As long as it does not want to put away its contrived faith, which it disgracefully conceals under the form of true faith, it can neither be counseled or assisted. The whole abuse consists in this: that no one among the Turks, heathens, Jews, and all unbelievers wants to come to faith in the same way. Rather, each one strains and purifies himself[8] with his faith and his works. And he knows neither the foundation nor basis of either [faith or works]. Therefore our coarse, clumsy fathers [the clergy] have consigned the whole world to the devil (excepting only themselves), and they grant honesty to no one. And with this [presumption] they have provided the cause for all sects and schisms. Because most [believers] have become divided on account of ceremonies and [external] ecclesiastical forms (regardless of whether [these reflect] contrived or true faith).

NINTH

In order to correct such a displeasing abomination in miserable, coarse Christendom, a stern preacher must first of all be heard, one who, together with John the Baptist, cries, pitiably and complainingly, at the barren, mad, and raging hearts of men, so that they learn the ways in which God works and how they may become sensitive to God's word after a manifold stirring [of their hearts]. After [this movement], the fountain of blessedness is announced, the son of God, who was like a mild lamb that did not open its mouth even as it was slaughtered and so bore the sins of the world. [Christ sacrificed himself] so that we, like sheep with him, should perceive our being killed the whole day, through and through. And we should perceive how, in our suffering, we should not murmur and growl like whining dogs. Rather, [we should be] like the sheep of his meadow [Ps. 95:7], for he brings us forward, with the salt of his wisdom, in suffering and not otherwise.

TENTH

The sheep are poisoned by a toxic meadow but nourished by the salt. To preach a sweet Christ to a carnal world is the most dangerous poison that has ever been given to the lambs of Christ. For a person who preaches this wants to be in conformity with God, but he never desires, and certainly does not clamor, to become conformed to Christ. At the very least, he is not true to himself. Rather, he is like a salamander or a leopard,[9] spotted in all his intentions, i.e., of mixed or impure intention because he wants to be saved, yet is unwilling to accept the suffering this entails. Therefore Christ deliberately said [Jn. 10:27], "My sheep hear my voice and do not follow the voice of strangers." And he is a stranger who allows the way to eternal life to run to seed, who lets the thorns and thistles grow, and who proclaims simply, "Believe, believe!" Rather, hold yourself firm, firm with a strong, strong faith with which one can drive pilings into the earth.

ELEVENTH

One should not climb in the window [see Jn. 10:1], and one should have no other basis for faith than the whole Christ and not the half. He who does not want to accept the bitter Christ will eat himself to death on honey. Christ is a cornerstone [Eph. 2:20]. And just as Christ was polished [in his final shaping] like a cornerstone, so the master craftsman [God] must deal with us, in order for us to grow in a rightly constructed life. In all of life not the slightest particle[10] may be found wanting, so that each lives just like Christ, through and through, and becomes like Christ to the greatest extent, according to his talent or measure [Lk. 19:12–27]. For he who does not die with Christ cannot be resurrected with him. How can he be truthful to his life who has not once taken off the old raiment? Thus, they who offer consolation before they bring grief are thieves and murderers. They want the results before Christ comes, and they do not know when to say yes or no.

TWELFTH

Christ, unchangeable with his father, proved to his elect no more joyous love than that he made the elect, according to his purpose, like sheep which are marked for the kitchen. The elect are unlike the damned, who see only that they will be driven out, killed, and their memory wiped from the earth.[11] And whoever regards the lamb [Christ] in this way, seeing how he takes away the sins of the world, will say, "I have heard with my own ears how the old patriarchs in the Bible dealt with God and how God dealt with them. None of them was united with God until he had triumphed over his suffering (which came to him from eternity)." This is the way the radiance of God comes: in the light, to the light. This is what the Lord says [Jn. 10:29], "The sheep which my father has given me, no one can tear from my hands." The [correct] interpretation of these words is the meadow of the sheep that are ordained for heaven. For after the whole slaughter, [the sheep] say, "Oh Lord, awake from your sleep! Why do you turn your gaze from me? Help me, for the sake of your name, to ensure that my feet rest on a foundation of stone [Is. 26:4]. For

then I will say, 'You have done it alone.' Then I will not let my lips be
sealed and I will proclaim in your great church the righteousness that you
alone begin."

THIRTEENTH

True Christendom, which is ordained for eternal life, will be built on a
foundation such as this, so that one learns, accordingly, to protect one's
self and to throw out the leaven of evil learned ones,[12] who make a
leaven of the pure word of God with their worm-eaten, lame jabbering.
For all their teachings make people falsely boast in a contrived way with
an untested faith and think that, with the scribes' promises, they can master every tribulation. But the scribes do not really teach how a person can
attain this mastery of tribulation.

FOURTEENTH

Examine thoroughly, you elect brother, every word of the sixteenth chapter of Matthew! There you will find that no one can believe in Christ
unless he has previously become like him. When the elected person
becomes conscious of his own unbelief, he abandons all his contrived
faith, all that he has learned, or listened to, or read in the manner of the
scribes. For he sees that an external testimony can produce nothing
genuine in him. Rather, he sees that an external testimony only serves
the purpose for which it was created.[13] Therefore, a member of the elect
does not turn to every saying of inexperienced people. Rather, he is zealous for revelation, like Peter who showed the way for all by saying [Mt.
16:16], "I know it to be true that Christ is the son of the living God." For
the unbelief concealed in my flesh and blood is almost completely overcome through the desire that the mustard seed and the good leaven con-
sume and penetrate[14] and that breaks through all unbelief. [Before this
breakthrough of faith], one must have suffered despair and the deepest
contradictions. First, hell itself must be suffered, if one is to guard one's
self against the trap of the devouring gates [of hell].

The damned and the elect do not have the same assumptions. The godless one accepts Scripture with infinite gladness. Since another suffers for
him, the godless one constructs a strong faith. But when it concerns perceiving the lamb who unlocks the book [see Rev. 5:6–8], a godless person
does not want to lose his soul, does not want to become like the lamb,
and wants to help himself in his comfortable way with clear texts of Scripture. This is false.

If the whole Scripture is set forth in human fashion for one of the
scribes, he still cannot grasp it, even if he cracks his head open trying. He

must wait until it is opened for him with the key of David [Is. 22:22] in the winepress [of tribulation; see Rev. 14:19]. For he must be crushed in all of his usual ways so that he becomes so poor in spirit that he finds absolutely no other faith in him except that he gladly wants the right faith. This is the faith that is as small as a mustard seed [Lk. 17:6]. Then the person must see that he patiently endures the action of God, so that he grows from day to day in the knowledge of God. Then the person is taught only by God, totally and completely, and not by any creature. What all creatures know becomes for him a bitter gall because it is based on an inverted way of knowing.[15] May God guard and save all of his elect from this false way after they have fallen into it. May Christ grant this. Amen.

<h2 style="text-align:center">[APPENDIX][16]</h2>

To his dear brother Hans Zeiss, official at Allstedt,

One thing, dear brother, was forgotten in my reply to [the claim, discussed above] that suffering should be imputed to Christ alone, so that we need not suffer after Christ truly suffered for our sins. It should be noted here from what tenderness this improper tranquility is falsely presented to us. Adam is a model of Christ in a negative way, but Christ is the opposite.[17] The disobedience of the creature is restored by the obedience of the word. The word was made flesh according to nature, like our carnal nature. Corresponding to the growth of faith, [the word] must partly diminish, just as happened to the whole Christ as the head. Thus, Christ atoned for the whole sin of Adam, so that the community would remain whole. As the holy apostle of God clearly says [Col. 1:24], "I fulfill that which the suffering of Christ still lacks." The church suffers as his body. Paul was not able to suffer for the church except as a member who performs his duty. We must all follow in the footsteps of Christ, armed with such thoughts. In this respect, no gloss on Scripture can help those people who judge themselves superior, in their comfortable way, to those seeking righteousness through works. In this way, they poison the world more with their contrived faith than the others do with their foolish deeds.[18] Because they do not know how to correctly distinguish [between true and contrived faith], they are still neophytes, that is, untested persons. They should not be pastors, but rather, for a long time yet, catechumens, that is, industrious students of his divine action. And they should not teach until they have been taught by God.

To publish this writing of mine for an insane world is still [at this time] inconvenient. I would have to explain every chapter of Scripture and in my own sections not think of Scripture as a tool for the destruction of the carnal scribes. For the contrived faith of the scribes has alloted a place for every evil. Thus this writing cannot be printed now, since it would be released without defenses against those who (in their own opinion) are well armed. You should also know that [these scribes] attribute this teaching of mine to the abbot Joachim [of Fiore].[19] They call it, with great mockery, the "Eternal Gospel." I have great respect for the testimony of the abbot Joachim, but I have only read his commentary on Jeremiah.[20] However, my teaching has a far higher source. I do not derive it from Joachim, but rather from the living speech of God, as I will prove at the appropriate time on the basis of the whole Bible. For now, let us leave it at that and let us always faithfully preserve copies of our writings. Given on the Wednesday after the feast of St. Andrew [2 December] in the year 1523.

Thomas Müntzer, your brother in the Lord.

5

Selected Liturgical Writings

The order and account of the German service at Allstedt, instituted last Easter by Thomas Müntzer, curate. 1523.
Printed at Eilenburg by Nikolaus Widemar, 1524.

The order and account of the German service at Allstedt, which has recently been introduced by the servants of God. 1523.[1]

A servant of God has the task of holding the divine service for the whole community[2] in an open or public way. His task is not to practice secret things, but rather to promote the elevation and edification of the whole congregation, which is fed by the true steward who distributes the full measure of wheat [God's word] at the appropriate time. The minister should not hide this wheat beneath a deceiving cover, but rather conceal or bury nothing before all of Christendom and also before the whole world. For those [clerics] who take away the key to the knowledge of God are accustomed to practice secret things. This key should be brought to each of the elect, in order to reveal to them, through Isaiah 22[:22], an understanding of how the eternal living God has spoken.[3]

[INTROIT][4]

Accordingly, we take the introit of the service from the Psalter, where the key of David is laid on the shoulders of Christ [Is. 22:22], in order to reveal everything that is recited. The whole psalm is recited, without fragmentation, so that one always sees its meaning clearly, as was practiced at the beginning of Christianity by the pious successors of the holy apostles.

[KYRIE]

After the general confession has been made before the altar at the start of the divine service and after the introit, then one proceeds to the *Kyrie eleison* so that the friends of God grasp his eternal mercy,[5] in order to praise his name to the highest.

[GLORIA]

Then follows the *Gloria in excelsis*, in which we give our thanks that we have been promoted by the son of God to eternal life and the highest divine goods and enabled to return to our origin.

[SALUTATION]

After this expression of gratitude, the people are consoled with the saying of Boas [Ruth 2:4], for he said to his mowers what we recite to the ripe wheat, the sons of God,[6] "The Lord be with you." Afterward, the whole parish wishes the servant of God [the minister], a pure spirit (as St. Paul taught his disciple Timothy [2 Tim. 4:22]), saying, "And with your spirit"—so that this needy assembly does not have a godless person as a preacher. For whoever does not have the spirit of Christ is not a child of God. How then can he know about the action of God when he has not suffered it? And if he does not know it, how then can he talk about it? With this kind of ignorance, one blind man is trying to lead another.

[COLLECT]

Therefore, next, in all our prayers, we pray for the complete unity of the larger Christian church and against the deeply rooted, miserable crimes that prevent the most worthy name of God from shining forth before the whole world.

[FIRST READING]

Next the people are reminded, through the holy reading of the gospel and the letters of the beloved apostles, that every member of the elect must yield to the action of God before God the father allows his dearest son to speak through the gospel.

[GRADUAL AND HALLELUJAH]

After this, the gradual and the hallelujah are recited. so that a person develops the courage to rely stalwartly on the word of God. For one sees, from the hymns that are taken from the psalms, how almighty God treats and regards his dear elect. The person sees that God draws the elect to him in his gracious way, in order to instruct them about their gratitude with fatherly punishment.

[SEQUENCE]

Instead of the *prosa* or sequences, the Fifty-first Psalm, "God be merciful to me . . ." is recited in *tono peregrino*.[7]

[SECOND READING]

Second. It should be known that we always read a whole chapter, instead of the traditional readings of the epistle and gospel, so that the former, piecemeal way of reading Scripture is abolished, so that the holy Scripture of the Bible becomes well known to the people, and so that the superstitious ceremonies or rituals in the Mass are abolished through constant listening to the divine word. But all this must occur in a gentle and gradual breaking[8] with the colorful ceremonies, so that any [appearance of] effrontery is mollified and people are led with accustomed songs in their own language, just as infants are nourished with milk [Col. 4:16]. And yet there must be no accommodation with their evil ways. Even though this causes much trouble [for us] among our opponents, the improvement [brought about by] this [new German] service is always more effective and silences our opponents. Therefore, in the service we also recite the epistle and the gospel in our own language, because the holy apostle Paul let his letters be read publicly, before the whole community. And Christ, our savior, ordered the gospel to be preached simply and plainly to all creatures, neither in Latin exclusively, nor with any additions. Rather, the gospel should be preached as each person understands or can understand it, in his own language, irrespective [of nation, culture,] etc.

[CREDO]

Third. The summary consensus of all the main articles of the faith is recited after the gospel on Sundays or feast days. In the creed, the coarse errors of the church are confronted, so that pseudo-Christians[9] may not assume that these articles of faith will be denied by us when our divine service is openly presented to the whole world.[10]

[SERMON]

Fourth. The sermon is preached next. It is situated at this point in the service so that the recitation of Scripture which has just been heard in the service is explained. For David [rather Daniel, cf. Dan. 2:21] says, "The explanation of thy words gives understanding to the little ones." After the sermon we recite, "Now we bid the holy spirit," etc.

[BENEDICTUS]

Then the *benedictus* is recited so that the preacher can collect himself, catch a breath, and praise God that the people have heard God's word. We do not hold an offertory in our service.[11]

[PREFACE]

Fifth. The preface is recited. Through it, Christendom is reminded to recognize [Christ] the first born among all creatures in the fullness and knowledge of the divine will and in the knowledge of God, which he, together with all of the elect, received from God himself.

[SANCTUS]

Sixth. The sanctus is recited so that it is explained in what condition the person should be who wants to take the sacrament [of communion] without harming his soul. Specifically, he should and must know that God is within him. He must know that he cannot contrive or imagine him as though God were a thousand miles away from him. Rather, he must know that heaven and earth are full, full of God, that the father gives birth to the son in us constantly, and that the holy spirit declares the crucified one in us only through heartfelt grief. In addition, what we lack is that, in our blindness, we refuse to recognize or perceive when God grants us the greatest honor through shame and grants us health of the spirit through sickness of the body, etc. For God appears in the greatness of his name only when our name is dishonored and slandered, without regard to all our deeds and omissions, etc.

[INSERTION]

Seventh. So that we can endure patiently such great, powerful tribulation [as that described above], we accept the manner in which Jesus Christ, the son of God, commanded his church to conduct itself. The church must think of his suffering during every affliction, so that our soul languishes and hungers for the food of life. Therefore, it is necessary for us to hold passionately to the most wonderful words of Christ. It is necessary to direct all people away from clinging to this life, through him who wants to have his memory, essence, and word in the soul of man, not in man as an animal, but as his temple, which he most dearly purchased with his precious blood.

[CONSECRATION]

Eighth. In the earliest beginning of the church, the words of the transformation [of the bread and wine] were said publicly. And this practice was abandoned only on account of a deception, which [supposedly] arose due to some shepherd boys in a field.[12] But now, to avoid the superstition that has entered the church through the misuse of the divine service, we recite these same words of transformation publicly, etc. For Christ, the son of God, did not whisper these same words to one person or conceal them; rather, he said them to all, as the text of the gospel clearly shows. For there Christ says many times, "Take and eat," etc. "Take and all drink therefrom," etc.

Besides, the consecration is also a transformation that does not occur because of only one person, but rather through the whole assembled community. With this assertion, we refute our opponents, who persecute us without just cause, since they claim that we also teach young stable boys in the field to say Mass. On the basis of this charge, every pious, good-hearted person can easily evaluate what our opponents think of the son of God. They act as if he were a painted puppet or a clown show. Since one banishes and enchants the devil with words, these opponents also think that one should enchant Christ, the son of God, with words, to and fro, wherever the insolence of men wishes. No, not in this way! Christ satisfies only those who are hungry in spirit, and he leaves the godless empty. But what can Christ do for people in the sacrament if he finds no hungry and empty souls among them? Thus, he must be perverse to the perverse and good to the good. What use is this symbol [the sacrament of communion] to one who denies its essence? Now, without a doubt, the whole congregation always contains many pious people. And because of the faith of such people, Christ truly comes [in the sacrament] to satisfy their souls, etc.[13]

Ninth. Therefore the formula of the transformation or the Lord's Supper is recited in the same tone as the preface, with the following words: "On the day before Jesus was to suffer, he took bread in his holy and worthy hands and raised his eyes to heaven, to you God, his almighty father, and gave thanks to you. And he blessed it and broke it and gave it to his companions, saying, 'Everyone take and eat of this!'" Raising his hand, [the minister] says, "This is my body which will be sacrificed for you." While turning, the minister takes up the chalice and says publicly to the common people, "In the same way, when they had eaten, Christ took the chalice in his holy, worthy hands and gave thanks to you [God]. And he blessed it and gave it to his companions, saying, 'This is the chalice of my blood, of the new and eternal covenant, a mystery of faith which will be shed for you and for many in forgiveness of sins.'" Turning back to the altar, the minister says, "As often and frequently as you do this, you should think of me in doing so," etc.

[OUR FATHER]

Tenth. Just after the elevation, the following is immediately recited in the same tone: "Therefore, let us all pray, as Jesus Christ, the true son of God, taught us, saying, 'Our father who art in heaven,'" etc. And then all the people chant, "Amen." Afterward, it is quiet, to catch a little breath, at which time the minister distributes the sacrament to the communicants and recites, "Through all eternity of eternity." To which the common people reply, "Amen."

[BLESSING OF PEACE]

The minister again recites, "May the peace of the Lord always be with you." To which the people respond, "And with your spirit."

[AGNUS DEI]

Soon after this, so that the death and resurrection of Christ are considered in our divine service and to further explain these things, all the people recite three times the testimony of John, the baptizer of Christ, "Oh, lamb of God who takes away the sin of the world," etc. And the Gospel of Luke 17[:13] is recited, "Have mercy on us!" And finally, "Give us your peace." For Christ died and was resurrected for the sake of our sins, so that he might justify us, which he alone did, and we must suffer being justified.

[COMMUNION]

In this faith, during the *Agnus dei* the people are given the most worthy sacrament, and without the papist, hypocritical confession. For the people are generally admonished in every sermon that each person must regret his old past life, so that he sees with how many carnal desires he has earned his cross, etc. The person sins, God sets the penance, and it is the person's duty to conform himself to this. No person can have a good, pure, and peaceful conscience before God if he has not completely acknowledged this. Therefore, the third *Agnus dei* ends with, "Grant us your peace," and "Let your servant, oh Lord, abide in peace, according to your word." For only patient people are worthy of the savior of life, etc.

Eleventh. The most worthy sacrament is distributed under both forms [wine as well as bread], without paying attention to the blabber of petty shopkeepers concerning this or that market,[14] this or that ecclesiastical division. For if we do not rightly understand the sacrament, the holy symbol, how do we then want to understand the essence of what the symbol signifies? After communion, the minister says, "God be thanked," and to the people, "May the Lord bless you," etc.

[BENEDICAMUS]

Lastly. No one should be surprised that we in Allstedt perform a German service. At another time, a better accounting of it will be given, with a more detailed explanation. It is certainly not only a matter of saying Mass in another manner than the papists, because the Milanese in Lombardy also have a very different way of saying Mass than at Rome. Each bishopric has its own special ceremonies or rites. Why then should we not do likewise, according to the nature of the times? Because we at Allstedt are Germans and not Italians, and we would gladly like to work our own way through the turmoil [of the times], so that we can know what we should believe. And this will only come about in the right way through what we do with the true word of God. The Croats are Roman Catholics, yet say Mass and all the services in their own language. The Armenians say Mass in their own language and they are a great nation. They show the people the sacrament on the paten. Again, the Bohemians say Mass in their own language and with many of their own customs. Again, Spanish Christians and Russians have many different rites, but because of this they are not devils. Again, in the land where the Christian faith originated there are some fourteen divisions, all of them having different rites than we do. Oh, what blind, ignorant people we are; on the basis of external rituals alone we presume to be Christians and then we fight over them like insane, animalistic people! Why may not each servant of the word of God have the power to teach his parishioners a way to be edified with psalms and hymns from the Bible? As St. Paul says with clear words, Ephesians chapter 5[:18ff.], "You should," he said, "be filled with the holy spirit and speak to one another with psalms, praises, spiritual songs, and hymns. And you should sing and perform for the Lord and always give thanks for everything."[15] He teaches the same thing in 1 Corinthians 14[:26]. If we wish to call German singing and reading in church unchristian, what then would we say if we were to present an account of the development of our faith, etc.?

ON THE PERFORMACE OF BAPTISM

If a child is baptized among us, the godparents are admonished, on the blessedness of their souls, to pay attention to what baptism means, so that later, when the child grows, they can explain it to him, and, in time, his baptism can be understood. Therefore, Psalm 69 is read in German. It tells that a poor man is born to fear and distress, that for him the waves reach to his throat, etc. In addition, we read Matthew 3[:13ff.] concerning the baptism of Christ. This text shows how Christ came to us, drowning people, and saved us from the raging waves. But Christ soon climbed out [of the water], and the waves did not overpower him, as they do us. In this way he provided the way for all justification.

For a long time we poor, miserable, pitiable people have made of baptism a pure fantasy and mere sprinkling of water. The infant is given salt and told, "N.,[16] take the salt of wisdom, to distinguish good and evil in the spirit of wisdom, so that you will not be trampled by the devil." Then the infant is told, "Come to Christendom, so that God finds you like the pure wheat." Then, in the baptism ceremony, the faith is proclaimed and the works, pomp, and cunning of the devil are renounced. When the infant receives oil on the breast and back, the priest says, "N., rejoice that you are in the eternal mercy of God." Then, when the priest administers baptism, he says, "Do you want to be baptized?" And the godparents say, "Yes." Then the priest says, "I baptize you in the name of the father and of the son and of the holy spirit, amen. May God, who generates you with his eternal love, grant you [the power] to avoid the oil of the sinner." And, as he puts on the baptismal cap, he says, "Put on the new garment and remove the old. Do not mend the old garment with a new patch [Lk. 5:36], so that you can pass the Last Judgment." Then the minister says about the candle, "N., let Christ be your light and take heed that your light is not darkness [Mt. 5:14ff.]. Let the life of Christ be your mirror, so that you have eternal life. Amen."

ON MARRIAGE

About marriage we do not make jests, but rather we read to the couple, in German, Psalm 128, "Blessed be all," and the Gospel of John 2[:1-11] concerning the marriage feast [at Cana], and we give them instruction, etc.

ON BRINGING THE SACRAMENT TO THE SICK

The sick are administered the sacrament as follows: [first] they make a general confession. Then the Gospel of Luke 12[:39ff?], "In whichever house you go," etc. is recited. Then the *Confiteor* is recited, "I believe in God the father. . ." and, afterward, the "Our Father." Then the words of the Lord's Supper are read in a loud voice, "The day before Christ suffered," etc. After the reception of the sacrament, the minister says, "Oh, lamb of God," etc. and gives thanks to God and admonishes the sick person to arm himself with the cross, etc.

ON THE BURIAL OF THE DEAD

We come for the dead while reciting the *benedictus* in German, without a prior night watch. All the people follow [in procession] behind the corpse and join in reciting the *benedictus*. Then, after the burial, the people recite, "In the midst of life," etc.[17] Then they go into the church, where the minister recites the epistle [1 Thes. 4:13ff.], "We do not wish to leave you in ignorance," etc., and the Gospel of John 5[:24–29], concerning the resurrection of the dead. The minister closes with the hymn "In the midst of life," etc.

Such is our service, but, if a child can give us better instruction, we would gladly accept it.

Prefaces to the German Evangelical Mass[18]

PREFACE TO THIS HYMNAL

Our true savior, Jesus Christ, prophesied all the harm that has come to Christendom, Matthew chapter 13[:25], "While the people" (whom he soon after called "angels") "slept, the enemy came and sowed tares among the wheat." Christ began Christendom in the right way, but the godless have polluted it through the negligence of all the lazy among the elect. Therefore, in the history of the apostles of God, Acts 20[:28–31], Paul says the following in plain terms: "Watch out for yourselves and for the whole flock, among whom the holy spirit has set you as guardians, to feed the community of God, which he has won by his own blood. For I know this: after my departure ravaging wolves will come among you who will not spare the flock. Men will also arise from among you who will proclaim a perverted teaching in order to attract the young. So beware!" But now, so that no one with a limited understanding changes the meaning of these words of Christ and Paul according to his own opinion, in order to lead the already damaged church to further harm, all the credible history books must be examined. It will certainly be evident then that the words of Christ and Paul and the words of all the holy prophets concerning the fall of Christendom have become absolutely and totally true.[19]

Josephus, a credible writer of history and a pupil of the apostles, in the fifth book of his *Explanations*[20] and Eusebius, in the fourth book of his

History of the Christian Church,[21] say straightforwardly that the holy bride of Christ remained a virgin until after the death of the pupils of the apostles, and that soon afterward the church became a fornicating adultress. In such clear historical books of this kind, it is not only to be noted in passing, but to be profoundly grasped, how Christendom has been afflicted since our forefathers came to the faith six hundred years ago.[22] The pious good-hearted fathers (who converted our land) did what they knew [to be effective] according to the circumstances of the people. They were Italian and French monks. Their arrival was acceptable [since it came] as an improvement. For it is indeed easy to see that they recited in Latin because the German language then was utterly undeveloped and because the people were being directed to an ecclesiastical unity; for all of Asia fell away [from this unity] because of the Lord's Supper.[23]

But it would indeed be an ironic joke if such a beginning could not be improved upon. For, in everyday matters, mankind thinks every reasonable change is a great improvement. And is God supposed to be so powerless that he cannot improve upon his work? No. Indeed, Christ says about this point—and commanded us to think about it seriously— Matthew 5[:14ff.] and 10[:27], "The city should appear publicly on the mountain. The light should not be hidden under a bushel. It should enlighten all who are in the house." What else should it do? For Paul says in 1 Corinthians chapter 14[:26] and Ephesians chapter 5[:19], "When the people come together, they should edify one another with hymns and psalms, so that all who go unto him [Christ] may be improved."

It is no longer tolerable that people ascribe power to Latin words, as magicians do, and that the poor people are allowed to leave church more uneducated than heathen. As God has always said, Isaiah 54[:13], Jeremiah 31[:34], and John 6[:45]: All of the elect must be taught by God. And Paul says, "The people must be edified by hymns." Thus, to bring about this improvement, I have translated the Psalms according to the German manner and pattern, but in the irrevocable mystery of the holy spirit and more according to the sense than the words. It is a filthy thing to [imitate and] paint one puppet after another,[24] when, at this time, we are still much in need of being modeled on the spirit, until we are educated beyond our usual ways.

There will be five services[25] to be recited over the whole year, in which the whole Bible will be recited instead of the traditional readings. The first service concerns the future coming of Christ and begins in October or at the feast of All Saints, when the prophets are to be read. The second service extends from the birth of Christ to the sacrifice in the temple. The third from the passion of Christ to Easter. The fourth from the resurrection of Christ to Pentecost. The fifth from [the descent of] the holy spirit [Trinity Sunday] to the feast of All Saints. Thus Christ, through the holy spirit in us, will be explained through the testimony about him—as he was announced by the prophets, was born, died, and was resurrected, [Christ] who reigns eternally with his father and the same holy spirit, and who makes us his pupils. Amen.

PREFACE

I, Thomas Müntzer, a servant of God, wish all truly elected friends of God grace and peace along with the pure, correctly developed fear of God. Recently some services and hymns in German have been published as a result of my work; these are liturgies which for a long time were recited in Latin by the papist parsons and monks, to the disadvantage of the Christian faith. This liturgy most greatly angered some scholars[26] who out of hateful envy of me zealously tried to hinder my work. Indeed, they drew inferences from it, accusing me of wanting to reestablish and help confirm old papist ceremonies, Masses, matins, and vespers—something which was never either my intention or disposition. Rather it was much more to rescue the poor, miserable, blind consciences of people, presenting briefly what for a long time was read and recited in Latin by deceitful, false parsons, monks, and nuns in churches and cloisters, and withheld from the poor mass of the laity, to the decline of the faith, gospel, and word of God—and contrary to the clear, brilliant teaching of the holy apostle Paul, 1 Corinthians 14[:1ff.]. Therefore, it is my earnest, good intention, even in these present days, to help poor, collapsing Christendom with German services, be they Masses, matins, or vespers, so that every person of good intention is able to see, hear and grasp how the despairing papist villains have stolen the holy Bible from poor Christendom, to its great harm, and how they have withheld a right understanding of Scripture. And at the same time the papists have evilly devoured the good [news] in Scripture for the poor people, as Christ says of them, Matthew 23[:2ff.], and St. Paul in 2 Timothy 3[:2–7], and indeed as the holy apostle Peter also says of their false works, 2 Peter 2[:1], together with all the beloved prophets.

But now, because the poor common man has based his faith on mere external forms, indeed on idolatrous rites in the churches, with reciting, reading, and papist black magic, it is fitting and proper, as the evangelical preachers themselves admit, that the weak should be cared for, 1 Corinthians 3[:1ff.]. And no better or more appropriate care can be found than to perform these same hymns in German, so that the poor weak consciences of people are not swiftly demolished, or satisfied with weak, untried songs, but rather [so that they are strengthened] with the transformation of Latin liturgies into German, with psalms and hymns to the word of God, and with the right understanding of the Bible, including the opinion of the apostolic writers who composed such hymns for the strengthening of the faith as well as its advent. [The apostles did this] so that it might come about—and indeed for this very reason—that, through such songs and psalms, the consciousness [of people] is directed away from the externals of the church and drawn to the word of God, which is contained in the Bible, so that their consciousness does not remain as coarse and uncomprehending as a butcher's block.

But the fact that I only published five services should not make anyone angry with me. For I wanted to develop a liturgy in which the services can be shortened or lengthened according to the circumstances. And the same with the hymns, be they the *Gloria* or the "Our Father," which are at times to be curtailed on account of the many methods of intonation, and which each may take or leave as he finds appropriate. With this liturgy I did not want to retain or reestablish the papist abomination. Each person may add to or reduce from what has been established by man, but not what God has established and commanded. Thus, one can also make changes here in the songs and notes. One may recite as much as one chooses about a liturgical feast[27]—as [for example] from Pentecost to Advent, from Advent to Christmas, from Christmas to Mary's purification [i.e., Candlemas, 2 February], from the purification of Mary through the passion of Christ to Easter, from Easter to Pentecost—as one thinks appropriate. The only requirement is that the psalms should be well sung and read to the poor laity. For the working of the holy spirit can be clearly recognized in the psalms—what one's attitude toward God should be and how one is to arrive at the source of the true Christian faith. Yes, also how faith must be reinforced with many tribulations. All this is clearly set forth by the holy spirit in the psalms. Therefore, St. Paul teaches how one should exercise and renew himself with spiritual hymns and psalms, Ephesians 5[:19]. But then the pampered parsons must exert themselves for the benefit of the poor people, or they will have to give up their priestly craft. Should they be lazy and only preach a sermon on Sunday and be Junkers the rest of the week? No, certainly not! But I know well how they will wrinkle up their noses at this view and mock it. But it is true. And they have no excuse for their mockery, because poor, coarse Christendom cannot be made upright unless the coarse, uncomprehending people have been educated out of their hypocrisy with German hymns. Each may say whatever he wants [but this still holds true].

Therefore, in no way should the common man turn to the lazy rogues, the parsons, who want to preserve their pampered ways and who proclaim that first they must give [spiritual] milk and that they seek to do so. Yes, they give dragon's milk![28] They want both to fear for their own skins and to be preachers of the faith and the gospel. When, then, will their faith be tested like gold in the fire, 1 Peter 1[:5]? A priest should conduct himself as St. Paul teaches and imitate Christ as Paul imitated Christ, 1 Corinthians 11[:1ff.]. Indeed, a priest should not heed the raging of tyrants, but publicly live the testament of Christ and recite and explain it in German so that the people may model themselves after Christ, Romans 8[:17]. When this happens, all the greed, usury, and deceitful tricks of the parsons, monks, and nuns will collapse with all their roots. These tricks now retard the faith under the appearance of good. May God help us all in this. Amen.

6

Sermon to the Princes (or An Exposition of the Second Chapter of Daniel)

An Exposition of the Second Chapter of Daniel the Prophet, preached at the castle of Allstedt before the active and dear dukes and rulers of Saxony by Thomas Müntzer, servant of the word of God.

Allstedt, 1524.

FIRST

The text of the abovementioned chapter of the prophecy of Daniel the prophet was set forth and translated [from the Vulgate] in its clear literal sense, and then the whole sermon, with the correct context, was set down as follows:

It is to be understood that poor, miserable, disintegrating Christendom can neither be counseled nor assisted unless diligent, indefatigable servants of God promote the Bible daily by reciting, reading, and preaching. But if this is done, either the head of many a pampered cleric must suffer a continuous rain of hard blows, or he will have to give up his profession. How can this be avoided when Christendom is being so terribly devastated by ravaging wolves?—as it is written about the vineyard of God in Isaiah 5[:1ff.] and Psalm 80[:9–14]. And St. Paul teaches in Ephesians 5[:19] how one should train oneself in the recitation of divine praises.

At the time of the beloved prophets Isaiah, Jeremiah, Ezekiel, and the others, the whole community of God's elect had fallen so totally and completely into idolatrous ways that even God himself could not help the people. Instead, he had to let them be led away into bondage and suffer long among the heathen until they again acknowledged his holy name, as it is written in Isaiah 29[:17–24], Jeremiah 15[:11–14], Ezekiel 36[:20ff.], and Psalm 89[:31–38]. And just as it was then, it is no less true that, in the time of our forefathers and in our own time, poor Christendom has become much more petrified and has only an inexpressibly slight resemblance to its divine name, Luke 21[:5], 2 Timothy 3[:5]. And the devil and his servants finely adorn themselves with this semblance, 2 Corin-

98

thians 11[:13ff.]. Indeed, they adorn themselves with it so attractively that the true friends of God are seduced by it, and, even with the most practiced zeal, they are scarcely able to recognize their error, as Matthew 24[:24] clearly shows.

All this has been brought about by the contrived holiness and hypocritical forgiveness of sins practiced by the godless enemies of God, since they assert that the Christian church cannot err. But to the contrary, in order to guard against error the church should be constantly built on the word of God and thus kept free from error. Yes, the true church should also acknowledge the sin of its own ignorance, Leviticus 4[:13f.], Hosea 4[:6], Malachi 2[1–7], and Isaiah 1[:10–17]. For it is surely true that Christ, the son of God, and his apostles—indeed, even his holy prophets before him—began a true, pure Christendom, for they cast the seed of pure wheat in the field. That is, they planted the true word of God in the hearts of the elect, as is written in Matthew 12 [see, rather, Mt. 13:3–23], Mark 4[:3–20], Luke 8[:5–15], and Ezekiel 36[:29]. But the lazy, negligent ministers of this same church have not wanted to maintain this work and bring it to fruition through diligent care. Rather, they have pursued their own selfish interests and not those of Jesus Christ, Philippians 2[:21].

Therefore, the clergy permitted the damage of the godless—that is, the tares—to spread in its strength, Psalm 80[:9–14]. For the cornerstone [Christ] referred to here in the second chapter of Daniel [Dan. 2:34–44] was still small. Isaiah 28[:16] also speaks of it. To be sure, it has not yet come to fill the whole world,[1] but it will soon fill it and make it full, ever so full. Thus, in the beginning of the new Christendom, the established cornerstone was soon rejected by the masons—that is, by the rulers, Psalm 118[:22f.] and Luke 20[:17f.]. Therefore, I say that the church, begun in this way, has become dilapidated everywhere, down to the present time of the divided world,[2] Luke 21[:10], and here Daniel 2[:35] and Ezra 4[1:–5]. For Hegesippus says, and Eusebius says in the twenty-second chapter of book IV on the Christian church,[3] that the Christian community did not remain a virgin any longer than up to the time of the death of the disciples of the apostles. And soon afterward it became an adulteress, as had already been prophesied beforehand by the beloved apostles, 2 Peter 2[:14]. And in the Acts of the Apostles, St. Paul said to the shepherds of the sheep of God with clear, ringing words, Acts 20[:28–31], "Take heed, therefore, unto yourselves and unto the whole flock, which the holy spirit has placed you to watch over, that you should feed the community of God, which he has purchased through his blood. For I know that after my departure ravaging wolves which will not spare my flocks will come among you. Also, from among yourselves men will arise who will promulgate perverted teachings to attract the younger disciples to themselves. Therefore, watch out!" The same thing stands written in the letter of the holy apostle Jude [Jude 4:19], and Revelation 16[:13f.] points to it as well. Therefore, our Lord, Christ, warned us to guard against false prophets, Matthew 7[:15].

Now, it is as clear as day—and may God hear our complaint —that nothing is as badly and as little respected today as the spirit of Christ. And yet no one may be saved unless this same holy spirit has previously assured him of his salvation, as it is written in Romans 8[:6], Luke 12[:8], John 6[:63] and 17[:2–31]. But how do we poor little worms expect to reach this while we regard the worthiness of the godless with such respect that unfortunately Christ, the gentle son of God, appears before the great titles and lineages of this world like a scarecrow or a painted puppet? And yet he is the true stone that will be cast down from the high mountain [Dan. 2:45] into the sea, Psalm 46[:3], because of the pompous opulence of this world. He is the stone who was torn from the great mountain without human hand, the stone who is called Jesus Christ, 1 Corinthians 10[:4]. He was born just at the time when the evil of slavery prevailed, Luke 1[:52] and 2[:1], at the time of Octavian, when the whole world was in motion and was being counted. Then Octavian, one who was spiritually without any power, a miserable scumbag, wanted to have power over the whole world, which was of no use to him except for his own luxury and arrogance. Indeed, he let himself think that he alone was great. Oh, how very small then was the cornerstone, Jesus Christ, in the eyes of men! He was banished to a stable, like an outcast among men, Psalm 22[:7]. Accordingly, the scribes rejected him, Psalm 118[:22], Matthew 21[:42–46], Mark 12[:10–12], Luke 20[:17–19], as they still do today.[4]

Indeed, since the death of the beloved disciples of the apostles, these scribes have even reenacted the Passion with him. They have turned the spirit of Christ into a laughingstock, and they continue to do so, as is written in Psalm 69[:11ff.]. They have most blatantly stolen him, like thieves and murderers, John 10[:1]. They have robbed Christ's sheep of their true voice and made the true crucified Christ into a completely fantastic idol. How has this come about? My answer is that they have rejected the pure knowledge of God and, in its place, they have set up a pretty, fine, golden image of God. Before it, the poor peasants smack their lips, as Hosea has clearly said in chapter 4[:6–13], and as Jeremiah said in Lamentations 4[:5], "Those who formerly ate fine spiced food have now received instead dirt and filth." Oh, how unfortunate is the pitiful abomination of which Christ himself spoke, Matthew 24[:15], foreseeing that he would be so wretchedly mocked by the devilish offering of Mass, the superstitious preaching, the ceremonies, and the manner of living. And even so, the whole time, there is nothing there but a mere wooden idol. Indeed, there is only a superstitious, wooden parson and a coarse, loutish, and rude people, who cannot grasp the slightest assertion about God. Is this not a pity, a sin, and a scandal? I believe most assuredly that the beasts of the belly, Philippians 3[:19], and the swine written about in Matthew 7[:6] and 2 Peter 2[:22] have trampled underfoot the precious stone, Jesus Christ, as completely and totally as they have been able. He has become a doormat for the whole world. For this reason all the unbelieving peoples, Turks, heathens, and Jews, have mocked us in the vilest way and taken us for fools—as one should regard senseless people who do not want to hear the spirit of their faith mentioned. Thus, the suffering of Christ is nothing but the baiting at a market festival and the disparaging of rogues, as Psalm 69[:11–12] says, which not even a lowly foot soldier has had to endure.

Therefore, dear brothers, we should come out of this filth and become true pupils of God, taught by God, John 6[:48], Matthew 23[:8–10]. Then we will need God's great powerful strength, which will be granted us from above, in order to punish and annihilate such unspeakable wickedness. This knowledge is the most clear wisdom about God, Proverbs 9[:10], which springs only from a pure, uncontrived fear of God.[5] This same fear alone must arm us with a mighty hand for revenge on the enemies of God and with the highest zeal for God, as stands written in Proverbs 5[:18], John 2[:17], and Psalm 69[:9,18,24]. There is certainly no excusing God's enemies with human or rational considerations, for the appearance of the godless is beautiful and deceptive beyond all measure, like the beautiful cornflower among the golden ears of wheat, Ecclesiastes 8[:14]. But the wisdom of God must recognize such deceit.

SECOND

We must examine more closely and correctly the abomination that despises this stone. But so that we correctly recognize the abomination in the godless, we must daily expect God's revelation. Oh, that has become the most precious and rare thing in this corrupt world! For [unless we expect revelations], the sly schemes of the clever ones could overcome us at any moment and keep us still more from the pure knowledge of God, Proverbs 4[:12], Psalm 37[:14–32]. Such a thing must be forestalled by the fear of God.

Only if this same fear is completely and purely anchored in us can holy Christendom easily return again to the spirit of wisdom and the revelation of the divine will. All this is encompassed in Scripture, Psalm 145[:18f.], Psalm 111[:5–10], Proverbs 1[:7]. But the fear of God must be pure, without any admixture of human or "creaturely" [i.e., materialistic and selfish] fear, Psalm 19[:10], Isaiah 66[:2], Luke 12[:4f.]. Oh, this fear is very necessary for us! For just as one can scarcely serve two masters, Matthew 6[:24], so one can scarcely fear both God and creatures. Nor may God himself have mercy on us (as the mother of Christ our Lord says) unless we fear him alone with our whole heart. Therefore, God says, "If I am your father, where then is the honor due me? If I am your lord, where then is fear of me?" Malachi 1[:6].

So, you dear princes, it is necessary in these most dangerous days, 1 Timothy 4[:1f.], that we apply the greatest diligence to combat such underhanded evil, as have all our beloved ancestors who are recorded in the Bible from the beginning of the world. For the time is dangerous and the days are evil, 2 Timothy 3[:1–8], Ephesians 5[:15f.]. Why? Only because the noble power of God has been so miserably disgraced and dishonored that the poor, coarse people are seduced by the great blubbering of unsaved scribes. The prophet Micah in chapter 3[:11] says about them that this is the nature of nearly all the scribes with very few exceptions: they teach and say that God no longer reveals his divine mysteries to his beloved friends through valid visions, his audible word, or other ways. Thus the scribes remain bogged down in their inexperienced ways, Ecclesiastes 34[:10]. And they have coined a gibe against people who go about with revelations from God, as the godless did to Jeremiah in chapter 20[:7f.], "Listen, has God spoken to you recently? Or have you directed your questions to the mouth of God lately and taken counsel with him? Do you have the spirit of Christ?" The scribes do this with great scorn and mockery.

Was it not a great thing that took place in the time of Jeremiah? Jeremiah warned [Jer. 20:4–5] the poor, blind people about the punishment of captivity in Babylon, just as pious Lot warned his sons-in-law, Genesis 19[:14]. But this warning appeared to the people to be most foolish. The blind people said to the beloved prophet, "Yes, yes, God should indeed warn the people in such a paternal way." But what happened then to the mocking crowd during the Babylonian captivity? Nothing, except that they were brought to shame by this heathen king, Nebuchadnezzar. Behold the text [of Dan. 2:47] here! Nebuchadnezzar had received the proclamation of God, and, nevertheless, he was a powerful tyrant and a punishing rod for the people of the elect who had sinned against God. But, because of the blindness and stubbornness of the people of God, the most exalted goodness of the world had to be proclaimed in such a way, as St. Paul in Romans 11[:22] and Ezekiel 23[:22–35] say.

Thus, for your instruction here, I, too, say that the omnipotent God not only revealed to the heathen king those things that were many years in the future—to the unspeakable disgrace of the proud among the people of God who did not want to believe any prophet. The untested people of our time are exactly the same—they are not conscious of the punishment of God, even when they see it right before their eyes. What shall almighty God then do with us? He must withdraw his goodness from us.

Now we come to the biblical text of Daniel 2, "The king Nebuchadnezzar had a dream which vanished from him," etc.

What should we say about this? It is an unspeakable, indeed an abnormal and hateful thing to speak about people's dreams. The reason for this is that the whole world, from the beginning down to the present time, has been deceived by dreamers and interpreters of dreams, as is written in Deuteronomy 13[:2ff.] and Ecclesiastes 34[:7]. So it is shown, in this chapter of Daniel, that the king did not want to believe the clever fortune-tellers and dream interpreters. For he said, "Tell me my dream and only then the interpretation. Otherwise you will tell me nothing but mere deception and lies." What happened then? They were not able to do this and could not tell him the dream. And they said, "Oh, beloved king, no man on earth is able to tell you your dream. Only the gods can do this, who have nothing on earth in common with human beings." Yes, to be sure, according to their understanding they spoke correctly and in a reasonable way. But they had no faith in God. Rather, they were godless hypocrites and flatterers, who said then what the rulers gladly wanted to hear, just as the scribes do now in our time, those who gladly want to eat tasty tidbits at court. But opposing them is that which is written in Jeremiah 5[:13–31] and 8[:8f.]. And how much more is written there! The text of Daniel says here [Dan. 2:28] that there must have been people then who had fellowship with God in heaven. Oh, for the clever ones that is a bitter herb to swallow. But St. Paul wants to have it so too, Philippians 3[:20]. And, nevertheless, such learned ones immediately want to explicate the secrets of God. Oh, the world has now had more than enough of these rogues, who publicly presume to do such things.

And God says in Isaiah 58[:2] about these scribes, "They want to know my ways just as the people do who have fulfilled my righteousness." Such scribes are like fortune-tellers, since they openly deny any revelation from God and hence assault the holy spirit in his handiwork. They want to instruct all the world. And what does not conform to their inexperienced understanding they immediately ascribe to the devil. And yet they are not even assured of their own salvation, although this assurance is necessary, Romans 8[:14ff.]. They can babble beautifully about faith and brew up a drunken faith for the poor, confused consciousness of the people. All this comes from their indecisive judgment and from the abomination. They have derived this view from the contemptible deception of the most damnable, poisonous monks' dreams,[6] through which the devil has effected all his plans. Indeed, this teaching has also irretrievably deceived many pious people among the elect. For, without any instruction from the spirit, they have given themselves over without hesitation to these visions and dreams of their crazy faith. And so from the revelations of the devil, monastic rules and sheer idolatry have been written down. St. Paul vigorously warned against this in his letter to the Colossians 2[:8]. But the damnable monkish dreamers have not known how they can become conscious of the power of God. Therefore, their perverted minds are hardened. And they are now shown before the whole world, more clearly from day to day, to be nothing except sin and shame—like do-nothing scoundrels. They are still blind in their stupidity. Nothing else has misled them, and nothing else even to the present day seduces them further than this superstition. This is so because, without any experience of the advent of the holy spirit—the master of the fear of God—they despise knowledge of God and fail to separate good from evil which is concealed under the appearance of good. God cries out about this through Isaiah 5[:20], "Woe unto you who call good evil and evil good!" Therefore, it is not the manner of pious people to reject the good along with the evil. For St. Paul says to the Thessalonians 5 [1 Th. 3:20f.], "You should not despise prophesying. Test all things but hold fast to what is good," etc.

THIRD

You should also know that God is so completely and totally well disposed toward his elect that if he could warn them in the smallest matters, Deuteronomy 1[:42] and 36 [see, rather, Dt. 32:6,29], Matthew 23[:37], he would most certainly do it—if they could receive this same warning despite the magnitude of their unbelief. For here this text of Daniel agrees with what St. Paul wrote to the Corinthians in chapter 2 [1 Cor. 2:9f.]—and is taken from holy Isaiah 64[:3]—saying, "What no eye has seen, what no ear has heard, and what has not come into any human heart, this God has prepared for those who love him. But God has revealed this to us through his spirit. For the spirit searches all things, yes also the depth of the godhead," etc.

In brief, it is an earnest conviction of mine that we must know and not only believe in an empty way whether what has been given us is from God or the devil or from nature.[7] If we want to be able to make our natural understanding of these same matters obedient to faith, 2 Corinthians 10[:5], then reason must be led to the ultimate limit of its capacity for judgment, as is shown in Romans 1[:16ff.] and Baruch 3 [see, rather, Jer. 45:3]. But natural reason can in good conscience make no certain judgment without God's revelation. For people will clearly find that they cannot attain heaven with their heads. Rather, they must first become in an interior way complete and utter fools [to the world], Isaiah 29[:13f.] and 33[:18], Obadiah 1[:8], 1 Corinthians 1[:18ff.]. Oh, that is a very alien message to the clever, carnal, and sensual world. For when it is received, there immediately follow pains like those of a woman giving birth, Psalm 48[:7], John 16[:21]. For Daniel and every pious person with him finds that it is just as impossible for him to acquire by natural reason a knowledge of God as it is for the rest of the common people. This is what the wise prophet means, Ecclesiastes 3[:11], for he says, "He who wants to discover the majesty of God will be crushed by his magnificence." For the more natural reason strives for God, the further the working of the holy spirit distances itself, as Psalm 139[:6] clearly shows. Indeed, if one understood the pretensions of natural reason, without a doubt one would not seek much help from stolen Scriptures, as the scribes do with a scrap or two of text, Isaiah 28[:10], Jeremiah 8[:8]. Rather, he would soon feel how the working of the divine word springs from his heart, John 4[:14]. Indeed, he would not need to carry stagnant water to the well, Jeremiah 2[:13], as our scribes now do. They confuse nature with grace, without drawing any distinction. They obstruct the way of the word, Psalm 119[:110], which arises from the abyss of the soul. As Moses says, Deuteronomy 30[:14], "The word is not far from you. Behold, it is in your heart," etc.

Now, perhaps you ask how it is that the word comes into the heart? The answer is: when the striving for truth is strong, it comes down to us from God above—which I will let stand for now and say more about at another time. And this striving for truth, whether what is called God's word is really God's or not, begins when one is a child of six or seven years of age, as is symbolized in Numbers 19[:19f.]. Therefore St. Paul cites Moses [Dt. 30:14] and Isaiah [65:1] in his letter to the Romans 10[:8]. And he speaks there of the inner word to be heard in the abyss of the soul through the revelation of God. And the person who has not become conscious of and receptive to this inner word, through the living testimony of God, Romans 8[:9], does not know how to say anything essential about God, even though he may have devoured a hundred thousand Bibles.

From this, anyone can easily measure how far the world really is from the Christian faith. Still, no one wants to see or hear it. Now, if a person should become conscious of the word and receptive to it, God must remove all his carnal desires. And if the impulse from God comes into his heart, so that he wants to kill all the desires of the flesh, it is necessary that the person then give way to God, so that he may receive his action. For a bestial person does not perceive what God speaks in the soul, 1 Corinthians 2[:14]. Rather, the holy spirit must refer him to the serious contemplation of the plain, pure meaning of the law, Psalm 19[:8]. Otherwise, he remains blind in his heart, and he fantasizes for himself a wooden Christ, and he misleads himself.

Therefore, look at how repugnant it became for beloved Daniel [Dan. 2:18] to interpret the vision to the king and how diligently he thus beseeched God and prayed to him! To have revelations from God, therefore, one must cut himself off from all diversions and have a serious desire for truth, 2 Corinthians 6[:17]. And through practicing such a [method of discovering] truth, he must learn to distinguish the undeceived vision from the false one. Thus, beloved Daniel says, in chapter ten,[8] "A person must have the right method of understanding visions in order to know that they are not all to be rejected," etc.

FOURTH

You should know that an elected person who wants to know which visions or dreams are from God and which are from nature or the devil must be severed in his mind and heart, and also in his natural understanding, from all temporal reliance on the flesh. And it must happen to him as it happened to beloved Joseph in Egypt, Genesis 39 [rather, Gen. 40:5–20], and also to Daniel here in this second chapter. For a sensual man, Luke 7[:25], will accept nothing but the pleasures of the world, which are thistles and thorns, as the Lord says, Mark 4[:7,18], and he will suppress the whole manifestation of the word that God addresses in the soul. For this reason, if God has already spoken his holy word in the soul, the person cannot hear it if he is inexperienced. For he does not look within or see into himself and into the abyss of his soul, Psalm 49[:21]. Such a man does not want to crucify his life, with his lusts and appetites, as Paul the holy apostle teaches [see Gal. 5:24]. Thus, the plowed field of the word of God remains full of thistles and thorns and full of much underbrush. These must all be removed for the work of God to take place, in order that the person is not found to be negligent or lazy, Proverbs 24[:30f.]. And, after these hindrances have been removed, one sees the fruitfulness of the field and finally the good crop. Only then does the person become aware that he is the dwelling place of God and the holy spirit for the duration of his days. Indeed, he sees that he has been truly created for one purpose only, that he should seek the testimony of God in his own life, Psalm 93[:4] and 119[:95–125]. He will perceive these testimonies at first only in part, through visual means, and then perfectly in the abyss of his heart, 1 Corinthians 13[:10ff.].

In the second place, he must take note that such visual images and symbols in dreams or visions approximate in every respect those which are testified to in the holy Bible, so that the devil does not intrude next to them and spoil the balm of the holy spirit with his diabolical sweetness, as the wise man says of the flies that die from this sweetness, Ecclesiastes 10[:1].

In the third place, the elected person must pay attention to the manner in which the visions occur. They must not pour forth swiftly through human machinations. Rather, they should simply flow out according to God's irrevocable will. And the elected person must take heed most carefully that not a particle of that which he has seen is lost, so that its effect can be fully reproduced. But when the devil wants to do something, he is betrayed by his lazy posturing, and his lies finally peek out, for he is a liar, John 8[:44].

In this chapter of Daniel the same point is clearly demonstrated by King Nebuchadnezzar and, afterward, is shown in fact in the third chapter. For the king quickly forgot the warning of God. Without a doubt, this was caused by his carnal desires, which he directed toward pleasures and creaturely things. It must always happen in this way when a person wants constantly to cultivate his own pleasures and yet also have something of God's action and not be in any tribulation. In this condition the power of the word of God cannot overshadow him, Luke 8[:12–14]. God the almighty shows true dreams and visions to his beloved friends most often in their deepest tribulation, as he did to pious Abraham, Genesis 15[:1–6] and 17[:1ff.]. God appeared to him as he shuddered in terrible fear. Similarly, as beloved Jacob fled with great tribulation from his brother, Esau, a vision came to him in which he saw a ladder extended up to heaven, with the angels of God climbing up and down on it, Genesis 28[:12]. Afterward, when he came home again, he had a tremendous fear of his brother Esau. Then the Lord appeared to him in a vision in which God crushed his hip and struggled with him, Genesis 32[:25f.]. And similarly, pious Joseph was also hated by his brothers, and, in this tribulation, he had two visions of danger, Genesis 37[:5–11]. And afterward, in his heartfelt tribulation while imprisoned in Egypt, Joseph was so greatly enlightened by God that he could interpret all visions and dreams, Genesis 39[:21], 40[:12–19] and 41[:25ff.].

More than all these examples, that other Joseph, in Matthew 1[:20–23] and 2[:13,19f.,22], should be held up before the untempted, pleasure-seeking swine who think they are such clever little ones. This Joseph had four dreams when he was terrified by his tribulation, and, through the dreams, he was reassured. So, also, in their sleep the wise men were instructed by an angel not to return to Herod [Mt. 2:12]. Similarly, the beloved apostles were diligently attentive to visions, as is clearly described in their history, the book of Acts. Indeed, it is a truly apostolic, patriarchal, and prophetic spirit that awaits visions and attains them in painful tribulation.

Therefore it is no wonder that Brother Fattened-swine and Brother Soft-life [Luther] rejects visions, Job 28[:12]. But if a person has not perceived the clear word of God in his soul, then he must have visions. So it was that St. Peter, in the Acts of the Apostles, did not understand the Mosaic Law of Leviticus, chapter eleven, and had doubts about the cleanliness of food and about whether to have anything to do with heathens, Acts 10[:10f.]. And then, in the fullness of his mind, God gave him a vision. In it he saw a linen cloth with four corners stretching down from heaven to earth, and it was filled with four-footed animals. And he heard a voice saying, "Slaughter and eat." The devout Cornelius had a similar experience when he too did not know what he should do, Acts 10[:3–6]. And when Paul came down to Troas, a vision appeared to him in the night. It was a man from Macedonia, who stood before him and greeted him and said, "Come down to Macedonia and help us." After he had seen such a vision, says the text of Acts 16[:8ff.], "Soon thereafter we tried to travel to Macedonia for we were certain that the Lord had called us there." And similarly, when Paul was afraid to preach in Corinth, Acts 18[:9f.], the Lord said to him through a vision in the night, "You should not be afraid," etc. "No one shall attempt to do you harm for I have many people in this city," etc.

And what need is there to bring forth the many other witnesses of Scripture? In such momentous and dangerous matters as those which true preachers, dukes, and princes have to deal with, it would never be possible to guard themselves securely against error on all sides, and to act blamelessly, if they did not rely on revelations from God—as Aaron heard from Moses, Exodus 4[:15] and David from Nathan and Gad, 2 Chronicles 29[:25]. For this reason, the beloved apostles were completely and totally accustomed to visions, as the text of Acts 12[:7ff.] proves. There the angel came to Peter and led him out of Herod's prison. And he thought he was having a vision. He did not know that the angel was accomplishing his release by this means. But if Peter was not accustomed to visions, how could it have occurred to him that this was a vision?

From this, I now conclude that whoever is inexperienced and an enemy of visions because of a carnal consciousness, and either accepts them all without any discrimination or rejects them all because the false dream interpreters of the world have done such harm by being greedy and selfish people, this person will not fare well. Rather, he will be in conflict with the holy spirit, Joel 2[:26f.]. For God clearly speaks, as in this text of Daniel, about the transformation of the world.[9] He will bring about this transformation in the Last Days, so that his name will be rightly praised. He will release the elect from their shame and pour forth his spirit over all flesh. And our sons and daughters shall prophesy and shall have dreams and visions, etc. For, if Christendom is not to become apostolic, Acts 27 [rather, Acts 2:16ff.], where Joel is cited, why then should one preach? To what purpose then are visions in the Bible?

It is true—and I know it to be true—that the spirit of God now reveals to many elected pious people that a momentous, invincible, future reformation is very necessary and must be brought about. Each one may protect himself against it as he wishes and yet the prophecy of Daniel remains undiminished, though no one believes it, as Paul also says to the Romans 3[:3]. This text of Daniel is thus as clear as the bright sun, and the work of ending the fifth empire of the world is now in full swing.

The first empire was symbolized by the golden head [of the statue in Nebuchadnezzar's dream]. That was the empire of Babylon. And the second empire was represented by the silver breast and arms, which was the empire of the Medes and Persians. The third empire was the empire of the Greeks, which resounded with its cleverness, indicated by the brass. The fourth empire was the Roman empire, which was won with the iron sword and was an empire of coercion. The fifth empire or monarchy is that which we have before our own eyes [i.e., the Holy Roman Empire] and it is also (like the fourth) of iron and would like to be coercive. But, as we see before our very eyes, the iron is intermixed with filth,[10] vain schemes of flattery that slither and squirm over the face of the whole earth. For he who cannot be a cheat [in our empire] must be an idiot. One sees now how prettily the eels and snakes copulate together in a heap. The priests and all the evil clergy are the snakes, as John the Baptist calls them, Matthew 3[:7], and the temporal lords and rulers are the eels, as is symbolized by the fish in Leviticus 11[:10–12]. For the devil's empire has painted its face with clay.[11]

Oh, you beloved lords, how well the Lord will smash down the old pots of clay [ecclesiastical authorities] with his rod of iron, Psalm 2[:9]. Therefore, you most true and beloved regents, learn your knowledge directly from the mouth of God and do not let yourselves be seduced by your flattering priests and restrained by false patience and indulgence. For the stone [Christ's spirit] torn from the mountain without human touch has become great. The poor laity and the peasants see it much more clearly than you do. Yes, God be praised, the stone has become so great that, already, if other lords or neighbors wanted to persecute you on account of the gospel, they would be overthrown by their own subjects. This I know to be true. Indeed the stone is great! The foolish world has long feared it. The stone fell upon the world when it was still small. What then should we do now, after it has grown so great and powerful? And after it has struck the great statue so powerfully and irresistibly that it has smashed down the old pots of clay?

Therefore, you dear rulers of Saxony, stand boldly on the cornerstone, as St. Peter did, Matthew 16[:18], and seek genuine perseverance, granted by the divine will. He will surely temper you on the stone, Psalm 40[:3]. Your path will be the right one. Seek unhesitatingly the righteousness of God at all times and bravely take up the cause of the gospel. For

God stands so close to you that you do not believe it. Why do you want to be frightened by the specter of man, Psalm 118[:6]?

Look closely at this text of Daniel! King Nebuchadnezzar wanted to kill the clever ones because they could not interpret the dream for him. This was deserved. For, with their cleverness, they wanted to rule his whole kingdom, and yet they could not even do what they had been engaged for. So also are our clergy today. And I tell you this truly: if you were able to recognize the harm that has befallen Christendom and rightly reflect on it, then you would win for yourselves as much zeal as Jehu the king, 2 Kings 9 and 10, and as much zeal as the whole book of the Apocalypse shows. And I know for sure that you would hold yourselves back from exercising the power of the sword only with great effort. For the pitiable corruption of holy Christendom has become so great that at present no tongue can fully express it.

Therefore, a new Daniel must arise and interpret your revelation for you.[12] And this same new Daniel must go forth, as Moses teaches, Deuteronomy 20[:2], at the head of the troops. He must reconcile the anger of the princes and that of the enraged people. For, if you were truly to experience the shame of Christendom and the deception of the false clergy and incorrigible rogues, then no one could imagine how enraged at them you would become. Without a doubt it would gall you, and you would fervently take it to heart that you had been so kind to them after they had led you to the most shameful opinions with the sweetest words, Proverbs 6[:1ff.], and against all established truth. For they have made fools of you, so that everyone now swears to the saints that princes are heathen people insofar as their office is concerned.[13] Princes, they say, should do nothing but maintain civil unity.

Oh, beloved ones, the great stone will indeed soon fall on and smite this view of your office and smash such rational schemes to the ground. For Christ says, in Matthew 10[:34], "I have not come to bring peace but the sword." But what should one do with these false spiritual leaders? Nothing but what is done with evildoers who obstruct the gospel: put them away and cut them off, if you do not want to be servants of the devil but servants of God, as Paul calls you in Romans 13[:4]. You should not doubt that God will smash to bits all your adversaries who undertake to persecute you. For as Isaiah 59[:1] says, "His hand is not yet hampered." Therefore God is still able to help you and will do so, just as he stood by King Josiah the elect [2 Kgs. 22–23], and the others who defended the name of God. Thus, you rulers are angels when you seek to act justly, as Peter says in 2 Peter 1[:4]. Christ commanded this very earnestly, Luke 19[:27], and said, "Take my enemies and strangle them for me before my eyes." Why? Ah, because they have spoiled Christ's government, and, in addition, they seek to defend their villainy under the guise of the Christian faith. And, with their deceitful infamy, they pollute the whole world. Therefore Christ our Lord says, Matthew 18[:6], "Whosoever does evil to one of these little ones, it is better for him that a millstone be hung about his neck and that he be thrown into the depths of the sea." He who wishes, turning [in his evasions] here and there, can gloss over this. But these are the words of Christ. Now, if Christ can say this about someone who does evil to one of the little ones, what should be said about those who do evil to a great multitude in their faith? For this is how archvillains act, who do evil to the whole world and make it deviate from the true Christian faith, and who say that no one shall know the mysteries of God. Each person should judge them according to their words and not according to their actions, Matthew 23[:3]. They say that it is not necessary for the Christian faith to be tested like gold in the fire, 1 Peter 1[:7], Psalm 140[:11]. But if this were the case, the Christian faith would be worse than the faith of a dog that hopes to get a scrap of bread while the table is being set.[14] False scribes present such an image of the faith to the poor blind world. This suits them, for they preach only for the sake of their belly, Philippians 3[:19]. From their hearts they can say nothing else, Matthew 12[:34].

Now, should you want to be true rulers, then you must begin government at the roots, as Christ commanded. Drive his enemies away from the elect, for that is your appointed task. Beloved ones, do not offer us any stale posturing about how the power of God should do it without your application of the sword. Otherwise, may the sword rust away in its scabbard on you. May God grant this!

Let any scribe say whatever he wants to you. Christ's words are sufficient, Matthew 7[:19], John 15[:2–6], "Every tree that does not bring forth good fruit should be uprooted and cast into the fire." If you now remove the mask from the world, then you will soon recognize it for what it is with a righteous judgment, John 7[:24]. Judge righteously, as God commands! You have sufficient help for the purpose, Proverbs 6[:16–23?], for Christ is your master, Matthew 23[:8]. Therefore do not permit evildoers, who turn us away from God, to live longer, Deuteronomy 13[:6]. For a godless person has no right to life when he hinders the pious. In Exodus 22[:1] God says, "You shall not permit the evildoer to live." St. Paul also means this, for he says that the sword of rulers is given for the punishment of evildoers and to protect the pious, Romans 13[:1–4].[15] God is your guardian and he will teach you to struggle against his enemies, Psalm 18[:35]. He will make your hands skillful in fighting and he will also sustain you. But in addition you will have to suffer a great cross and temptation, so that the fear of God is made clear to you. This cannot happen without suffering. But it will cost you no more than the danger that is risked for the sake of God's will and the useless prattle of your opponents. Although pious David was driven from his castle by Absalom, nevertheless, he finally regained it when Absalom was hanged and stabbed [2 Sam. 15:10–18 and 18:9–15]. Therefore, you dear fathers of Saxony, you must risk it for the sake of the gospel. For God will chastise you in a friendly way, as he does his most beloved sons, Deuteronomy 1[:31], when he is burning with his momentous wrath. Then blessed are all those who rely on God. Say freely with the spirit of Christ, "I will not fear a hundred thousand, even if they have surrounded me."

At this point I imagine that our scribes will hold up to me the kindness of Christ, which they claim for themselves and use hypocritically. But in contrast to this, they should also look at the wrath of Christ, John 2[:15–17], Psalm 69[:10], with which he tore up the roots of idolatry, as Paul says to the Colossians 3[:5–9]. Because of these scribes, the wrath of God cannot be removed from the community. If, according to our view, he cast down those guilty of lesser offenses, then without a doubt he would not have spared idols and images if they had been there.[16] As he commanded through Moses in Deuteronomy 7[:5f.], where he says: "You are a holy people. You shall not have pity on the idolatrous. Break up their altars. Smash their images and burn them so that I am not angry with you." Christ has not abrogated these words. Rather, he will help us to fulfill them, Matthew 5[:17]. The visual symbols are all explicated by the prophets, but these are bright clear words that must remain for eternity, Isaiah 40[:8]. God cannot say "yes" today and "no" tomorrow. Rather, he is unchangeable in his words, Malachi 3[:6], 1 Samuel 15[:10–22], Numbers 22[:6]. But if it is objected that the apostles did not destroy the idols of the heathen, I reply as follows: St. Peter was a timid man, Galatians 2[:11ff.]. He was hypocritical with the heathen. He was also symbolic of all the apostles in this respect, so that Christ said of him in the last chapter of John [Jn. 21:15–19] that he had a very strong fear of death. And it is easy to figure out that Peter acted in this way because he did not want to give the heathen any reason to kill him. But St. Paul spoke out most firmly against idolatry, Acts 17[:16–31]. And, if he had been able to carry out his teaching resolutely among the Athenians, without a doubt he would have utterly cast out idolatry, as God commanded through Moses, and as also happened afterward through the martyrs, according to trustworthy histories.

Therefore the deficiency or negligence of the saints gives us no reason to allow the godless to continue in their ways. Since they profess God's name with us, they should choose one of two alternatives—either repudiate the Christian faith entirely or put away their idolatry, Matthew 18[:8f.].

But then our scribes come along and, referring to the text of Daniel, say in their godless, stolen way that the Antichrist will be destroyed without a hand being lifted. This is too much! Anyone who says this is already as fainthearted as the Canaanites were when the elect wanted to enter the promised land, as Joshua [5:1] writes. Joshua nevertheless did not spare them from the sharpness of the sword. Look at Psalm 44[:4] and 1 Chronicles 14[:11]. There you will find the same solution: the elect did not win the promised land with the sword alone, but rather through the power of God. Nevertheless, the sword was the means, just as for us eating and drinking are the means for sustaining life. Thus the sword is also necessary as a means to destroy the godless, Romans 13[:1–4].

But for this use of the sword to occur as it should and in the right manner, our dear fathers who confess Christ with us—that is, the princes—should do it. But if they do not do it, then the sword will be taken away from them, Daniel 7[:27].[17] For then they confess Christ with words and deny him in their actions, Titus 1[:16]. Thus the princes should offer peace to the enemy, Deuteronomy 2[:26–30]. But if the princes want to be "spiritual" and not render an account of their knowledge of God, 1 Peter 3[:12–17], they should be gotten rid of, 1 Corinthians 5[:13]. I, together with pious Daniel, bid them not oppose God's revelation. But, if they do take the contrary course, may they be strangled without any mercy,[18] as Hezekiah [2 Kg. 18:22], Josiah [2 Kg. 23:5], Cyrus [2 Chr. 36:22f.], Daniel [Dan. 6:27], and Elijah, 1 Kings 18[:40] destroyed the priests of Baal. Otherwise, the Christian church will not be able to return to its source. The tares must be pulled out of God's vineyard at the time of harvest. Then the beautiful golden wheat will gain lasting roots and come up right, Matthew 13[:24–30,39]. The angels who sharpen their sickles for the cutting are the earnest servants of God who fulfill the zeal of divine wisdom, Malachi 3[:1–6].

Nebuchadnezzar perceived this divine wisdom through Daniel [Dan. 2:46f.]. He fell down before him after the mighty truth had overpowered him. He was blown like a straw in the wind, as chapter 3[:26–30] proves. Similarly, there are now innumerable people who accept the gospel with great joy as long as everything is going well for them in a pleasing way, Luke 8[:48]. But when God wants to put such people in the crucible or when he puts them into the fire of a crucial test, 1 Peter 1[:7], oh, then they are angered by the smallest word of the gospel, as Christ proclaimed in Mark 4[:17]. By the same token, without a doubt many untested people will be angered by this booklet, because I say with Christ, Luke 18 [see, rather, Lk. 19:27], Matthew 18[:6], with Paul, 1 Corinthians 5[:7,13], and with the instruction of the whole of divine law, that godless rulers, especially the priests and monks, should be killed. They tell us the holy gospel is a heresy, and, at the same time, they want to be the best Christians. Just as their hypocritical, false goodness will turn to rage and become infinitely bitter, it will also defend the godless and say that Christ killed no one, etc. And because the friends of God, most lamentably, are without effective power, the prophecy of Paul is fulfilled, 2 Timothy 3[:1ff.]. In the Last Days the lovers of pleasure will indeed have the appearance of virtue, but they will deny its power. Nothing on earth has a better form and mask than false goodness. Thus, all the corners of the earth are full of absolute hypocrites, among whom none is so bold as to be able to proclaim the real truth.

In order that the truth may really be brought to light, you rulers—God grant that you do not willingly do otherwise—must act according to the conclusion of this chapter of Daniel [Dan. 2:48]. That is, Nebuchadnezzar elevated holy Daniel to office so that the king might carry out good, correct decisions, inspired by the holy spirit, Psalm 58[:11f.]. For the godless have no right to life except that which the elect decide to grant them, as is written in the book of Exodus 23[:29–33]. Rejoice, you true friends of God, that the enemies of the cross have crapped their courage into their pants. They act righteously, even though they never once dreamed of doing so. If we now fear only God, why should we recoil before vacillating, incapable men, Numbers 14[:8f.], Joshua 11[:6]. Only be bold! He to whom is given all power in heaven and on earth [Christ] wants to lead the government, Matthew 28[:18]. To you, most beloved, may God grant eternal protection. Amen.

7

Special Exposure of False Faith

Special Exposure of False Faith, set forth to the unfaithful world through the witness of the Gospel of Luke, in order to remind suffering pitiable Christendom of its false life.

Ezekiel 8[:7–10], "Beloved companions, let us widen the gap, so that the whole world can see and grasp who our mighty ones are, who have so viciously made God into a painted puppet."

Thomas Müntzer, with a hammer.

Mühlhausen, 1524.

Jeremiah 1[:9f.], "Behold, I have set my word in your mouth. Today I have set you over the people and over empires, so that you may root out, break up, disperse, and destroy. And so that you may build up and plant."

Jeremiah 1[:18f.], "An iron wall has been set up between the kings, princes, and parsons, on the one hand, and the people on the other. They will contend and the victory will be wonderful due to the defeat of the strong, godless tyrants."

PREFACE TO POOR DISPERSED CHRISTENDOM

The spirit of the strength and fear of God be with you, you pitiable community. After the libelous writings[1] [of Luther] have made you partly fearful—and also most impudent—it is exceedingly necessary for me to counter the rising evil with a demonstration of Christian mastery. At the present time, this mastery cannot be shown except through an exposition of holy Scripture, especially the teachings of the spirit of Christ, and through a comprehensive comparison of all the secrets and judgments of God. For all knowledge contains within itself its diametrical opposite. But where passages of Scripture have not been grasped in their context, no individual passage may be completely and totally understood (no matter how bright and clear it is) without damaging unspeakably the other passages. This error is the basic cause of every evil schism in the Christian community.

For the sake of such an important cause [as scriptural integrity], I, an inadequate person, have advanced on the fortress [in which the godless have barricaded themselves] in order to widen the breach in the wall[2] and with the expectation of suffering all the evils that the godless despoilers

115

usually impose on the servants of Christendom. They impose these evils after. they have elaborately embellished their literalistic faith and denied (this too is palpable) the gracious power of God. And so they want to make God dumb, insane, and fantastic with their false word and false faith. Therefore, the arrogant practice of every abomination among all the communities of the whole world has also made people so proud that from day to day they engage in nonsensical resistance [against true faith]. Thus, a fundamental consideration of the holy Christian faith must turn back the wild upsurge of the rising waves (as described in Psalm 93[:3]). Because no one else wants to grasp the rudder of the ship on account of the difficult effort involved, I cannot release the rudder, since the water of every ruination has penetrated into the souls of the friends of God, Psalm 69[:2]. I must faithfully uncover the poisonous damage which has spread so far. I will gladly do this with all mercy where my critique is accepted. But, where it would redound to the disadvantage of the spirit of Christ, my patience will not conceal the disgrace of anyone whatsoever.

At the beginning of this explanation and exposure of false faith, I always want to let each section follow the other naturally and so allow sufficient space and time [to vindicate myself against] my opponents. But I have only shunned the dangerous corner [of a private disputation][3] for the reason that the situation demands it. In the same way, Christ himself shunned the viperous scribes, John 7[:32ff.], and would give Annas in a private conversation no other justification for his teaching than that he referred him to his listeners, the common people, John 18[:19–21]. He spoke clearly to Annas: "Why do you ask me? Ask my listeners." Our learned ones would gladly like to give the witness of Jesus' spirit a higher education. They will completely fail in this because they are not educated enough to teach so that through their teachings the common man may be brought up to their level. Rather, the learned ones alone want to pass judgment on the faith with their stolen Scripture, although they are totally and completely without faith, either before God or before men. For everyone perceives and realizes that they strive for honors and worldly goods. Therefore, you, the common man, must become learned yourself, so that you will be misled no longer. The same spirit of Christ will help you in this which will mock our learned ones to their destruction. Amen.

EXPLANATION OF THE FIRST CHAPTER OF LUKE

The whole Gospel of Luke gives Christendom a precious testimony in order for it to realize that the holy Christian faith has become such an alien, strange thing that it would not be surprising if a good-hearted person, one who has correctly perceived the blindness of Christendom, were to weep blood. Christ himself spoke about this in the Gospel of Luke

18[:8], saying, "Do you think that if the son of man were to come, he would find faith on the earth?" Isaiah, too, complains about this in chapter fifteen [see, rather, Is. 65:1ff. or 53:1.], and Paul in his Letter to the Romans 10[:16,20f.].

Therefore, it is an inexpressible calamity and a completely awful abomination that the unfaithful (as anyone can see with his own eyes) want to preach the Christian faith to the people—a faith that they themselves have not felt and experienced. Nor do they know the feelings of a believer. They think, or deceive themselves into thinking, that faith is as easy to attain as they all blabber about very boastfully.

Therefore, my most beloved brothers, we must earnestly take to heart this first chapter of Luke from start to finish. For, indeed, we will clearly find in it how unbelief is laid bare in all of the elect. Zechariah did not want to believe the word of the angel Gabriel [Lk. 1:11–19], and he reproached Gabriel because what he said was impossible. Mary, the bearer of our savior, who is therefore praised by the children's children, is also most worthy of consideration [Lk. 1:48]. She wanted to have good reasons and supporting information [for believing what the angel said]. Zechariah and Mary did not attain their faith, as the insane world now believes, in a rosy way. They did not merely go on and say, "Yes, I will simply believe that God will make everything all right." With such an easy source of belief, the drunken world concocts a poisonous faith, which is much worse than that of the Turks, heathen, and Jews. But Mary and Zechariah were terrified in the fear of God, until the faith of a mustard seed [Mt. 17:20 and Lk. 17:6] conquered their unbelief. This process is experienced with great trembling and affliction.

Even God cannot increase the faith of anyone and look upon him as saved unless this person has patiently endured the source [of real faith] with the greatest trembling and fear. God himself says this through holy Isaiah 66[:2]: "Whom should I scrutinize except the lowly and those who are terrified before all my sayings." Thus Paul says to the Philippians 2[:12], "You must strive for your salvation with trembling and fears." Oh ho, the fear of God at the beginning of faith is an unbearable thing to human nature. Moses heard God himself speak. Nevertheless, he did not want to heed his word, since God told him to go into Egypt, Exodus 4[:1ff.]. Moses had to experience the power of God in the abyss of his soul, as he later testified, Deuteronomy 30[:9–14]. Otherwise he would not have gone to Egypt. God promised the patriarch Jacob many goods and infinite security. Nevertheless, he quarreled with God. He had to fight for a victory over God before he could accept the blessings that faith brings with it, Genesis 32[:25–30].

Thus, every diligent person finds testimony throughout the whole of Scripture, especially in the Book of Judges 6[:13ff.], 7[:7],and 8[:4ff.], of how faith continually contends with unbelief. Gideon had such a firm, strong faith that, with it, he conquered a huge army with only three hundred men. But, before he was willing to accept such a faith, he said to the angel of God, just as one chastises a habitual liar: "You say the Lord is with you, you almighty man. How can that be when we must suffer so much misfortune?" The person of untrained faith, at the first encounter with God, has no other basis for acting than to be fearful of everything and to be unreachable by the best arguments. For he who easily believes has an easygoing heart. But the fear of God gives the holy spirit an abode, so that God may protect the elect—God, whom the world most foolishly fears, with irreparable harm to its "wisdom."

Thus, in this Gospel of Luke, one should especially note the beginning and the end, where the protection that comes through the holy spirit is treated, which teaches us faith through the pure fear of God. This fear engenders great amazement at the seemingly impossible work of faith. For the power of the All-Highest (which Luke describes in the first and last chapters) rejects all false, secret unbelief in the most radical way. This unbelief will be discovered through the putting on or breaking through of the divine spirit in the abyss of the soul. Paul says, "You should put on Christ" [Rom. 13:14]. Then false faith can have absolutely no place. But whoever has not experienced this breakthrough knows absolutely and utterly nothing of faith. For he only retains his unexperienced faith in his hardened spirit, like an old beggar's cloak, which the false, doubt-producing scribes think they can darn most masterfully with a new patch, as the Gospel of Luke 5[:36] affirms. And for this patching, they employ nothing other than their stolen Scripture. If they are questioned as to how they came to such a high faith, since they so incessantly blabber about it, or why they would not rather be heathen, Jews, or Turks, or what kind of revelations they have had—since they so threateningly assail the world and so steadfastly defy it—then they come back with an infinitely insipid and stale smirk and simply say without shame: "Behold, I believe the Scripture!" And then they become so jealous and hateful that they simply snarl straight out, saying: "Oh ho, this one denies Scripture!" For, with their vices they most eagerly want to plug the snouts of all people. Like the fool—the pope, with his butter-boys[4]—they merely want to appease the great unrest and the heartfelt suffering of the elect, or to assign this unrest and suffering to the devil, without any refutation. Our scribes, the learned clergy, usually declare that Christ rejected the godless scribes, so that one might think they are also similar to him. They stick out their forked little tongues and say in a soft way, "Search the Scriptures, for in them you think you have eternal life and they are that which testify of me" [Jn. 5:39]. Therefore, the poor, needy people are so greatly deceived that no tongue can complain about it enough. With all their words and deeds our scribes make sure that the poor man cannot learn to read, because he is worried about his sustenance. And they shamelessly preach that the poor man should let himself be sheared and clipped by the tyrants. The scribes say: "When will the poor man then learn to read Scripture? Yes, dear Thomas, you gush such nonsense. The scribes should read the beautiful books and the peasants should listen to them, for faith comes through hearing."[5] Oh yes, there they have found a fine dodge. He [Luther] would set up many more evil rogues to replace the priests and monks than the world has known since the beginning.[6] God be blessed, however, that a great many of the elect recognize the root of unbelief where it has long been concealed. And, even today, this root would gladly like to grow wild, preventing the wheat from coming up. Therefore, shortly before the above-mentioned words [of Jn. 5:39], Christ spoke to those "pious" people, the scribes, "My word does not abide in you." And indeed why not? On account of unbelief, which will make absolutely no room for the true root of undeceivable faith, Matthew 13[:3ff.], Mark 4[:3ff.], Luke 8[:5ff.], John 9[:22], and Isaiah 6[:9f.].

Now, if such a harmful root is to be rooted out, one must be on guard against the godless ways of the scribes, with whom Christ himself in no way compromised. For they make a shameful cloak out of Scripture, a cloak that hinders the true nature of Christian faith from manifesting itself before the whole world, Matthew 5[:16] and 10[:5ff.].

The son of God has said, "Scripture gives testimony." But the scribes say, "It gives faith." Oh no, most dearly beloved, look much further about you! Otherwise you will have the most foolish faith on earth, like that of apes. In this way, the poor masses are seduced by the arrogant, itinerant scholars. Therefore, the concealed truth, which has slept for so very long, must once come to light boldly. And it must appear in such measure that, when a Christian speaks among the poor masses, saying he has learned the Christian faith from God himself, he would not be believed (as we are still today ready to believe) if he did not agree with Scripture in his account of the faith and that all of the elect should be taught by God, John 6[:45], Isaiah 54[:11f.], Jeremiah 31[:33f.], Job 35, and Psalm 18[:29], 25[:14], 33[:12–22], 71[:17], and 94[:10]. These and many other passages of Scripture force all of us to the conclusion that we need to be taught by God alone.

Now, if one has neither heard nor seen the Bible his whole life long, he could still possess an undeceived Christian faith through the correct teaching of the spirit, as all those had who wrote the holy Scripture without any books. And he could also be most highly assured that he has derived such a faith from the undeceivable God, and not from the image of the devil, nor drawn it from his own nature. Therefore, to gain this certainty, he must render an account of this faith, together with all its origins, before those people who also have a tested, uncontrived faith, responding to all their demands—just as gold is tested in the fire of the greatest sufferings of the heart. Otherwise a mere mockery and a completely flattering,   ghing matter would be made of faith before the pampered ones, whu nave never once in their whole life seriously striven for true faith with the smallest thought. For they merely think that one should believe, like archseducers proceeding further with their fabrications.

Now, should we Christians unanimously agree, Psalm 72 [see, rather, Ps. 68:33], together with all of the elect among all religious divisions or every kind of faith (as the clear text of the Acts of the Apostles 10[:1ff.] gives testimony), then we must know how one feels who has, from his youth on, grown up among unbelievers and has experienced the right action and teaching of God without any books.

To this end, one should use Scripture so that one instructs with a friendly attitude each and every one, be he Jew or Turk, about such excellent works and the testimony of such people and teaches them how to judge which spirits are divine and which are devilish, 1 John 4[:1ff.]. Here our learned ones intrude and want to have miracles,[7] as the godless scribes usually do, Matthew 12[:38]. With their too hasty judgment, the scribes give over to the devil the people who speak a single word against them, and they make a mockery out of the spirit of Christ. And they are so brazen that they dare to scream and write: "Spirit here, spirit there. I praise my own writings. I have done it," etc. And, so that they alone are acknowledged, they strive, day and night, with all their intrigues to kill those who say one word about the spirit of God. They do this just as the scribes did before they brought Christ to the cross. They said to Christ that he was not prophesied in the law of God.

And now our scribes say the same thing, indeed in a more perverted way. They say one should not take the spirit of Christ as the basis of faith. One should not even mention this idea. For whoever does mention it is marked with the first essential sign of a false prophet. Scripture (they say) should give faith. But the godless, pampered ones do not know any clear reason why holy Scripture should be accepted or rejected, only that it has been accepted by tradition, that is, by many people. The Jews, Turks, and all peoples also have such a greasy-ape way of verifying their faith.

But Mary and Zechariah, Abraham, Joseph, Moses, and all the patriarchs tell us about the opposite way of verifying faith, those who, in the abyss of their hearts, clung firmly to the stimulus of the holy spirit, and who absolutely and completely rejected the temptations of the desperate, unvirtuous godless ones, as Isaiah 8[:12] says. Thus, the agreed opinion and counsel of the godless describe the activity of the spirit of God as a disgrace.

The scribes speak as follows without becoming embarrassed: "The holy Christian Church has accepted this and that. This article, this teaching is heresy." And, nevertheless, they do not have the least inkling about real heresy. Nor do they know the least reason to justify why they are more attracted to the Christian faith than to any other. Therefore, the hireling clerics are such evil comforters of the poor, miserable, sad, heart-afflicted people.

SECOND

Each and every person should observe most carefully, and then he will certainly find that the Christian faith is an impossible thing for a man of the flesh, 1 Corinthians 3[:1]. Indeed, he will find further, everywhere in the texts of Scripture, that all right-believing people like Mary, Zechariah—Elizabeth, too, was one—found faith to be impossible. And it is also impossible for every sober, patient, serious, earnest, experienced person. Whoever pays attention to this will feel the hair on his head stand on end. Heed it precisely in this text of Luke 1. The angel spoke to the mother of God, "For God nothing is impossible" [Lk. 1:37]. Why is this, my most dearly beloved reader? In truth, because according to nature bearing the son of God was an impossible, an inconceivable, and an unheard of thing, 1 Corinthians 2[:9], Isaiah 64[:3f.]. And all of us must have just this experience of impossibility in the beginning of faith. And we must hold to it that we carnal, earthly men shall become gods through the incarnation of Christ as man. And so we will be pupils of God with him, being taught and deified by God himself. Yes, indeed, even more, we should be completely and totally transformed into him, so that earthly life revolves around into the heavenly, Philippians 3[:20f.].

Behold what an impossible thing this [deification] was to all the godless and the hesitant among the elect, John 10[:25ff.], Psalm 82[:5ff.]. They wanted to stone Christ to death because he spoke this message. Ah, dear lords, how meaningless the world will become when the voice of God reproaches you in the right way with the impossibility of faith and you must endure this impossibility until finally faith arrives, Psalm 40[:2].

So, why does Brother Soft-life and Father Pussyfoot [Luther] become so worked up and very angry, Job 28[:15ff.]? Indeed, he thinks that he would gladly like to direct all his intended desires into works. He would like to maintain his pomp and riches and simultaneously have a tested faith. The son of God accused the scribes of just this with clear words, John 5[:44], when he said, "How is it possible that you can believe when you seek your own honor?"

Further, an additional impossibility concerning true faith is also set forth in Matthew 6[:24], with Christ saying to the disbelieving pleasure-seekers, "You cannot serve both God and mammon." He who takes these same honors and earthly goods as his master must finally be left empty of God for eternity, as God says, Psalm 5[:10]. Their hearts are vain, and, therefore, the mighty, self-centered and unbelieving people must be thrown off their thrones. Because, as soon as the holy and true Christian faith seeks to begin, with all its true origins, they seek to prevent it, both in themselves and in the whole world. Thus, for example, when the grace of God was announced through the birth of John the Baptist and the conception of Christ, Herod was ruling—that "pious" blue blood that the nobility of this world dripped out of its sack, so that the most precious and highest good [Christ] could be clearly and easily recognized as the opposite of that godless one.

So, now, in our times, God also sends his light into the world. And this is proven by the government and authority of godless and nonsensical people who most arbitrarily and with all physical coercion rage and rave against God and all his anointed ones, Psalm 2[:1ff.], John 2[:16–20]. And these rulers have only now seriously begun to oppress and exploit their people. They threaten in this way all of Christendom. And they punish and blasphemously kill both their own people and foreigners in the most aggressive way, so that, after the struggle of the elect, God will neither be able nor wish to witness this affliction any longer. And he must shorten the days of suffering for his elect, Matthew 24[:22]. Otherwise, because the people lack time for proper reflection, they could not accept the incarnation of Christ and would become mere devils and heathen. And there would be more vexing sects than before the beginning of Christianity.

Therefore Paul says, 1 Corinthians 10[:13] that God is so entirely true to his beloved elect that he does not impose more on them than they are able to bear, even though human nature always thinks that too much is put upon it. The good, omniscient father does not lay aside the rod of chastisement until the child has recognized his guilt, for which he has deserved this treatment because of the coarseness of both rulers and subjects.

What, most dearly beloved, is the source of this meaning in the Gospel of Luke? Behold, it stems from Herod, in whose reign Christ and John the Baptist were conceived and born, and also from what this text [Lk. 1:52] says without any ambiguity, "He cast down the mighty from their thrones"—because, at present, the mighty take it upon themselves to rule the Christian faith, and they seek to set Christ up as a lord, one about whose advent they never have to think of preparing themselves. Nor do they allow anyone else to prepare himself for this advent. Nevertheless,

our rulers want to condemn all people, and they want to remain the supreme authority, but only so that they are feared, prayed to, and held in
honor above all people. And what is more, they always want to condemn
the gospel in the worst ways they can think of. This makes clear the real
art of Herod,[8] the essence of worldly government, as holy Samuel, 1
Kings 8[:5–22] together with truly illustrious Hosea 13[:11] prophesied,
"God gave the world lords and princes in his wrath and he will get rid of
them again in his vehemence."

Since man fell from being a god to being a creature, it has become the
most widespread commonplace to think that one must fear the creature
(to one's own harm) more than one fears God. It is for this reason that
Paul says to the Romans 13[:3] that princes do not exist to produce the
fear that leads to good works, but to generate a fear of evil based on
death. Therefore, rulers are nothing but hangmen and corpse renderers.
This is their whole craft. But what is an evil work except that now one
prefers a creature to God, and with awe and dignity? Oh, how did this
come about? Because no one places God alone first (as is plainly evident), with his active strictness and all that he does and lets happen. Oh,
the fear of God can and will not grow pure because of a greater respect
for a human than for God, Psalm 19[:10]. Christ gave a very great and
difficult command about just this, Luke 12[:4f.,8f.], and previously
through Moses in Deuteronomy 6[:1–9]. In the same way, Mary also described the source of her faith (in order to support all the elect), saying,
"His mercy descends from generation to generation among those who
fear him" [Lk. 1:50].

If the spirit of the fear of God is properly cultivated among the elect,
the whole world will have to fear a righteous zeal for the majesty of God,
whether it wants to or not, as David described in the first book of the history of the patriarchs, chapter 14 [1 Chr. 14:17]. But he who does not fear
God alone out of the depths of his heart cannot be treated graciously by
God, as each and every one learns from the contrasting words of Mary.
Neither can we be saved by the hand of all those who hate us, nor can the
heartfelt mercy of God enlighten our unacknowledged ignorance as long
as the fear of God has not emptied us for the onset of unending wisdom.
This is clearly written in Psalm 145[:19], "The Lord does the will of the
God-fearing," and they are filled with this will in the wisdom and the
understanding and the knowledge of God, Colossians 1[:9].

However, the world will not open its eyes to the source of faith. For
this reason, all unenlightened people have to exhaust their reason with
great, mighty efforts in order to serve a poor, miserable, wretched sack of
gunpowder[9] and to shamelessly elevate it above God. Therefore, the
world is too coarse to perceive God's judgment. Consequently, wisdom
about God, the right Christian faith, has become such an alien, rare, hid-

den, unknown thing, and so completely impossible to attain that no eye can sufficiently lament and weep about it, nor can any tongue say enough about it. A dismayed man may not hear or read enough that the right, precious knowledge of God, the Christian faith, has been dishonored and shamed. This has come about because those who are spiritless, who have no fear of God, have been assimilated into Christendom and must be publicly prayed to, as no one with eyes that see can deny.

Abraham in Gerar,[10] as is described in Genesis 20[:11], ordered all his affairs according to the fear of God, through which the angel also recognized him, as is written in the same book [Gen. 22:11f.]. Abraham was infinitely awed, and where he did not act out of divine fear, he could not distinguish between the impossible and the possible. It was also the same for Zechariah and Elizabeth [Lk. 1:5–25], although they were righteous people before God and the world. They feared God above all things. Nevertheless, they could not distinguish between the possible and the impossible, because the spirit of the fear of God, which is necessary for the advent of faith, was not revealed to them. Thus, Zechariah could not believe the angel. Indeed, from the very nature of the case, this was to be expected. For his wife was old and besides she was unfruitful. It could not seem otherwise; she could never become pregnant.

Oh, dearest brothers, of what else does this Gospel of Luke remind us? Only that faith, with all its sources, presents us with impossible things, which the tender ones believe will never come to pass in reality. The whole insane, fantastic world sets forth instead a false path to faith, relying on glosses on Scripture, and the world says with a little forked tongue: "Yes, one can indeed preach the Gospel, fear God alone, and yet also hold in honor the unreasonable rulers, even though they strive against all justice and do not accept God's word. Oh, for God's sake, one should be obedient to them in all things, those good Junkers." Yes, welcome, you [i.e. Luther] defender of the godless! How fine, how very fine it must be to be able to serve with praise two masters who strive against one another, as the advisors of the rulers truly do! Oh, how skillful clever reason thinks it is! In its hypocrisy, it uses love of neighbor to dress up and ornament itself in the most imposing manner.

Yes, it is completely impossible in our time, much more so than at any other time since the beginning of perverted government, that the whole world can survive the force [of this contradiction].[11] Yes, this teaching of mine seems to countless people to be utter fanaticism. They can only judge that it is impossible that such a play[12] could be presented and performed, knocking the godless from their thrones and raising up the lowly and the coarse [Lk. 1:52]. So they do not want to listen to Mary, although she is their most beloved Madonna, for they do not want to allow her to speak. Oh Mary, how can your words produce so much unhappiness in those who pray to you, those whom others want to rule. And yet, in an emergency, these rulers could not even bring order to a louse on their chest.

The world, and the untried scribes who are its top layer of scum, think that it is the most impossible thing of all that the lowly should be raised and separated from the evil ones. Yes, that is the true, weighty, and whole difficulty. The scribes do not want to give credence to the text of Matthew 13[:47–50] about the separation of the godless from the elect. From this text, they have imagined, visualizing from an old image of a scale's balance-beam, that angels with long spears will separate the good from the bad at the Last Judgment.

I think that the scribes could tweak the nose of the holy spirit himself. They shamelessly say that God does not reveal his judgment to anyone. Therefore, they deny that such angels, who are true messengers, will separate the good from the bad in the near future, as Malachi says [Mal. 3:1–5]. But our pious people, the scribes, cannot be accused of anything, as all can truly see, for they are "impartial"—that means excellent archhypocrites who can easily bear the yoke of serving two masters on both shoulders. They speak, these highly credulous people, straightforwardly: "No one can know who is among the elect or among the damned." Oh yes, they have such a strong faith, which is so powerfully certain that it has absolutely and completely no understanding of anything except defending the godless. Yes, nevertheless, it is a fine faith! It will yet bring about much good. It will certainly produce a subtle people, as Plato the philosopher speculated (in *The Republic*), and Apuleius, the author of *The Golden Ass*, and as Isaiah 29[:8] says concerning the dreamer, etc.

The scribes cite St. Paul, 2 Timothy 2[:19], to support their arbitrariness and to cloak their hypocrisy, as is their constant habit. They say, "The Lord knows his own." This is true, dear companion, but you must give up your piecemeal way of understanding Scripture and also give credence to the following words of the text [2 Tim. 2:19], which say, "He who seeks the name of God avoids evil deeds." A member of the elect may be a sinner, if he pleases. Nevertheless, he is guided by the consciousness of his sins if he merely perceives the sorrowful agitation of his heart, as Psalm 40[:12] attests. But the consciousness of the godless does not do this, as Psalm 36[:2–5] says. The consciousness of the godless strives constantly after vice and after greed and arrogance. No evil is too much for this consciousness. Therefore, it ultimately shows its real face. This consciousness can never be an enemy of evil, even though it, along with Judas, has a gallows repentance at Passion Week.[13] However, at the bottom of its heart, the consciousness of the godless strives for nothing other than the same thing as the rich man in this Gospel of Luke 12[:16–

21]—for a long and pleasure-filled life. And it always wants to have a good time. This form of consciousness thinks that it has been created exclusively for pleasure.

THIRD

One must perceive how the heart of a member of the elect is constantly moved to the source of his faith by the power of the Supreme Being. Thus, one of the elect usually says, Psalm 51[:5], "Oh Lord, my sin is always before my eyes. Do not take from me your holy spirit." For the spirit of God is most highly revealed through fear, so that the heart is completely and totally prepared for the reception of God's gift. For God cannot despise the repentant heart that has become humble. He must yield to it because such a good sacrifice is made from it. And this heart is redolent of the sweetness that, in its fullness, is most deeply hidden from many God-fearing people on account of their misunderstanding, Psalm 31[:10–14], until the time of a meaningful tribulation. Then, this sweetness is revealed to them, Psalm 34[:19], 1 Peter 2[:9].

Behold how Zechariah went into the temple [Lk. 1:8f.], according to the requirement of the law. This was nothing but that which is set forth in the Fifth Psalm [Ps. 5:7f.]: "I will go into your house. I will pray before your holy temple in fear of you, so that you will lead me in the path of righteousness for the sake of my enemies." Zechariah himself explained what this means in his present song of praise [Lk. 1:74f.], that we can serve God in his holiness and righteousness without fearing man. This takes place with an uncontrived, experienced faith that is very pleasing to God. Now, what is this faith in its clearest form? Each and every person should delve into himself and, in doing this, simultaneously perceive, on the basis of his turmoil, how he is a holy temple, 1 Corinthians 3[:16f.] and 6[:19] belonging to God from all eternity. Each person should also note that he has been created only in order to have the holy spirit as the teacher of his faith and to perceive all the spirit's effects, John 14[:26] and 16[:13], Romans 8[:14]. And each should also note that this same temple has been infinitely ravaged by ignorant parsons. Oh, every creature should indeed feel pity that no one wants to recognize such an outrage in the holy place. The poor people cannot attend to their hearts themselves due to the poisoning of the godless. Each one still stands outside the temple and awaits the time when it will finally be holy.

The common people think today—and have never thought differently—that the priests know the faith because they have read many beautiful big books. Therefore, the poor commoner says: "Oh, they are fine men with their red and brown university berets. Should they not know what is right and wrong?" In truth, the people (even though they want to be Christians) have a foolish judgment, despite the fact that Christ commanded his followers most emphatically to distinguish the false from the true servants of God and to recognize each, Matthew 7[:15]. No one pays attention to anything except the accumulation of many earthly goods. Therefore, each one tarries before the temple and cannot enter into his heart due to his great unbelief, which he does not want to acknowledge on account of his preoccupation with sustenance. The holy spirit complains about this in Jeremiah [Jer. 5:4]. If, in addition to this, the people have completely relied on the parsons and scribes, then the people are dumb idols. They know much less of God than does an oaken block and a flint pebble. The prophecy of the Thirty-first Psalm [Ps. 31:18] is fulfilled, "The lips of the deceitful become dumb."

So Jeremiah runs around in circles, through all the streets, and would gladly like to hear a man who zealously applies himself to obtain God's judgment and faith. Jeremiah comes to the poor peasants and asks them about the faith. They refer him to the parsons and scribes. Yes, the poor miserable peasants know nothing about the faith after they have relied on the most poisonous people.

So the prophet Jeremiah 5[:4] thinks: "Oh God, the peasants are hardworking people. They have spent their lives with the totally painful labor of obtaining sustenance, with which they have also filled the throats of the arch-godless tyrants. What, then, should the poor unlettered people know?" Jeremiah 5[:5] says further: "I thought, wait! wait! I will go to the mighty ones. They will surely care for the poor people and bring them the faith and knowledge of God with words and deeds, like good shepherds. I will speak with them about it and without a doubt they will know." Yea, yea, in truth they knew much less than the lowliest.

This is what the holy spirit prophesied through Hosea 4[:6]: the godless do not wish to have the right way to the knowledge of God available on earth. Thus, as the people are, so too is the priest, Isaiah 24[:2]. One blind person always leads another in this way, and both fall together over a bump into the ditch of unknowing corruption, Matthew 15[:14]. In this case, each one wants to puff himself up beautifully with the filth of another. And it is still the fault of all men that the whole Christian community prays to a dumb God.

Where else did this situation come from except that each peasant has wanted to have his own priest so that he has prosperity? At present, they do not wish it, for the whole world is not willing to help attain a good priesthood. Indeed, the world is accustomed to beheading good priests. Oh, a good priest's office tastes to the world like bitter gall. One must tell the truth. In relation to the nobility of our souls, we are much coarser than an unreasoning animal. This is because almost no one has an understanding of anything except usury and the other tricks of this world.

When something is said about God, then the slogan of Solomon [Prov. 23:9] applies, "If you preach to a fool, then at the end of the sermon he says, 'Hey, what did you say?'" It is just as if one addresses a sleeping man. So we poor, suffering, miserable Christians can express nothing about God except that which each has stolen from the Bible according to his own opinions. And, if the Bible were taken from us (which is possible), then one would be totally unable to help this coarse Christendom. Is that not the greatest misery? Yet no one wants to take it to heart. It is thought best that one remain silent about it. Oh, what gigantic, miserable blindness! Oh, that everyone has learned to see with but half an eye! John 9[:39ff.], Isaiah 6[:10].

FOURTH

If Christendom is to be truly made upright on another foundation, the usury-seeking scoundrels must be done away with and turned into the servants of dogs, although they can scarcely serve as such—and yet they are supposed to be prelates of the Christian church. The poor common people must nurse the memory of the spirit, and so learn to sob, Romans 8[:1–11], to plead, and to wait for a new John the Baptist, for a preacher rich in grace who has experienced every aspect of the faith through his own lack of faith. For he must know how an archunbeliever feels. And he must know that the measure of active desire corresponds to the measure of faith, Ephesians 4[:7f.], Psalm 68[:19]. If this does not happen, then this unexperienced Christian faith of our times will become much worse than the devil's blasphemy against God in the abyss of hell. Therefore, one must arise who shows people the revelations of the divine lamb in the form of the eternal word emanating from the father. You can surely see here [Lk. 1:21] that the people had an opinion about why Zechariah was in the temple so long. For the people could surely figure out and accept that, because of his long presence in the temple, he must have seen a vision. At that time, the people were not so absolutely and completely hardened as Christendom has now become through the evil scribes. In no way does Christendom want to believe that God is so near, Deuteronomy 4[:7], Jeremiah 23[:23], and capable of revealing his will to it. Oh ho, how shy the people have become about revelations, as Micah prophesied in chapter three [Mic. 3:6f.]!

Nearly everybody says: "Yes, we are satisfied with Scripture. We do not want to believe in revelations. God does not speak any more." What do you think? Had such people lived at the time of the prophets, would they have believed the prophets or preferred to kill them? Are they so blinded by holy Scripture that they do not want to see or hear how these

Scriptures totally and powerfully insist that one should and must be taught by God alone? Should someone wish to be filled in another way than reading Scripture with the eternal divine gifts, then, after long chastisement through his suffering and his cross, he must be emptied for revelations, so that he may be filled according to the measure of his faith with the greatest treasures of Christian wisdom, Colossians 2[:1–3], Ephesians 4[:7ff.]. Each must receive the knowledge of God, the true Christian faith, not from the stinking breath of devilish scribes, but rather from the eternal powerful word of the father, in the son, with the enlightenment of the holy spirit, and thus be filled in his soul, in its length, width, and breadth, and in its depths and heights, Ephesians 3[:18].

In short, it cannot be otherwise. Man must smash to bits his stolen, contrived Christian faith through powerful, enormous suffering of the heart, through painful grief, and through an amazement that cannot be rejected. Through this, man becomes very small and despicable in his own eyes. The elect sink down while the godless arm themselves and mightily puff themselves up. Then the elect can raise God up and make him mighty, and, after experiencing heartfelt grief, the elect can rejoice from their whole heart in God, their savior. Then the mighty ones must give way to the small people and be ruined by the small. Oh, if the poor rejected peasants knew this, it would be most useful to them. God despises the powerful and mighty, the likes of Herod and Caiaphas and Annas, and he accepts for his service the small, like Mary, Zechariah, and Elizabeth. For that is God's way of working, and down to the present day he does not act otherwise, 1 Corinthians 1[:26–29], Matthew 11[:25], Luke 10[:21].

Zechariah was a despised man since his wife was unfruitful. According to the substance of the law, Mary was equally despised, Matthew 13[:55]. Oh, dear friends, they were not mighty people with splendid titles, such as the church of the godless now has, Psalm 26[:4–6]. Many poor coarse people think that the great, fat, plump, chubby cheeks[14] must possess true knowledge about the source of the Christian faith. Oh no, most dearly beloved. What can such people know who deny us all living development of the faith and who damn and persecute everything that opposes them in the most despicable way? For they have consumed their whole life with animalistic gobbling and swilling. From their youth on, they have been trained for the gentlest ways, and they have had no difficult day their whole life long. Yet they do not want or think of accepting a single difficult day for the sake of experiencing the truth, nor do they want to reduce their rents by a penny.[15] And yet they want to be the judges and protectors of the faith. Oh, you poor Christendom! How you have been totally turned into a chopping block by your foolish rulers! How truly poorly they have provided for you!

FIFTH

If the holy church is to be renewed by the bitter truth, then a servant of God, rich in grace, must step forward in the spirit of Elijah, Matthew 17[:3], 1 Kings 18[:1], Revelation 11[:3], and he must bring all things into the right momentum. Truly, many of these servants of God must be awakened, so that, with the greatest zeal and through passionate rigor, they cleanse Christendom of godless rulers. First, the people must also be sternly reprimanded on account of their disorderly desires, those who so luxuriously wile away their time without any steadfast interest in a rigorous consideration of the faith. Therefore, very few people know what to say about the first movement of the spirit. Yes, this initial movement is so distasteful to them that they have not even endured the ennui[16] through which alone God's action is to be found, Psalm 40[:2]. In the first place, God's action is experienced through the sprinkling, Numbers 19[:19], where the waters of divine wisdom stir, Ecclesiastes 15[:3]. There the sad person perceives that God has begun a most rapturous thing in him. Thus, for the first time, he is terrified by God's name, which is revealed to him in the first movement of the divine action. He has no peace his whole life long, seeking this same name with his whole heart until he has received the grace from God to recognize that his name has been written in heaven from all eternity, Luke 10[:20]. Without this recognition, he can obtain no peace, joy, and righteousness in his conscience, even though they are due him, as is described in Romans 14[:17], John 17[:3], and Ephesians 1[:4].

Unless this happens, he stumbles after the true God in darkness and the shadow of death until his feet, after many attempts, are directed onto the path that leads to peace through the greatest discontent. All passions are directed toward this first sprinkling, caused by the blowing breath of the holy spirit, which arises from the deepest grief with the greatest groaning. If one expends all his efforts for this, then he can have no rest before the driving of the holy spirit, which never leaves him in peace in order to show him the way to the eternal good [God]. The holy spirit cannot make an insensitive person understand this except after the most coarse, foolish sins, for the coarse person comes to feel the gnawing, devouring thorns of his conscience without respite, as Psalm 32[:4f.] says. Then he must turn to God and away from the sins and become their enemy. After all the pleasures of the flesh have been overcome, man must turn to God. Otherwise human nature cannot hold out. Then man first confesses his lack of faith and cries for the doctor [God], who on account of his solicitude can never neglect to help such a spiritually impoverished person. There is the source of all good, the true kingdom of heaven. Then he is first assured of his blessedness and clearly perceives that God, through his unchanging love, has driven him from evil to good through the sin by which unbelief is perceived. Then he has become completely liberated. This process is described in Jeremiah 31[:3].

Thus, true faith must win the victory, 1 John 5[:4], after it has triumphed over the world, a victory that is many thousandfold more abundant in the heart than externally. After such a rigorous recognition of unbelief, the exuberance of faith is no longer prevented from increasing in the person. Here you may weigh it and recognize, you literalistic fellow [i.e., Luther], how heavy your talent really is [Lk. 19:12–27]. But you cannot weigh it until you have at your disposal the scales of divine judgment for the examination of your heart, Psalm 119[:75]. However, if you want to make a mockery of the increase of holy faith, then you will be mocked, to your downfall and on account of your chubby cheeks, Proverbs 1[:24ff.]. How will faith be found? According to the scribes, one must only believe the Scriptures, without any discovery of the most certain witness of the spirit. And one should hide in the most covetous way of life, through which the godless hang onto each other like toads, as Psalm 55[:11f.] makes evident. No one can come to faith through usury and taxes and rents. The more that the shame of the world becomes longer and broader and deeper, the more the road is closed to human faith. Reasonable judgments are not to be disclosed in this way. If we do not improve ourselves in the near future, we will also have lost our natural reason, which we all still apply to the pleasures of the flesh because of our own selfishness, Psalm 32[:1], Isaiah 1[:4]. Thus, John the Baptist called the people who were on the side of the scribes a generation of vipers, Matthew 3[:7], Luke 3[:7]. For nothing but pure venom results when one preaches to lustful people. They select the worst things out of the best, just as later contemporary Christians have done with the precious faith.

It would have been better for them to have remained heathens with their forefathers. What is preached to them is said to the swine in the mud, Matthew 7[:6], 2 Peter 2[:22]. They run into the bog and are choked, Matthew 8[:32]. One may tell them as much as one wishes, or how they may yet obtain faith, but this is absolutely no help to them. They excuse themselves with their lame, insipid smirks: "Yes, we are poor sinners. But if Christ did not despise sinners, how can this pharisaic spirit despise us?"

If I tell them about the faith that they have stolen out of Scripture, then they answer me with talk about sin in order to excuse themselves and to justify themselves with their appearance of faith and love, after which they deny the trial by God. For they do not want to accept the cure of blessedness proclaimed through the mouths of all prophets from the beginning of the faith. Therefore, they will be left empty, without faith and love, of which they have not a particle although they praise both in the most stately fashion. Since they can be such impressive hypocrites, everyone swears to the most holy that they are pious Christians. But they really are so full of all kinds of insidiousness that they thrust faith down on every occasion. How is it possible that one who is full of every lie can have divine faith, as the scriptural thieves seek to convince the whole world, Jeremiah 8[:8f.]?

Thus, Christ was conceived by a pure virgin through the holy spirit, so that we might recognize the shame of sin in all its origins. For sin has come from our first parents through lust for the fruit of the forbidden tree, Genesis 3[:1ff.]. The human body has been disordered as a result of this. And on account of this, all bodily pleasures are also a hindrance to the working of the holy spirit, Proverbs 9[:13ff.]. All the days of a human life are nearly too short, Ecclesiastes 2[:1–11?], to recognize this shame and to avoid it with rigorous renunciation. If someone is negligent in these matters and, with all his riches, wants to look like a prim man who has just vomited, and says without hesitation, "Believe! believe! until the snot bubbles from your nose," then that person belongs to the family of swine and not to mankind.

Each may gabble whatever he wants about faith. The lustful and ambitious are in absolutely no way to be believed, for they preach what they themselves have not tried. Therefore Christ says, John 10[:5], "The sheep should not listen to the voice of a stranger." The faith is foreign to the lustful and ambitious, and they to it, for they are far removed from salvation, Psalm 119[:155]. Therefore, they are also animals of the belly, Philemon 3[:19]. They preach what they want, but they still seek to fill the belly. Oh ho, to maintain their stomach they gladly take golden guilders with great devotion. They hardly need a hundredth part of what they take and nevertheless they want to be our evangelists. Consequently, their teaching also has no power, Matthew 7[:29]. Their teaching will be practiced in absolutely no way except for the sake of the freedom of the flesh. Therefore, they poison holy Scripture for the holy spirit. One hears at various times that they walk along the right path. But that does not last long. None of them can improve himself, for their teaching is stolen, Jeremiah 23[:30]. In this way no one finds access to his heart.

John the Baptist, however, is a very different preacher, a confessing angel of Christ, who is represented in every true preacher. Each preacher should be praised, like John, not on the merit of his works, but on account of his rigor, which is born of persevering abstinence and which strives for a separation from pleasure, by which the powers of the soul are laid bare, so that the abyss of the spirit becomes visible in all these powers. For there, in the abyss of the soul, the holy spirit must persuade, Psalm 85[:9ff.]. For such a baring of his soul, a preacher must be trained in a wonderful way, from his youth on, in the withering away of his own will. Therefore, John was sanctified in his mother's womb as a model for every preacher. Paul says [Gal. 1:15f.] that John was ordained in his mother's womb to proclaim the inestimable riches of Christ. For this reason, preachers must know who always sends them out for the harvest, Matthew 9[:38], John 4[:35–38]. And they must know for what harvest God has sharpened them, like a strong scythe or sickle, from the beginning of their life. Not everyone can fulfill this office. For, even if he has also read nearly every book, he must first know the certainty of his faith, as did those who wrote the Scriptures. Otherwise preaching is a thief's prattle and a war of words.

SIXTH

What is never acceptable, accordingly, is the shameless defense of false preaching by the malicious archhypocrites who want to be kinder than God himself, insofar as they defend godless, damned, false preachers. They proclaim: "A parson may be good or evil. Nevertheless he can handle God's secret [the Eucharist] and preach the true word." These perverted defenders of the godless, indeed their companions (one raven does not claw out the eyes of another), are clearly hardened against the clear, ringing text of Exodus 23[:7], where God surely says of a more insignificant matter, namely, worldly jurisdiction, "I am not well disposed to the godless. You shall not adorn their affairs." Accordingly, they violate still much more openly Psalm 50[:16f.], where it speaks of the ordination of the servant of God and of his word, and God says to the godless preacher, "Who has called you to preach my righteousness? You take my attested covenant in your mouth and you have hated virtue." And he would say today, "Are you going to preach my dear crucified son to the world for the sake of your belly? Do you not yet know how one must become like him" Romans 8[:29]? "You have not learned the knowledge of God and yet you want to be a schoolmaster to others?"

Therefore the totally abandoned person[17] must be awakened by God from the desert of his heart. He must break out of this condition and strive to receive the truth among the lustful soft ones, who are really harder than diamonds. Through a tested life, he must have taken up the cross from his youth on, revealed it to others, and called out in miserable deserts to the erring hearts of those who fear God, since they now begin to seek the truth there, Luke 12[:36ff.].

Oh, these God-fearing people wish very much for the right faith, if they could only meet it. The desire of such people is described in Psalm 63[:2f.]: "Oh God, my God, because of the light I have waited for you. My soul thirsts for you. Oh, in how many ways has my body struggled in the desert without a path or water. There I recognized myself and that I must experience your strength and praise in this way." Thus, the power of God must be sought in the shadow of God. One may gladly rejoice over true preachers and that God wants to give them to the world in our times, so that the right testimony of the faith comes to light. Therefore, this text [Lk. 1:14] says, "Many will rejoice on his account," etc. The hearts of many will be disturbed on account of their negligence, which makes them persist in their unbelief. And they will reject this same negligence and exercise great care in the true faith through the unanimously discovered testimony of Christ.

You must always bear in mind here the whole context [of Lk. 1], one word after another, if you want to understand correctly what I say about faith and its impossibility. The elected friend of God discovers a wonderful rapturous joy when his brother has also come to faith through the same process as he. Therefore, the mother of God gives testimony to Elizabeth, and she in turn to Mary. We must do this as well. Peter and Paul conversed with each other. They discussed the gospel that Peter had received through the revelation of the father, Matthew 16[:17], and Paul had received through a heavenly disclosure, Galatians 2[:2]. But the poisonous black raven [i.e., Luther] mocks revelations, as you may see in his slanderous booklet.[18]

In a short time, each will have to give an account of how he has come to the faith. The separation of the godless from the elect would indeed bring about a true Christian church. What can the godless know of true faith, since they have never been saddened by unbelief and have also never acknowledged it? What, then, can they know of true faith?

SEVENTH[19]

The present church, by contrast, is truly an old whore, one that must still be judged with fervent zeal if the chaff is to undergo its separation from the wheat. But the time of the harvest is certainly here, Matthew 9[:37]. Dear brothers, the chaff everywhere now screams that it is not yet harvest time. Ah, the traitor betrays himself. The true Christians of the present time will gain the correct momentum for change after every vexation, Matthew 18[:7ff.]. For improvement follows vexation, after the harm and the suffering of unbelief have reached their end. The gospel, Matthew 8[:10–12], will be much more perfectly realized than at the time of the apostles. Many diverse members of the elect from many lands and foreign nations will be far superior to us lazy, negligent Christians.

Oh, dear lords, do not be so bold with your insane faith that you give over all your subjects (excepting yourselves alone) to the devil, as is your custom. For the profit-hungry evangelists who hoist their names so high now begin to damn others to the greatest extent. They think that no one may be a Christian unless he accept their literalistic faith.

Behold how, in former times, Jewish comrades were lifted from the mass of the heathen: Rahab of Jerico; a woman of Salma from whom was born Boas, Matthew 1[:5]; Naeman of Syria who was brought to faith through Elias; Job was chosen by God from the Edomites; Jethro was brought to faith through Moses; Cornelius through Peter; a Roman official through our Lord Jesus, Luke 7[:1ff.], an official who was preferred far ahead of Israel on account of his great faith. The heathen woman was far preferred to the Jews at Jerusalem, Matthew 15[:21–28].

Even so, there are now many who will be chosen from the wild, strange heathen, to the shame of the false scriptural thieves. For, as I have heard from these heathen, they are astonished beyond measure at our faith, and they are held back from converting by our loose impudence. They are often perplexed by hyperrational afflictions, and yet, as a result, are sure that they are inclined and ordained to eternal life, Acts 13[:48]. They lack only the true testimony of the faith, as do we all as well. Otherwise, innumerable heathen and Turks would become Christians. You can surely realize that if any Jew or Turk should be living among us and should be improved at all through this faith that we profess at present, then he would gain from it as much value as a gnat can carry on its tail, indeed much less. For there is no people under the sun that so pitifully hereticizes, damns, and dishonors its own laws as do present-day Christians. And especially the literalistic rogues are the leading cause of every evil, and nevertheless they still want to justify the whole world. But they do not even believe that God might bestow or grant them goods worth a penny. Thus, every corner is full of the greedy and the treacherous, Psalm 55[:12].

And those who should preside most supremely over Christendom, since they are called princes, supremely prove their lack of faith in all their actions and plans. And the princes also prove that they are afraid to do right before their fellow rulers, Isaiah 1[:23]. They think that they would be driven out of their principalities if they were to stand by the truth, which they have only accepted *pro forma* and only for as long as no persecution has befallen them. They also want to be called "most Christian" and to strut about here and there, straightforwardly defending the godless and their followers. They do not want to intervene when their subjects are persecuted by their own vassals for the sake of the gospel. They want merely to be the hangers of thieves and good, majestic corpse renderers. The so-called pious people, the princes's parsons who preach the gospel to them, marry old women with great wealth,[20] for they are worried that they might finally have to look for their own bread. Yes, truly, they are fine evangelical people! They surely have a firm and strong faith! Whoever relies on their plausible façade and on their prattle, with their monastic idols, will prosper. For they brag a great deal about this. And they puff up their literalistic faith far more than anyone can say.

I say to you, most dear brothers, it is not possible for me to be silent about this. I would rather instruct heathen, Turks, and Jews with the most trivial word, speaking of God and his ordering of creation, giving an account of God's rule over us, and ours over other creatures. For the most clever scriptural thieves fundamentally deny this, so that what Jude and Peter say in their letters [Jude 10:2, 2 Pet. 2:12] will become true for them too: "What they know, therein they corrupt themselves, like irrational animals. Yes, they even repudiate it." They have neither sense nor understanding because of their insane faith. And they malign everything that they do not wish to accept. They want neither to hear nor see it when I admonish them in a friendly way to take up the Bible and learn about God's rule over us and ours over creatures. So, for them, all this is fanaticism. Therefore, I say that, if you scribes do not want to learn to truly take up the Bible, you will not understand and assimilate the truth concerning either God or creatures (to the praise of God's true name). And God will disgrace you in the most evident way through the heathen, who will prosper, so that those Christians who come later will spit on you, when you are even remembered.

If our scribes, along with their mortal idols [the princes], now want to snarl and fume mightily about what I say, they can nevertheless find their error in this Gospel of Luke by comparing it with the whole of holy Scripture. Jesus was conceived in Galilee, at Nazareth, and brought up in the same place, Matthew 3[:13]. The apostles have described it very exactly. So if anyone makes a synopsis to harmonize all four gospels, he will recognize this scribal error in the clearest fashion and not without excellent and powerful reasons, as anyone can see in the Gospel of John 7[:50ff.]. The rabid, furious, nonsensical thieves of Scripture believed in their carnal brain that Jesus of Nazareth could not in any way be the Christ, since he grew up in Galilee. They held to Scripture without the spirit of Scripture, as the godless ones down to the present day are accustomed to do. They punished poor Nicodemus due to his simple faith [Jn. 7:50ff.]. They referred him to Scripture and thought they had settled the matter. But God led them around by their noses. Consequently, they were not able to grasp Scripture in the context of its wholeness, due to their great blindness. And they paid no attention to the wonderful work of God, just as now our envious fantasts seduce the people to all kinds of presumptuousness, as anyone can see with his own eyes. But to prevent just this, holy Scripture was left to us negligent ones as our sole consolation here on earth.

If Scripture were not dear to the scriptural thieves on account of their bellies etc., then they could certainly have known the time of Christ's birth from Daniel [2:44 and 12:1ff.], and from Micah [5:1] the name of the city that had been selected for the birth. And through Isaiah [7:14ff., 9:5, 11:1f.] and others they could have known of the coming of our savior.

For the scribes then (as for the world now), everything turned on the fact that Christ was a lowly person, of unimportant parents. And nevertheless, he wanted too much to instruct and punish the mighty chubby-cheeks and the lustful people. He so clearly preached the wisdom of his heavenly father that the scribes could not refute it. And he worked such miracles that they could not reject them, John 9[:32f.]. Then one scribe said to another, "Whence does he receive the wisdom and the power? He is a carpenter's son. Is not his mother called Mary? From where then could he receive all this?" And they were angry with him, Matthew 13[:55ff.], Luke 4[:22,28]. The godless react this way down to the present whenever anyone punishes them for their façades, their pomp, and their false hair-splitting wisdom. Oh, how often has the eternal word concealed itself in the elect, in our Nazareth within Christendom—that is, in the burgeoning elect, who are renewed and who sweetly prosper in the wisdom of the cross. And every lustful pussyfoot has regarded them as crazy and nonsensical. This is the world's evil way. People anger themselves most about that which should improve them. Oh, most dearly beloved, this is the wisdom of the cross, with which God greets his elect. One should not anger himself over the condition of the world and see nothing good in any corner. And the whole world gets angry at the effect of the highest good and says that it is a diabolical apparition.

EIGHTH

The elect would be filled beyond measure with the grace of God if they immediately set aside their own will and made room for God's will. Christ says with clear words, "Who does the will of my father there, he is my mother," Matthew 12[:50], Mark 3[:35], Luke 8[:21]. For our sake, on the cross, he entrusted his mother to the care of his followers as our companion. Like her, we are also terrified by God's greeting, when God wants to deify us with the incarnation of his son and when he tests our faith like gold in a fire. We think, "Oh, what is going to happen?" Mary was suspicious of the angel, in accordance with human nature, just as we are suspicious of acknowledging truthful preachers who explain and present to us the cross and the impossibility of faith, so that we recognize that therein is the true kingdom of David; there Christ rules from the cross, and we are crucified with him. There the house of Jacob [Lk. 1:33] is as well, the empty soul, emptied by the crushing of its loins—that is, by the removal of its lusts. There [in the cross] the power of the almighty brings forth the impossible work of God, in our suffering and through the ecstasy of the holy, ancient covenant. And God's power will be completely illuminated by the light of the world, who is the true and unfeigned son of God, Jesus Christ.

The whole of this first chapter of Luke is about the strengthening of the spirit in faith. This means only that almighty God, our dear Lord, wants to give us the most exalted Christian faith by means of the incarnation of Christ. God does this so that we emulate Christ in his suffering and life through ecstasy in the holy spirit, against whom the world rages in a bitter and carnal fashion and mocks in the coarsest way. Thus, faith will be given only to the poor in spirit (who also recognize their unbelief).

This conclusion is confirmed by every word of the whole first chapter of Luke, and especially in the most wonderful songs of praise of Mary and Zechariah, which speak so clearly of the heartfelt mercy that will be received through the spirit of the fear of God. This is the holy covenant which God swore to Abraham and to all of us, Romans 4[:13]. To keep this covenant, we should serve him in holiness and righteousness, a righteousness that God will also exercise over us. Whoever does not truly fear God cannot be renewed from day to day in the knowledge of God. But this knowledge is necessary for man to understand the faith and the work of God in him. Nor can one who does not fear God learn to render an account of the faith. Because the fear of God is presently despised, faith is a rare thing that God will grant and enlarge only in tribulation. May the spirit of Christ, which mocks the godless, help you. Amen.

8
Highly Provoked Defense

Highly provoked defense and answer to the spiritless, soft-living flesh at Wittenberg, who has most lamentably befouled pitiable Christianity in a perverted way by his theft of holy Scripture.

By Thomas Müntzer, Allstedter.[1]

From the caverns of Elijah, whose zeal spares no one, 3 Kings 18 [see, rather, 1 Kg. 19:9ff.], Matthew 17[:1ff.], Luke 1[:11, 26f.], and Revelation 11[:3].

Written in the year 1524.

"Oh God, save me from the false accusations of men so that I may keep your commandments. And so that I may proclaim the truth that was born in your son, lest the stratagems of the evildoers endure longer."[2]

To the most illustrious, firstborn prince and all-powerful lord, Jesus Christ, the gracious king of all kings, the brave duke of all believers, my most gracious lord and faithful protector—and to his troubled, only bride, poor Christendom.[3] All praise, name, honor, and dignity, title, and all glory are yours alone, you eternal son of God, Philippians 2[:9–11], because your holy spirit has constantly had the fate of seeming to those graceless lions, the scribes, to be a most enraged devil, John 8[:48], even though you possessed this spirit beyond measure from the beginning, John 3[:14]. And all of the elect have received this spirit from your bounty, John 1[:16], and thus it lives in them, 1 Corinthians 3[:16] and 6[:19], 2 Corinthians 1[:21f.], Ephesians 1[:13], and Psalm 5[:12f.]. You give the spirit to all who approach you, according to the measure of their faith, Ephesians 4[:7], Psalm 68[:10–12]. And he who does not have Christ's spirit, so that he can give an unmistakable testimony of it from his own spirit, does not belong to you, Christ, Romans 8[:9]. You have the invincible testimony, Psalm 93[:3–5].

So it is scarcely a great surprise that the most ambitious scribe of all, Doctor Liar,[4] increasingly as time passes, becomes an arrogant fool and clothes himself in your holy Scripture, without his own name and comfort withering away at all. And Luther uses Scripture in a most deceptive way and actually wants to have nothing to do with you, Isaiah 58[:1ff.], as if through you he had attained the gates of truth to knowledge of you. And,

139

thus, he is insolent in your presence and fundamentally he despises your true spirit. For he betrays himself clearly and irrevocably in that, out of raging envy and in the bitterest hatred, he mocks me, a member of the community that is integrated to you. He does this without sincere and true cause before his flattering, mocking, and most ferocious associates. And, before the simple people, he describes me in uncalled-for anger as a Satan or devil. And he slanders and mocks me with his perverted, vicious judgment.

But in you, Christ, I am blissful, and, through your mild comfort, I am totally satisfied, just as you also most sweetly told your dearest friends, saying in Matthew 10[:24], "The disciple does not have it better than the master." Oh, innocent duke and comforting savior, since they have blasphemously called you Beelzebub, how much more will they insult me, your untiring foot-soldier, after I expressed my views about the flattering rogue at Wittenberg and followed your voice, John 10[:4f.]? Indeed, this will always happen if one does not want to let these soft-living people, who follow their own arbitrary opinions, get away with their contrived faith and pharisaical tricks, but instead wishes to see their fame and pompousness collapse. In the same way you, Christ, were not accorded recognition by the scribes. The scribes also had the illusion that they were more learned than you and your disciples. Indeed, with their literalistic pigheadedness they were probably more learned than Doctor Mockery[5] could ever be. Even though they had reputation and fame enough throughout the whole world, it was still not right that they proceeded against you rationalistically and sought to prove you wrong with clear Scripture, as they previously rejected Nicodemus, John 7[:50ff.], and spoke of the Sabbath, John 5[:9f.] and 9[:16]. They cited the whole Scripture against you in the most extreme manner, arguing that you should and must die because you freely confessed yourself to be the son of God, born of the eternal father, just as we confess ourselves to be born of your spirit. Thus the scribes said, "We have a law according to which he must die." And they misapplied to you the text of Deuteronomy 13[:1–6] and 18[:20] and did not wish carefully to explore this text any further, just as the cunning scriptural thief [Luther] now does to me. There, where Scripture reveals itself most clearly, he mocks with fervent envy and calls the spirit of God a devil.

The whole of holy Scripture (as all creatures also prove) speaks only of the crucified son of God. Because Christ himself began to explain his mission or office [in the succession] beginning with Moses and extending on through all the prophets, therefore he had to suffer in such a way [i.e., by crucifixion] in order to enter into the glory of his father. This is clearly described in the last chapter of Luke [Lk. 24:25ff. and 44–47]. And Paul also says that he can only preach the crucified Christ, 1 Corinthians

1[:23]. After Paul searched the law of God more deeply than all his con-
temporaries, Galatians 1[:11–16], he could find in it only the suffering son
of God, who said, Matthew 5[:17], that he did not come to revoke the law
or to destroy the covenant of God, but much more to perfect, explain,
and fulfill it.

The spiteful scribes were not able to acknowledge all this for they had
not searched Scripture with their whole heart and spirit as they should
have done, Psalm 119[:2], and as Christ commanded them, John 5[:39].
They were learned in Scripture like apes who want to imitate a cobbler
making shoes and only ruin the leather. Oh, why is this? They want to receive the consolation of the holy spirit, and yet in their whole life, they
have never, as they should, come to the foundation of their existence
through sadness of heart. For only in this way can the true light illuminate
the darkness and so give us the power to become children of God, as is
clearly written, Psalms 55[:2–9] and 63[:1ff.], John 1[:4f.].

If then Christ is merely accepted through the testimony of the old and
new covenant of God and is preached without the enlightenment of the
spirit, a far more badly confused monkey business results than there was
among the Jews and heathen. For everyone can clearly see that present-
day scribes act no differently than the Pharisees previously did, insofar as
they, too, build their reputation with holy Scripture, scribble and spatter
all their books full, and they always babble more and more, "Believe! Believe!" And yet they deny the source of faith, mock the spirit of God, and
in general believe nothing, as you plainly see. None of them will preach
unless he is paid forty or fifty guilders. Indeed, the best of them want
more than one hundred or two hundred guilders. And thus in them the
prophecy of Micah 3[:11] is fulfilled: "The priests preach for the sake of
rewards." And they want comfort, pleasant leisure, and the greatest prestige on earth. And still they boast that they understand the origin of
faith! Yet they are driven into the greatest contradiction, for under the
cloak of holy Scripture they upbraid the true spirit as a false spirit and a
Satan. Christ also experienced this, as, in his innocence, he proclaimed
the will of the father, which was much too exalted and irksome for the
scribes, John 5[:16–18] and 6[:41f.].

You will find that things have not changed down to the present. When
the godless are trapped by divine law they say with great lightness, "Well,
now it has been set aside." But, when it is explained to them how the law
is written in the heart, 2 Corinthians 3[:3], and how one must be attentive
to its teachings in order to see the right path to the source of faith, Psalm
37[:32], then the godless one [Luther] attacks the righteous and drags
Paul around with such an idiotic comprehension that even to a child it
becomes as ridiculous as a puppet show, Psalm 64[:8]. Nevertheless,
Luther wants to be the cleverest fellow on earth, and he boasts that he

has no equal. Beyond this, he also calls all the poor in spirit "fanatics," and he does not want to hear the word "spirit" spoken or even whispered. He has to shake his clever head. The devil does not like to hear it either, Proverbs 18[:2]. If anyone tells Luther about the source of faith, he is rejected. Thus Luther employs deception, 2 Corinthians 11[:13–15]. He sings in the highest register what he takes out of Paul, Romans 12[:16], "One must not concern himself with such high things, but rather make them equal to trivial things." The pap tastes good to Luther mixed in this way and not otherwise—but he dreads clear broth for breakfast.[6] He says that one should simply believe, but he does not say what is necessary for this. Thus, Solomon says of such a man that he is utterly foolish, as it stands written in Proverbs 24[:7], "To the fool the wisdom of God is much too remote."

Christ began, like Moses, with the source of faith and explained the law from beginning to end. Thus, he said, "I am the light of the world" [Jn. 8:12]. His preaching was so true and so perfectly composed that he captivated the human reason of even the godless, as the evangelist Matthew describes in chapter 13[:54f.], and as Luke also gives us to understand in chapter 2[:47]. But, since the teaching of Christ was too elevated for the scribes, and the person and life of Christ were too lowly, they became angered with him and his teaching. They openly said that he was a Samaritan and possessed by the devil. For their judgment was made according to the flesh. As this false judgment pleases the devil in such circumstances, it must reveal itself as diabolic, for the scribes did not displease the worldly powers, who appreciate a Brother Soft-life [Luther], Job 28 [see, rather, Job 27:13–20]. The scribes did all they could to please the world, Matthew 6[:1–5] and 23[:5–7].

The godless flesh at Wittenberg does the same to me, now that I strive for the clear purity of the divine law, Psalm 19[:8–11], through the right approach to the Bible and the right ordering of its first part [i.e., the Pentateuch]. And I explain, through all the pronouncements of the Bible, the fulfillment of the spirit of the fear of God, Isaiah 11[:1ff.]. Nor will I allow Luther in his perverted way to treat the new covenant of God without declaring the divine commandment[7] and the onset of faith, which is only experienced after the chastisement of the holy spirit, John 16[:8]. For the spirit punishes unbelief only after there is a knowledge of the law, an unbelief no one knows unless he has previously acknowledged it in his heart passionately, like the most unbelieving heathen. Thus, from the beginning, all of the elect have recognized their unbelief through the exercise of the law, Romans 2[:12] and 7[:6f.]. I affirm Christ, with all his members [i.e., the true church], as the fulfiller of the law, Psalm 19[:7]. For the will of God and his work must be fundamentally fulfilled through the observation of the law, Psalm 1[:1f.], Romans 12[:2]. Otherwise, no one could distinguish faith from unbelief unless he did so in a false way, as did the Jews with their Sabbath and Scriptures, without once perceiving the foundation of their souls.

I have done nothing to the malicious black raven [Luther] (which Noah symbolically released from the ark [see Gen. 8:6ff.]) except that, like an innocent dove, I have spread my wings, covered them with silver, purified them in a sevenfold manner, and let the feathers on the back become golden, Psalm 68[:14], and I have flown over and despised the carcass on which the raven gladly sits. For I want the whole world to know that, as you see in his pamphlet against me, he flatters the godless rogues [i.e., the Saxon princes], and he wants to defend everything about them. It is clearly evident from all this, then, that Doctor Liar does not dwell in the house of God, Psalm 15[:4], for the godless are not despised by him. Rather, for the sake of the godless, many God-fearing people are insulted as devils and rebellious spirits. The black raven knows this well. In order to get the carcass, he picks out the eyes of the swine's head. He blinds the pleasure-seeking rulers to their obligations because he is so docile and so that he will be as full as they of honors, goods, and especially the highest titles.

The Jews continually wanted to slander and discredit Christ, just as Luther now does me. He rebukes me mightily, and, after I have preached the rigor of the law, he throws before me the kindness of the son of God and his dear friends. I preached that the punishment of the law has not been removed for godless transgressors (even though they be rulers). Rather, I preached that the law should be enforced with the greatest strictness, as Paul instructs his disciple Timothy, and through him all pastors of souls, 1 Timothy 1[:9–11], to preach the strictness of the law to people. Paul clearly says that the law's rigor should visit those who struggle and fight against sound teaching, as no one can deny. This simple clear judgment is contained in Deuteronomy 13[:9–12], and Paul also renders it on the unchaste transgressors, 1 Corinthians 5[:1–5].

I have let this message go forth in print, just as I have preached it before the princes of Saxony,[8] without any reservations. I have demonstrated to the princes out of Scripture that they should employ the sword [to punish evildoers] so that no insurrection may develop. In short, transgression of divine law must be punished. And neither the mighty nor the lowly can escape it, Numbers 25[:4].

Then, right away, along comes Father Pussyfoot [Luther], oh that docile fellow! And he says that I want to make a rebellion, which he supposedly interpreted from my letter to the journeyman miners.[9] He talks about one part of the letter, and he stays silent about the most decisive part, namely how I proclaimed before the princes that the entire community has the power of the sword,[10] just as it also has the keys of remitting sin. Citing the text of Daniel 7[:27], Revelation 6[:15–17], Romans 13[:1–4], and 1 Kings 8[:7], I said that princes are not lords but servants of the sword. They should not simply do what pleases them, Deuteronomy 17[:18–20]; they should do what is right. So, according to good, old, customary law the people must also be present if one of them is to be rightfully judged according to the law of God, Numbers 15[:35]. And why? If the authorities seek to render a perverted judgment, Isaiah 10[:1f.], the Christians present should deny this judgment as wrong and not tolerate it, for God demands an accounting of innocent blood, Psalm 79[:10]. It is the greatest monstrosity on earth that no one wants to defend the plight of the needy. The mighty ones do as they please, as Job 41[:24ff.] describes [the Leviathans].

Luther, the poor flatterer, wants to conceal himself beneath a false kindness of Christ that is contrary to the text of Paul, 1 Timothy 1[:7]. He says in his booklet on commerce[11] that the princes should make common cause with thieves and robbers. But in this same writing he is silent about the source of all theft. He is a herald who wants to earn thanks through the shedding of the people's blood for the sake of temporal goods—which God has certainly not intended. Behold, the basic source of usury, theft, and robbery is our lords and princes, who take all creatures for their private property. The fish in the water, the birds in the air, the animals of the earth must all be their property, Isaiah 5[:8]. And then they let God's commandment go forth among the poor and they say, "God has commanded, 'Thou shalt not steal'." But this commandment does not apply to them since they oppress all men—the poor peasant, the artisan, and all who live are flayed and sheared, Micah 3[:2f.]. But, as soon as anyone steals the smallest thing, he must hang. And to this Doctor Liar says, "Amen." The lords themselves are responsible for making the poor people their enemy. They do not want to remove the cause of insurrection, so how, in the long run, can things improve? I say this openly, so Luther asserts I must be rebellious. So be it!

Luther is totally incapable of shame, like the Jews who brought to Christ the woman taken in adultery, John 8[:3ff.]. They tested him. If he had transgressed the strictness of the father's law, then they would have easily called him an evildoer. But had he allowed the woman to go free without a decision, they would have said that he was a defender of injustice. In the gospel, Christ revealed through his kindness the strictness of the father. The kindness of God extends over all the works of his hands, Psalm 145[:9]. This kindness is not diminished by the rigor of the law, which the elect do not attempt to flee. As Jeremiah [Lam. 3:31–40] and Psalm 7[:9] say, the elect want to be punished with righteousness but not with wrath, which from eternity God has never possessed. Rather, a wrathful God springs from a perverted fear of God on men's part. Men are horrified by the rigor of the law and do not understand how God, after all the rigor, leads them through the deceptions of fear to his eternity. All those who, through original sin, have become evildoers within common Christendom must be justified through the law, as Paul said [Rom. 2:12], in order that the rigor of the father can clear out of the way those godless Christians who struggle against the saving doctrine of Christ. In this way, the just may have the time and space to learn the will of God. It is not possible that a single Christian can devote himself to contemplation in such a tyranny [as the prevailing political order], where the evil that should be punished by the law goes free and where the innocent must let themselves suffer. That is how godless tyrants justify themselves to pious people. They say, "I must make martyrs of you. Christ also suffered. You should not resist me," Matthew 5[:39]. This is an enormous depravity. Why the persecutors want to be the best Christians must be carefully analyzed.

The devil slyly strives to attack Christ and those who belong to him, 2 Corinthians 6[:14] and 11[:14], sometimes with flattering mildness, as Luther presently does when he defends godless rulers with the words of Christ. And sometimes the devil does it with terrifying strictness, in order to show his corrupted sense of justice concerning temporal goods. Nevertheless, the finger of Christ, the holy spirit, 2 Corinthians 3[:3], does not imprint this kind of rigor on the friendly strictness of the law or on the crucified son of God, who sought to reveal God's will through the strictest mildness, insofar as both kindness and strictness harmonize when brought into their proper relationship, 1 Corinthians 2[:6]. Luther despises the law of the father and plays the hypocrite with the most precious treasure of Christ's kindness. And he scandalizes the father with his interpretation of the strictness of the law by invoking the patience of the son, John 15[:10] and 16[:15]. Thus Luther despises the distinction of the holy spirit between law and grace. And he uses one to corrupt the other to such an extent that there is scarcely any true understanding of them left on earth, Jeremiah 5[:31]. He hopes that Christ will only be patient, so that godless Christians can truly torment their brothers.

Christ was called a devil when he pointed out the work of Abraham to the Jews [see Jn. 8:39–52] and gave them the best criteria for punishing and forgiving—namely, to punish according to the proper rigor of the law. Therefore, he did not abolish the law, since he said in John 7[:24], just before going on to chapter eight, "You should render a righteous judgment, and not according to appearances." They had no other basis for judgment than to hold as valid that which was written in the law and to judge according to the spirit of the law. Even so, with the gospel, transgression is to be forgiven in the spirit of Christ, for the promotion and not the hindering of the gospel, 2 Corinthians 3[:6] and 13[:10]. But then, through such a false distinction, Doctor Liar, with his scribes, wants to make me a devil. Luther and his scribes say: "Have I not taught rightly with my writings and dictations? But you have brought forth no other fruit than insurrection. You are a Satan, and indeed an evil Satan, etc. Behold, you are a Samaritan and possessed by the devil."

Oh Christ, I consider myself unworthy to bear such precious suffering in the same cause as you, however much the judgment of the enemy finds favorable, perverted support. I say with you, Christ, to the proud, sly, puffed-up dragon: "Do you hear? I am not possessed by the devil. Through my office, I seek to proclaim the name of God, to bring consolation to the troubled, and to bring corruption and sickness to the healthy,"[12] Isaiah 6[:8], Matthew 9[:12] and 13[:18–23], Luke 8[:11–15] and 4[:18f.]. And if I were to say that I would cease from this because of the bad name with which I am tarnished by lies, then I would be like you, Doctor Liar, with your perverted slander and viciousness. Indeed, at first, you could not do otherwise than quarrel with the godless. But now that you have succeeded in this, you have set yourself up in place of the scoundrels whom you have so skillfully attacked. Since you now realize that things might go too far, you want to saddle your name, since it is so bad, on another who is already an enemy to the world; and you want to burn yourself pure, as the devil does, so that no one becomes openly aware of your evil.[13] For this reason the prophet, Psalm 91[:13], calls you a basilisk, a dragon, a viper, and a lion, because first you flatter with your poison, and then you rage and howl, as is your manner.

The guiltless son of God rightfully compared the ambitious scribes to the devil. And he left us, through the gospel, the criteria to judge them— by using his immaculate law, Psalm 19[:8]. The desire of the scribes was simply to kill him, for they said, John 11[:48]: "If we let him have his way, the people will all believe in him and cling to him. Behold, they already run to him in great crowds. If we allow him to complete his task, we will have lost, and then we will become poor people." Then Caiaphas came also, Doctor Liar, and gave good counsel to his princes. He had things well in hand and was worried about his countrymen near Allstedt. But in truth it is simply that, as the whole territory bears witness, the poor thirsty people so eagerly sought the truth that the streets were all crowded with people from every place who had come to hear how the service, the reciting, and the preaching of the Bible were conducted in Allstedt.

Even if Luther racked his brains he could not have done this at Wittenberg. It is evident in his German Mass[14] how jealous he was of my liturgy. Luther was so irked that, first of all, he persuaded his princes that my liturgy should not be published. When the command of the pope of Wittenberg was ignored, he thought, "Wait! I can still salvage things by breaking this pilgrimage to pieces." The godless one has a subtle head for devising such things, Psalm 36[:4]. For his plans were, as you can see, to promote his teachings through the laity's hatred of the clergy. If he had a true desire to punish the clergy, he would not now have set himself up in place of the pope. Nor would he flatter the princes, as you see clearly written in Psalm 10[:7–11]. He has interpreted this Psalm very nicely, so that it applies to him too and not only to the pope.[15] He wants to make carrion renderers out of St. Peter and St. Paul in order to defend his princely executioners of thieves.

Doctor Liar is a simple man—because he writes that I should not be prohibited from preaching. But he says to the rulers, "You should see to it that the spirit of Allstedt keeps his fists still." Can we not see, dear brothers in Christ, that he is truly learned? Yes, obviously he is learned. In two or three years, the world will not yet have seen what a murderous, deceitful scandal he has caused. But he also writes, innocently, that he wants to wash his hands of the matter, so that no one will notice that he is a persecutor of truth. For he boasts that his preaching is the true word of God since it calls forth great persecution. It astonishes one how this shameless monk can claim to be terribly persecuted, there [at Wittenberg] with his good Malvasian wine and his whores's banquets. He can do nothing but act like a scribe, John 10[:33]: "On account of your good works we do not want to do anything against you, but on account of your blasphemy, we want to stone you to death." Thus, the scribes spoke to Christ as this fellow speaks against me: "You should be driven out not on account of your preaching, but because of your rebellion."

Dearest brothers, you believe it is truly not a bad thing that is going on now. Anyhow, you have no special knowledge of the matter. You imagine that, since you no longer obey the priests, everything is straightened out. But you do not realize that you are now a hundred—a thousand—times worse off than before. From now on you will be bombarded with a new logic deceptively called the word of God. But against it you have the commandment of Christ, Matthew 7[:15f.]. Consider this commandment with your whole heart and no one will deceive you, even though he may say or write whatever he wants. You must equally pay attention to what Paul warned his Corinthians, saying in 2 Corinthians 11[:3], "Take heed that your senses are not confused by the simplicity of Christ." The scribes have applied this simplicity to the full treasure of divine wisdom, Colossians 2[:3], in violation of the text of Genesis 3[:3], where God warned Adam with a single commandment against falling into sin in the future, in order that he not be led astray by the multiplicity of material desires, but rather that he find his pleasure in God alone, as it is written, "Delight yourself in God" [Ps. 37:4].

Doctor Liar wants to advance a powerful argument against me—how sincere his teaching is. And he maintains that this sincerity will lay everything open. Yet, in the last analysis, he puts no weight on preaching, for he thinks there must be sects. And he bids the princes not to prevent me from preaching. I hoped for nothing else than that he would act according to the word, give me a hearing before the world, and abide by his decision to act according to nothing but the word. Now he turns it around and seeks to involve the princes. It was a prearranged scenario, so that no one could say, "Wait, do those at Wittenberg now want to persecute the gospel?" The princes should let me preach and not forbid it, but I should restrain my hands and refrain from putting anything in print. That is indeed a fine thing! Saying, just like the Jews, "We do not want to do anything to you because of your good works, but because of your blasphemy" [Jn. 10:33]. And truly pious people have always said, "Even if he swears an oath, unless he swears by the sacrament of the altar it does not count for anything." This same trick the scribes used very often, Matthew 23[:18], Luke 11[:39]. Nevertheless, they were "pious" people. Indeed, they did no harm—if you only believe that the weak must be spared being troubled.

Blasphemy could make no impact on the hearts of the Jews, as you can gather from the gospel. Likewise, good works did not concern them much at all, as is also true of Luther. Therefore God held up to the Jews the work of Abraham, John 8[:39]. But there was a cruel hatred in those Jews who wanted to have a good reputation with the people, just as Virgin Martin does now. Oh, the chaste Babylonian woman, Revelation 18[:2]!

Luther wants to deal with everything for the sake of the word. But he does not want to begin to justify or condemn my case with the word. He only wants to make a bad case for me among the mighty, so that no one follows my teaching because it is rebellious. Whoever wants to have a clear judgment here must not love insurrection, but, equally, he must not oppose a justified rebellion. He must hold to a very reasonable middle way. Otherwise he will either hate my teaching too much or love it too much, according to his own convenience. I never want this to happen.

If I were to instruct the poor with good teaching, it would be more useful than to get myself involved in a dispute with this blasphemous monk. He wants to be a new Christ who has gained much good for Christendom with his blood. And what is more, he did this for the sake of a fine thing—that priests might take wives. What should I answer to this? Perhaps I will find nothing to answer, for you have anticipated and defended yourself against everything (or at least you allow yourself to think so)! Behold, how elegantly you have sacrificed poor parsons on the butcher's block in your first explanation of the imperial mandate![16] There you said that the mandate should apply to the priests, etc.[17] so that your initial teaching would not be brought to trial. Then, hypocritically, you were perfectly willing to allow the priests always to be driven out. Thus you would always have produced new martyrs and you would have sung a little hymn or two about them.[18] Then you would really become an authentic savior! Naturally you would sing in your true manner, "*Nunc dimittis*," etc. [see Jn. 8:54]. And they would all sing in imitation of you, "Monk, if you want to dance, the whole world will pay court to you."

But if you are a savior, you must truly be a peculiar one. Christ gives his father the glory, John 8[:54], and says, "If I seek my own honor, then it is nothing." But you want to have a grand title from those at Orlamünde.[19] You seize and steal (in the manner of a black raven) the name of the son of God, and you want to earn the gratitude of your princes. Have you not read, you overlearned scoundrel, what God says through Isaiah 42[:8]: "I will not give my glory to another." Can you not call the "good" people [i.e., the rulers] what Paul calls Festus in Acts 25[:1]?[20] Why do you call them most illustrious highnesses? Does not the title belong, not to them, but to Christ, Hebrews 1[:3f.], John 1[:11] and 8[:12]? I thought you were a Christian, but you are an archheathen. You make Jupiters and Minervas out of the princes. Perhaps [you think they were] not born of the loins of women, as is written in Proverbs 7[:2], but sprang from the forehead of the gods. Oh, what is too much is too much!

Shame on you, you archscoundrel! With your hypocrisy you want to flatter an erring world, Luke 9[:25], and you have sought to justify all mankind. But you know well whom you can abuse. Poor monks and priests and merchants cannot defend themselves, so you can easily slander them. But [you say that] no one should judge godless rulers, even if they trample Christ underfoot. In order to satisfy the peasants, however, you write that the princes will be overthrown through the word of God. And you say in your most recent commentary on the imperial mandate, "The princes will be toppled from their thrones."[21] Yet you still look on them as superior to merchants. You should tweak the noses of your princes. They have deserved it much more, perhaps, than any others. What reductions have they made in their rents and their extortions, etc.? Even though you have scolded the princes, you still gladden their hearts again, you new pope. You give them monasteries and churches, and they are delighted with you. I warn you that the peasants may soon strike out.

But you always talk about faith and write that I fight against you under your protection.[22] In this claim, one can see my integrity and your foolishness. Under your protection I have been like a sheep among wolves, Matthew 10[:16]. Have you not had greater power over me here in Allstedt than anywhere else? Could you not anticipate what would develop out of this? I was in your principality so that you would have no excuse [for failing to show your true colors]. You say: under "our" protection. Oh, how easily you betray yourself! I mean, are you a prince too?

What do you mean boasting about this protection? In all my writings, I have never sought the elector's protection. I have taken care to prevent him from picking a quarrel with his own people on account of the goat-stall and the Marian idolatry at Mallerbach.[23] He wanted to make incursions into villages and towns without considering that poor people have to live in danger day and night for the sake of the gospel. Do you think that a whole territory does not know how to defend and protect itself? May God have mercy on Christendom if it does not have as a protector he who created it, Psalm 111[:6].

You say that three years ago I was expelled from Zwickau and wandered about. And you say that I complained about much suffering. But look what is actually the case. With your pen, you have slandered and shamed me before many honest people. This I can prove against you. With your vicious mouth, you have publicly called me a devil. Indeed, you do the same to all your opponents. You can do nothing but act like a raven, cawing out your own name. You also know well, together with your unroasted Lawrence of Nordhausen,[24] that evildoers have already been paid to kill me, etc. You are not a murderous or rebellious spirit, but like a hellhound you incite and encourage Duke George of Saxony to invade the territory of Prince Frederick[25] and thus disrupt the common peace. But no, you make no rebellion. You are the clever snake that slithers over the rocks, Proverbs 30[:18f.]. Christ says, Matthew 10[:23] and 23[:34], "If they persecute you in one city, flee to another." But Luther, this ambassador of the devil, certainly his archchancellor, says that, since I have been driven out [of Zwickau], I am a devil and he will prove it with Matthew 12[:43]. And he has obtained this understanding of Matthew contrary to the holy spirit, which he mocks and about which he flaps his cheeks, Psalm 27[:12].

Luther makes a mockery and an utterly useless babble out of the divine word. And then he says that I call it a heavenly voice and that the angels talk with me, etc. My answer is that what almighty God does with me or says to me is something about which I cannot boast. I proclaim to the people out of holy Scripture only what I have experienced through the testimony of God. And if God wills it, I seek not to preach my own cleverness from my own ignorance. But if I do preach improperly, I will gladly allow myself to be punished by God and his dear friends, and I am ready to assume responsibility. But I owe nothing to this mocker, Proverbs 9[:7f.]. I will not eat the jay, an unclean bird, Leviticus 11 [see, rather, Lev. 1:19], nor swallow the filth of the godless mocker. I am only curious about your true colors. Since you are from the region of the Harz Mountains, why do you not call the secret of God's word a heavenly bagpipe?[26] Then the devil, your angel, would pipe your little song for you. Monk, if you want to dance, all the godless will pay court to you.

I speak of the divine word with its manifold treasures, Colossians 2[:3], which Moses offers to teach in Deuteronomy 30[:11–14] and Paul in Romans 10[:8]. Psalm 85[:9] says that the word of God shall be heard by those who are converted with their whole heart and who strive to find in the teaching of the spirit all knowledge about the mercy and, equally, the justice of God. But you deny the true word and hold before the world only an outward appearance of it. You turn yourself most powerfully into an archdevil since, from the text of Isaiah [see Is. 40:2,6] and contrary to reason, you make God the cause of evil. Is this not the most terrible punishment of God on you? You are deluded, and, nevertheless, you want to be a leader of the blind for the world. You want to make God responsible for the fact that you are a poor sinner and a venomous little worm with your shitty humility. You have done this with your fantastic reasoning, which you have concocted out of your Augustine. It is truly a blasphemy to despise mankind impudently, [which you do in your teaching] concerning the freedom of the will.[27]

You say that I want my teaching believed right away and forced on others, and that I do not want to give anyone time to reflect. I say, with Christ [Jn. 8:47], "He who is of God hears his word." Are you of God? Why do you not hear it? Why do you mock it and condemn what you have not experienced? Are you still trying to work out what you should teach to others? You should much more truly be called a crook than a judge. It will become evident to poor Christendom how your carnal reason has indeed acted against the undeceivable spirit of God. Let Paul render judgment on you, 2 Corinthians 11[:13–15]. You have always treated everything with simplicity—like an onion with nine skins, like a fox. Behold, you have become a rabid, burning fox that barks hoarsely before dawn. And now that the right truth is proclaimed, you want to upbraid the lowly and not the mighty. You do just as we Germans say [in the legend of "Reynard the Fox"]: You climb into the well, just like the fox who stepped into the bucket, lowered himself, and ate the fish. Afterward he lured the stupid wolf into the well in another bucket, which carried him out while the wolf remained below. So the princes who follow you will be defeated, as well as the noble highwaymen whom you set upon the merchants. Ezekiel renders his judgment on the fox, at 13[:4], and on the beasts and wild animals, at 34[:25], that Christ called wolves, John 10[:12]. They will all share the fate of the trapped fox, Psalm 73[:18ff.]. When the people first begin to await the light of dawn, then the little dogs, Matthew 15[:27], will run the foxes to their dens. The little dogs will not be able to do more than snap at the fox. But the rested dog will shake the fox by the pelt until he must leave his den. He has eaten enough chickens. Look, Martin, have you not smelled this roasted fox that is given instead of hare to inexperienced hunters at the lords' courts?[28] You, Esau, Jacob has deservedly thrust aside. Why have you sold your birthright for a mess of pottage? [Gen. 25:28–43].

Ezekiel 13[:3–9] gives you the answer, and Micah 3[:5–8]. You have confused Christendom with a false faith. And now that distress grows, you cannot correct it. Therefore you flatter the princes. But you believe that all will be well so long as you attain a great reputation. And you go on and on about how, at Leipzig, you stood before the most dangerous assembly.[29] Why do you want to blind the people? You were comfortable at Leipzig, leaving the city gate with a wreath of carnations and drinking good wine at the house of Melchior Lother. And although you were [interviewed by Cardinal Cajetan] at Augsburg, you were in no real danger for Staupitz the Oracle[30] stood by you, although he has now forsaken you and become an abbot. I am certainly worried that you will follow him. Truly, the devil does not stand for truth and cannot give up his tricks. Yet, in Luther's pamphlet on rebellion,[31] he fears the prophecy of his downfall. Therefore he speaks about new prophets as the scribes did against Christ, John 8[:52]. So I have used nearly the whole chapter [of John 8] for my present condemnation of Luther. Paul says about prophets, 1 Corinthians 14[:1–5], "A true preacher must indeed be a prophet even if he appears to the world as a mockery." How can you judge people when, in your writing about the monk-calf,[32] you renounce the office of prophet?

When you tell how you punched me in the snout, you do not speak the truth; indeed you are lying from the bottom of your throat. For I have not been with you now for six or seven years. But if you made fools of the good brothers[33] who were with you, this will come out. In any case, your story does not make sense. And you should not despise the little ones, Matthew 18[:10]. As for your boasting, one could be put to sleep by your senseless foolishness. It is thanks to the German nobility, whose snouts you have petted and given honey, that you stood before the Holy Roman Empire at Worms.[34] For the nobility thinks only that with your preaching you will give them "Bohemian gifts,"[35] cloisters and foundations, which you now promise the princes. If you had wavered at Worms, you would have been stabbed by the nobility rather than set free. Indeed, everyone knows this. Surely you cannot take credit unless you want once again to risk your noble blood, about which you boast. You, together with your followers, employed wild trickery and deception at Worms. At your own suggestion, you let yourself be taken captive, and you presented yourself as unwilling.[36] Those who did not understand your deceit swore to the saints that you were pious Martin. Sleep softly, dear flesh. I would rather smell you roasted in your own stubbornness by the wrath of God in a pot over the fire, Jeremiah 1[:13]. Then, cooked in your own suet, the devil should devour you, Ezekiel 23[:46]. Your flesh is like that of an ass, and you would have to be cooked slowly. You would make a tough dish for your milksop friends.

Most dearly beloved brothers in Christ, from the beginning of the quarrel I have been wearied by the unavoidable trouble it would give to the poor masses. But if Doctor Liar had let me preach, or defeated me before the people, or let his princes judge me when I was before them at Weimar,[37] where they interrogated me at the request of this monk, then I would not have had this problem.

It was finally decided that the prince [i.e., Duke John] would leave the matter to the decision of the strict judge [God] at the Last Judgment. The prince did not want to resist the other tyrants, who wanted, for the sake of the gospel, to let the case remain in his sphere of competence.[38] It would be a fine thing if the matter were remanded to this eschatological jurisdiction. The peasants would gladly see this happen. It would be a fine thing if everything were postponed to the Last Judgment. Then the peasants would also have a good precedent, when they were supposed to do the right thing. When it came to their judgment, they could say, "I am saving it for the divine judge." But in the meantime, the rod of the godless is their chief hindrance.

When I returned home from the hearing at Weimar, I intended to preach the strict word of God. Then members of the Allstedt city council[39] came and wanted to hand me over to the worst enemies of the gospel. When I learned this, I could remain in Allstedt no longer. I wiped their dust from my shoes.[40] For I saw with open eyes that they paid much more attention to their temporal oaths and duties than to the word of God. They assumed that they could serve two masters, one against the other. They did this even though God, most clearly, stood behind them. And God, who had saved them from the powerful clutches of the bears and lions, would also have saved them from the hands of Goliath, 1 Kings 17[:36f.]. Although Goliath relied on his armor and sword, David taught him a thing or two. Saul also began something well, but David had to bring it to a conclusion after a long delay. David is a symbol of you, oh Christ, in your dear friends, whom you will diligently protect for eternity. Amen.

In the year 1524.

"Sly fox,[41] with your lies you have saddened the hearts of the righteous, whom the Lord has not deceived. And you have strengthened the hands of your wicked ones, so that they do not turn from their evil life. Because of this you will be destroyed and the people of God will be freed from your tyranny. You will see that God is lord," Ezekiel 13[:22f.].

This should be translated: oh Doctor Liar, you sly fox. Through your lies you have made sad the hearts of the righteous, whom God has not deceived. Thereby you have strengthened the power of the evildoers, so that they remain set in their old ways. Thus your fate will be that of a trapped fox. The people will be free. And God alone will be lord over them.

9
Selected Letters

#14. To his father.[1] Place unknown, probably in 1521.

First of all, salvation in Christ, my dear father.

I did not expect to discover in you such unfaithfulness, which you so unjustly demonstrate in your behavior to me in that you want to refuse me my natural rights, as though I was a bastard—indeed, as though I was a heathen. It greatly amazes me that I must pay for the lack of faith that you have long had for God, because you have been unable to sustain yourself. My mother provided you enough [in her dowry?]. Many people in Stolberg and Quedlinburg[2] have told me this. Indeed, she earned her bread three times over. You have her. . . .[3]

**#31. To Philipp Melanchthon. Place unknown,
27 March 1522.**

To the Christian man, Philipp Melanchthon, professor of sacred Scripture, from Thomas Müntzer, messenger of Christ.

Greetings, tool of Christ. I embrace your theology with all my heart, for it has liberated many souls of the elect from the snares of the hunters [Psalms 90:3, 123:7]. I approve your priests taking wives, so that the Roman mask [of false piety] does not continue to oppress you. But I disapprove of this: You pray to the mouth of God as mute, and on account of your ignorance, you do not know whether the number of the elect or the reprobate is growing. As a result, you reject totally the future church, in which knowledge of the Lord will bloom most fully. This error of yours, most dearly beloved, stems entirely from ignorance of the living word. Consider Scripture, on which we rely to disparage the world. It says most clearly that man does not live by bread alone, but by every word which proceeds from the mouth of God [Deut. 8:3, Mt. 4:4, Lk. 4:4]. See, it comes from the mouth of God and not from books. To be sure, testimony about the true word comes from books. But unless it arises from the heart, it is the word of man—which condemns the cunning scribes [Jer. 8:8], who steal the holy oracles, Jeremiah 23[:30]. The Lord has never spoken to them, yet they usurp his words.

Oh, most dearly beloved, see to it that you prophesy [1 Cor. 14:1], otherwise your theology is not worth a penny. Regard your God as close by and not far away [Jer. 23:23]. Believe that God is more inclined to speak than you are prepared to listen. We are full of desires. They impede [God's] living finger, and he is not able to inscribe his tablets [i.e., human hearts].[4]

With your counsel, you drag people to marriage, even though the marriage bed is no longer an immaculate one [Heb. 13:4], but a whorehouse of Satan, which damages the church as severely as the most damned oils of the priesthood. Does not suffering these desires impede your sanctification? How can the spirit be poured out over your flesh, and how can you have living discourse with God, if you deny such things? No commandment (if I may call it this) constricts Christians more tightly than our sanctification. For, according to the will of God, [this commandment] first releases the soul, since the soul can never let inferior pleasures falsely rule it. We are to deal with wives as if we did not have them [1 Cor. 7:29]. Pay what is owed, not as the heathen, but in the knowledge that God speaks to you, orders and admonishes you, so that you certainly know how much must be paid for elected descendents, and so that the fear of God and the spirit of wisdom subdue animal concupiscence, lest you be destroyed.

The bowl of the third angel (I fear and I know) has already been poured into the water fountain [Rev. 16:4], and a whole stream of blood has arisen; indeed, their word has been changed into flesh and blood. Some are elected, but their reason cannot be opened, for the reasons already mentioned. Thus, their works are like those of the reprobate, except for the fear of God, which differentiates them from the latter. Two people lie in one bed [see Lk. 17:34] and perform an act of pleasure. Such acts, namely, I find among you, as long as there are disputes among you about abolishing the Mass.[5] I praise and applaud it that some people curse the abomination of the papal sacrifice. They are inspired by the holy spirit. But they are caught up in errors in that they have not followed apostolic usage as their guideline. For those who have scattered seed at the Lord's command must harvest; preachers must examine their listeners when they have finished speaking, and those who bear fruit of their understanding must be shown to the people. And they must be given bread and drink. For those to whom it is given to understand the testimonies of God have the true possessor [God], and not dead promises from books but living ones.

Our most beloved Martin acts ignorantly because he does not want to offend the weak, who are still as weak as children a hundred-years old, who were cursed [Is. 65:20]. No, to the contrary, the affliction of Christians has begun. I do not know why you think it is still to be expected. Dear brothers, delay no longer; the time is here! Do not delay; summer is at the door [Mt. 24:32]. Do not have anything to do with the reprobate, for they prevent the word from being effective with great strength [1 Thes. 2:13]. Do not flatter your princes; otherwise you will witness your ruination [2 Tim. 2:14]. May blessed God prevent this. If you deny Christian purgatory, you show your ignorance of Scripture and the work of the spirit. But I do approve your rejection of the papal bogeyman. No one can rest unless the seven levels of reason are opened by the seven spirits.[6] The error of denying purgatory must be avoided. Be warned! If you wish, I will support all my views from Scripture, the order of things, experience, and the clear word of God. You pampered scribes, do not be unwilling [to listen]; I cannot do otherwise.

Live well. Written on the Thursday after Mary's Annunciation [27 March], Thomas Müntzer, a messenger of God.

[P.S.] Do not ask the god of Ekron [2 Cor. 1:2], your [Johann] Lang, for advice. He is a reprobate who in his monsterous pride has persecuted the servant of God.[7]

#38. To unknown associates in Halle. 19 March 1523.[8]

May salvation and God's constant, eternal mercy be with you, my most dearly beloved brothers. I beg you not to get angry on account of my expulsion,[9] for, in such tribulation the abyss of the soul is cleansed, so that it is increasingly enlightened and recognized as worthy of obtaining the insuperable witness of the holy spirit. In order to discover God's mercy, one must be forsaken, as Isaiah clearly [testifies] in chapters 28[:19] and 54[:7]: "For a brief moment I forsook you and in great mercy I have gathered you." This is also what Christ, our savior, says about this [Jn. 16:7]: "If I go away, the consoler will come, the holy spirit," who can only be given to those without consolation.

Thus let my suffering be a model for your own. Let all the tares bloom as they will; they must pass under the thresher with the pure wheat. The living God makes his scythe so sharp in me that, afterward, I will be able to cut the red corn roses and the little blue flowers.

With this [letter] I give you my greeting. Be commended to God. Let he who is able share with me the wages of the gospel: "The wage laborer is worth his wages," Matthew 10[:10]. He who gets angry over this should give me nothing. It would be better to die than to besmirch the honor of God with sustinence that is given in anger. The whole winter I have had only two guilders, which I got from the abbess.[10] Of these, I gave one to the youth [Ambrosius Emmen],[11] the second, and more, I owe on a debt.[12] This youth is faithful to me.

Written in the misery of my persecution on the day of St. Joseph [19 March] in the year of Christ 1523.

Thomas Müntzer, a willing messenger of God.

#40. To Martin Luther. Allstedt, 9 July 1523.

Greetings, you most upright person of all.

My devotion to your worthy person was never so slight that I would have listened to deceitful insinuations. For I knew for certain from the beginning that you were leading not your own cause but that of all people. So it surprises me that in your letter you have recommended to me that most evil instigator of harm, Egranus.[13] For from daily contact with him, I knew for sure ahead of time that sooner or later this raven would reject his stolen feathers and devour his putrid cadavers and that he had no desire for the ark of righteousness.[14] He accurately painted his own portrait as a pampered beast of the belly in his unusual booklet on confession,[15] in which he so eruditely recommends the church of the evildoers [Ps. 26:5] that he could not have been of greater service to the godless than this. You want to reconcile me to such an ambitious person so that your enemies do not attack you in hordes. I have set myself up as an insurmountable wall against them [Jer. 1:18] in order to honor the name of God. With a resolute spirit I have contradicted "him of haughty glance and insatiable heart; I am not able to share a meal with him" [Ps. 101:5, 1 Cor. 5:11].

Concerning the effort to blame me for the insurrection in Zwickau,[16] everybody, except for the blind city councilors, knows that at the time of the uprising I was taking a bath, with no knowledge of such matters. And if I had not intervened against it, the whole council would have been killed the following night. Today I am ready to explain everything. The repugnant beasts spread numerous lies about me concerning revelations. I have never wasted a word replying to these absurdities. But now I want to tell you my views frankly. Knowledge of the divine will, with which we must be filled through Christ with wisdom, spiritual insight, and an undeceivable knowledge of God (as the apostle [Paul] teaches the Colossians [1:9f.]), must be present in everyone, so that we are found to be taught from the mouth of the living God, through whom we know most certainly that the teaching of Christ has been given to us without trickery, not by a human being, but by the living God. For Christ himself wants us to make a judgment about his teaching. And the Lord wants to prevent the opposite, for otherwise the flies will spoil the sweetness of our salve (which teaches all). John 7[:17] clearly says, "If someone wants to do his [God's] will, he will know whether my teaching is from God or whether I am expressing my own opinion." No mortal knows the teaching or Christ, knows whether he is lying or telling the truth, if his will does not agree with the will of the crucified one, if he has not previously borne the waves and surges of the waters [Ps. 93:3] that pour down on the souls of the elect from every side. They often sink in the storm, but rise again with effort and call with burning throats [Ps. 69:4] that they believe in hope where there is no hope [Rom. 4:18]. And after long expectation, on the day they go home, they fulfill his solitary will. Then their feet will be planted on the rocks [Ps. 40:3], and the Lord will miraculously appear in the distance [Jer. 31:3], and there will be credible witnesses of God. Someone who underestimates this and persists [only] in expecting the Lord, contradicts all of Scripture. And those people should not be believed who boast about Christ if they do not have his spirit, Romans 8[:16]. "Their spirit testifies that they are sons of God," Isaiah 8[:16]. What is more, no one is a child of God if he does not share his suffering [Rom. 8:17] and is constantly a sacrificial lamb [Ps. 44:22], so that God does not spare him and abandon him even for a short time [Ps. 54:7]. The person finally obtains certainty that no created thing can separate him from the living God and the truthful testimony of Scripture [Rom. 8:39]. Relying on this great certainty, the person distinguishes through divine revelation between the action of God and that of evil spirits. He will be nourished in special ways by the most undeceivable visions and signs. He investigates deep mysteries from God's mouth, 1 Corinthians 2[:10]; Isaiah 8[:19ff.]: "People will bid their God for a vision on behalf of the living and the dead, for a law, and for testimony," etc.; "Whoever mocks this, will curse his king and his God," etc. Dearest patron [Luther], you know Thomas personally and by reputation.[17] I acknowledge neither ecstacies nor visions if God does not lead me to do so; indeed, I do not believe those which are generally acknowledged if I have not seen the action. Nor should I be found so great that I am thought to represent a perfect person, corresponding to the measure of Christ's gifts. Why should I be worthy? The evident meaning of Scripture at many places is that the holy spirit proclaims future events to us, John 16[:33]. The holy spirit shields everything that it reveals in fire [Prov. 30:5]. I acknowledge only what is contained in the testimony of Scripture.

You think that I do not know what Moses said in the two passages explained by Jesus Sirach, Ecclesiasticus 34: "An unreasonable person deceives himself with empty hopes and lies, and dreams inspire only fools," etc. [Ec. 34:1]; "Dreams have led many people into error" [Ec. 34:7]. A little further on, he gives the reason for the error, which I have set forth above. Because they have not added wisdom to the testimony of God, they have deserved night instead of a vision of God, Micah 3[:6]. In this matter I am not so presumptuous that I do not wish to be justified and taught by your higher testimony, so that we walk the path of love together.

You were infuriated about Marcus [Thomae] and Nicholas [Storch].[18] They themselves should see what kind of people they are, Galatians 2[:6]. I tremble at divine proclamations of judgment. I do not know what they told you or what they did. You objected that certain words make you want to vomit—I do not know, but presume [you mean such words as] "patience," "spiritual tribulation," "talent," etc. Good father, I know that the apostle has given me the basic principle of avoiding unspiritual, useless gossip and false, so-called knowledge [1 Tim. 6:20]. Believe me, I will say nothing that I cannot base on a most clear and appropriate text [of Scripture]. If I fail in this, you may consider me unworthy of life.

May the Lord protect you, and let our old love begin anew. Greet Philipp [Melanchthon], [Andreas] Karlstadt, [Justus] Jonas, Johann [Agricola?] . . .[19] and the others in your community, and live well in the Lord. I do not believe that you really meant it, but said it only in conflict, when you said that Christ is not able to be present at a wedding. In fact, one must always ask the mouth of the Lord, above all concerning such a mystery [as marriage]; otherwise the clay urns remain [full of water] and this cannot be changed into wine [Jn. 2:7–9].[20] Perhaps here I appear to be like Origen in chapter two.[21]

Again, live well! So that this letter is not endlessly long, I sound the withdrawal.

From Allstedt in the year [1523], on 9 July.

Thomas Müntzer, pastor at Allstedt.

#43. To Andreas Karlstadt. Allstedt, 29 July 1523.

To his most beloved brother, Andreas Karlstadt, a peasant in Wörlitz.[22]

Greetings, brother in the Lord! I do not know what has prevented you from writing me, for you promised that you would write me often. I do not know if you are a layman or a cleric, dead or alive, for you have told me nothing, even though you had couriers at your disposal at Orlamünde. Explain why you have not renewed our old love even slightly? I will always reply to your letters. Your complaint about letters being intercepted is nothing [to worry about], for the Lord is taking care of our cause. I am sending to you this man, Nicholaus [Rukker],[23] a brother in the Lord. Help him in the matter of our paupers. For the people have stopped paying dues to our nuns in order to distribute them to the needy.[24] He himself will tell you the details. You may question him as though interrogating God; he will not fail you, as you know. Believe this man. He is sincere in the spirit of God. Farewell. Perhaps the Lord wants you to be a manager [of alms] so that you may expiate what you have done in the pompous regime of Antichrist. To you, most beloved, I speak as to myself. Again, farewell. Dated in the year of our Lord 1523, on the 29th of July.

Thomas Müntzer, parish priest of Allstedt.

[P.S.] Greet your wife in Jesus the Lord. I am oriented to God in the original rigor.[25]

#44. To Count Ernst of Mansfeld. Allstedt, 22 September 1523.[26]

Written in a Christian way to the noble, wellborn count, Lord Ernst of Mansfeld and Heldrungen.

Greetings, noble, wellborn count. The official [Hans Zeiss] and the council of Allstedt have shown me your letter,[27] according to which I am said to have accused you of being a heretical rogue and an oppressor. This is true to the following extent. I definitely know, and it is common knowledge in the territory, that you have brutally ordered your subjects, by public mandate, not to attend my "heretical" Mass or sermons. To this I have said, and wish to complain about it to all Christian people, that you are exceedingly audacious in allowing yourself to forbid the holy gospel. And if you persist (may God prevent this) in such raging and senseless prohibiting, then, from this day on, as long as my heart beats, I will not only describe you [as a heretical rogue and oppressor] before Christendom, but also I will let my writings against you be translated often into many languages. And I will denounce you to the Turks, heathens, and Jews as a foolish, stupid person. I will proclaim this and put it on paper. You should also know that when it comes to such mighty and righteous causes, I do not fear the whole world. Christ raised the hue and cry about those who take away the key to the knowledge of God, Luke 11[:52]. But the key to the knowledge of God is that people are so ruled that they learn to fear God alone, Romans 13, for the beginning of true Christian wisdom is the fear of the Lord.[28]

But since you want to be feared more than God—as I can prove from your actions and mandate—you are the one who takes away the key to the knowledge of God, who forbids people from going to church, and who is incapable of improvement. In performing the liturgy and the preaching that I have undertaken here, I will support what I say with the holy Bible, even in the smallest matters that I recite or say. If I am not able to do this, then I am ready to lose body and life and all worldly goods. But if you are incapable of any reply except violence,[29] then may you abstain from this, for the sake of God. And if you persist, like often before, in your persecution, then you should not forget a future of conflict without end.[30] The prophet says, "No violence or intrigue help against the Lord." I am a servant of God just as much as you, so go gently in what the whole world must bear patiently! Do not make boastful trouble, otherwise the old garment will tear.[31] If you force me to publish against you, I will give you a hundred thousand times more trouble than Luther gave the pope. Be my gracious lord, if you can bear and suffer it; if not, I will let God be my ruler. Amen.

Written at Allstedt on the day of St. Maurice [22 September], in the year 1523.

Thomas Müntzer, a disturber of the unfaithful.[32]

#45. To Frederick the Wise. Allstedt, 4 October 1523.[33]

To the most illustrious, highly born prince and lord, Frederick, elector and high marshal of the Holy Roman Empire, duke of Saxony, count of Doringen, and margrave of Meissen, my most gracious lord.

Jesus, the son of God.

Most illustrious, highly born prince and lord, may the righteous fear of God and the peace that is alien to the world be with you, your electoral grace. Most gracious lord, since almighty God has made me a resolute preacher, I have tried to blow the [Lord's] loud, moving trumpets,[34] so that they resound with zeal for the knowledge of God, and to spare no man on earth who strives against the word of God, as God himself commanded through the prophet Isaiah 58[:1]. Therefore my name (as is self-evident) must necessarily be most awful, ugly, and useless to the clever ones of the world, Matthew 5[:11], Luke 6[:22]. To the poor, needy masses, my name is a sweet smell of life, but to lustful people it is a displeasing abomination of swift corruption, 2 Corinthians 2[:15]. And my life verifies that fervent zeal for the sake of poor, miserable, pitiable Christendom has consumed me. So the abuse of the godless has often fallen on me, Psalm 69[:10], has unjustly driven me from one city to another, Matthew 23[:24], and has mocked my response [to this abuse] most hatefully, Jeremiah 20[:7f.].

As a result of all this, I have thought day and night, Psalm 1[:2], about how I can cast myself as an iron wall[35] for the [protection of the] needy, Jeremiah 1[:18], Ezekiel 13[:5]. And I have seen that Christendom cannot be saved from the mouth of the raging lion unless the ringing, pure word of God is brought forth, putting aside the bushel or cover with which it has been concealed, Matthew 5[:15], so that biblical truth is openly discussed throughout the whole world, Matthew 10[:27], testifying to both the humble and the mighty, Acts 26[:22], presenting to the world only Christ the crucified, 1 Corinthians 1[:17ff.], and singing and preaching [the truth] in an undisguised and indefatigable way. Performing my office of preaching so that the time does not pass in vain, but rather so that the people are edified with psalms and hymns of praise, Ephesians 5[:19] and 1 Corinthians 14[:15], provides proof for the basis of the German liturgy.

All my reasonable reproaches have been of no help to me and have not prevented the wellborn Count Ernst of Mansfeld, through the whole summer and thereafter, from constantly forbidding his subjects [from coming to Allstedt], even before the emperor's mandate was published.[36] And, through this prohibition, he has caused our people and his to revolt. Since, in the long run, I could not prevent this rebellion through my efforts to persuade [the people otherwise], on the Sunday after the birth of the Virgin [15 September 1523], I pleadingly warned him publicly from the pulpit and eagerly invited him to visit my flock, saying: "I bid Count Ernst of Mansfeld to appear here—with the clergy of the bishop—and to prove that my teaching or liturgy is heretical. But if he fails in this (may God prevent this), then I will regard him as an evildoer, a rascal, a rogue, a Turk, and a heathen. And I will prove this with the truth of Scripture." This is exactly what I said, and nothing else, as I can prove.

He has treated me improperly, and now he refers to the imperial mandate, as though his affair was included in it, although it is evident that it is not. He should have brought his learned ones with him and instructed me kindly and modestly. Had I been defeated [in debate with them], then he should have accused me before your electoral grace and, only then, forbidden his subjects from attending my services. If it becomes acceptable to stop the gospel with human commands, Isaiah 29[:13], Matthew 15[:7ff.], and Titus 1[:14ff.]—and if, in addition, the language of the mandate is not formally observed[37]—this will drive the people crazy. For the people should love princes more than fear them. Romans 13[:3f.]: Princes do not frighten the pious.[38] And if it turns out that [the princes do make the pious fear them], then the sword will be taken from them and given to the ardent masses in order to defeat the godless, Daniel 7[:18]. Then that noble treasure, peace, will be removed from the earth, Revelation 6[:2]: "He who rides the white horse will triumph, and this is not fitting." Oh, highborn, gracious elector, much zeal is necessary here, until our savior, at the right hand of God on the day of his wrath (when he shall tend the sheep himself and drive the wild animals from the flock), mercifully destroys the kings, Psalm 110[:5], Ezekiel 34[:10]. Oh, may it please God that this destruction is not caused by our negligence.

I have not wanted to conceal this from your electoral grace with a long speech, Ezekiel 3[:17ff.]. And I greatly exhort you with an additional request—that you look favorably on my letter and allow me to be examined according to divine law [in order to determine] whether I am righteous in my defense. If I should now yield, my conscience and my conduct could not stand before Christendom, 1 Timothy 3[:9f.]. Your Electoral Grace must also be bold in this matter. Do you not see that, from the beginning, God has stood unceasingly by your Electoral Grace? May God protect you and your people forever. Amen.

Written at Allstedt in the year of our Lord 1523, on the day of St. Francis [4 October].

Thomas Müntzer of Stolberg, a servant of God.

#47. To Christoph Meinhard at Eisleben. Allstedt, 11 December 1523.[39]

To his most beloved brother in the Lord, Christoph Meinhard.

First of all, I wish you the grace and peace of the gentle savior, Jesus Christ, my brother who is eager for the truth of God. I am not able to restrain myself from presenting to your conscience the powerful truth that God announces through David [Ps. 40:1–10]: "I will not let my lips be slack," in announcing your truth to all people, so that their desire [for God] may be founded on hard rock. It should be known that I want to present [my message] according to the teaching of Paul and that I want to prove decisively with numerous passages of Scripture that no one can be saved unless he endures God's realizing the whole of Scripture in him,[40] Matthew 5[:18]. Christ did not come to redeem us without our suffering spiritual poverty (through the removal of all that delights us). It is his sole mission[41] that only the poor shall be consoled and that the untried shall be handed over to their punisher [the devil]. For he who does not become one with the son of God is a murderer and an evildoer, for he would rather be resurrected with Christ than to die with him. And such a person will never succeed in being a sheep of the true meadow.[42] [The real Christian] must observe with the greatest seriousness and sincerity how God, from outside, shatters his life, and how he grows from day to day in the knowledge of God. Each one should truly put off the old man [Eph. 4:22] and not do as the untempted scribes do, who put a new patch on the old garment [Mt. 7:16]. They steal a saying or two from Scripture and do not compose the teaching that springs from a truthful foundation. They are people who think that one can master the knowledge of God in a moment, but they do not see how much effort it costs to endure God's actions. Especially, they do not see what it costs to bear the fear of God to the most intense degree, like that borne by a murderer on the cross.

[The scribes randomly cite] one scriptural saying or another, as they might occur to them in sleep, as though the whole Scripture was not composed through strong comparisons.[43] I publicly proclaim with all my strength, against all the untempted scribes, that the whole Scripture must become true in every person, according to the capacity of each, before he is saved. To whomever denies these words of mine, I will prove openly that he does not believe a single word of the Bible and bears [instead] a stolen word, Jeremiah 23[:30].

I have consoled you [by telling you] that you should not pray for the dead[44] and that, according to the content of Scripture, the unwise ones are commanded to come to the court and law of God without a superstitious judgment. It must not be concluded from such writings that I have yielded the least thing to the papal evil, for I certainly know that all the wealth of the blasphemers of God rests on a contrived [doctrine of] purgatory. I have scarcely drawn a breath about my studies concerning the dead. Do my dear friends think that I want to reaffirm purgatory? One can clearly see what kind of experienced people they are, who do not know how to measure a single mile of the justification from faith to faith [Rom. 1:17]. Since the faith of a mustard seed [Mt. 17:20] has never once been planted in them, how then can it grow? My teaching may not and cannot permit the judgments of the miserable, pitiable one to stand unchallenged, Psalm 69[:30]. Passionate zeal consumes me about this— and devours the scribes. You have been told enough: Scripture does not teach you to pray for the dead. What God does with the inexperienced among the dead,[45] you should leave to his judgment. Matthew 24[:32] provides you with good instruction—that you should respect all creatures and that, just as creatures are subordinate to you, you should be subordinate to God. And if God wants to make his gospel true in you, in this time of temptation you should not retreat into your house seeking to escape this tribulation. You should commend yourselves to God from the housetop [Mt. 24:17] when you experience rapture, and you should commend yourselves to him freely and without any clinging [to earthly goods]. Let your suffering be a lesson and an exercise in the decline of your unfaith, through Jesus Christ, the son of God. May he protect you, amen, with your children, wives, and so on.

Allstedt, in the year 1523, on the sixth day after the Conception [11 December]. In the spirit and soul of 1 Thessalonians 5.

Thomas Müntzer, a servant of God.

#49. To Christoph Meinhard in Eisleben. An Exposition of the Nineteenth Psalm. Allstedt, 30 May 1524.

Thomas Müntzer to his dear Christoph Meinhard.

May the spirit of wisdom and the knowledge of the art of knowing God be with you, cordial brother.

I detect in your letter a most keen desire for truth, since you have expended so much effort in asking about the right way. This you will recognize most certainly in the pure fear of God, according to Psalm 19, "The heavens are telling the glory of God," etc.

There you are told by the holy spirit how you must first learn to have your eyes opened by suffering the action of God as it is declared to you in the law. You must always keep one word of Scripture next to the other and direct the attention of your heart to where the sun rises from its true source after the long night, Psalm 130[:6]. He who has not suffered the night cannot have knowledge of God, which the night announces to the night and only after which the true word is shown in the bright daylight, John 8[:12] and 11[:9ff.]. They must be heavenly people, who seek God's prize to the disadvantage of their own name. Every moment must be lived for killing the flesh, especially so that our name stinks hideously to the godless.[46] For only a tested person can preach God's name, and the listener must previously have heard Christ preach in his heart through the spirit of the fear of God. Then a true preacher can give him sufficient testimony. The actions of the hands of God must first have convinced one that God is something inconceivable. Otherwise all preaching and writing is in vain. Whoever constantly practices such things can perceive all speech with a blameless judgment. And the designated teaching of such men must resound throughout the whole world, to all the frontiers of the godless, so that with their nonsensical power they are shocked by him who will instruct them with the Second Book of Jehu [2 Kings 9]. God is a friendly bridegroom to his beloved. At the very beginning, he lets them be rejected serving maids, until he protects them. For he has regard for lowly things and rejects the mighty, Psalm 113[:6ff.], 1 Samuel 2[:4–9], Deuteronomy 32.

It appears as though the godless will maintain political power forever. But the bridegroom will come from the bedchamber like a powerful man who is very drunk and who has slept through all that his servants have done, Psalm 78[:65]. Oh, we must pray—I mean, the time is at hand to cry, "Arise. Why are you sleeping?"[47] For the Lord has indeed slept in the small boat, while the storming wind of the impudent godless ones has nearly capsized the small boat. But then the bridegroom rises from his bedchamber, when the voice of the true owner [God] is heard in the soul, John 3. Then all of the elect rejoice with Jesus, saying, Luke 12[:50], "I must be baptized other than with the baptism of John, and I am very constrained until I have accomplished this." This entirely agrees with Psalm 19: "He is happy as a hero. He is joyous, like a hero wandering his streets."

If a person is to be true to his origins, when he is in the midst of vacillations in the wild sea of his encounters, he must do what a fish does which dives from the stagnant water on the surface, then turns, swims, and climbs from the depths of the waters, so that he is able to return to his initial point of departure. The elect cannot get too far from God, or he sends out his fire, Luke 12[:50], from which no one can hide, so that their heart, their conscience is not driven [by sin]. Even though the elect commit enormous sins, the fire of their conscience drives them to revulsion and an abomination of their sins. If they willingly keep in mind such sadness and abomination, then they cannot sin. I term this condition ennui [*Langweil*[48]], which is unpleasant to the noses of the lustful swine. They condemn the Old Testament; dispute a great deal about works, citing St. Paul; insult the law to the greatest extent; and nevertheless they do not possess the views of St. Paul, even if they get so worked up they explode.[49]

The law of God is clear, enlightens the eyes of the elect, totally blinds the godless, and is an irreproachable teaching if, through it, the spirit of the pure, right fear of God is declared. This happens if a person risks his neck for the truth, as Christ says, Luke 12. St. Paul required such works of the law. In brief, works of the law are necessary, even though the godless present a sophistic and contrived version of St. Paul. It is their allegation that St. Paul did not dream even once.[50] "To the devil with such preachers!," says St. Paul about the empty rubbish with which the godless try to seduce the elect. Then come our impudent followers of Bacchus[51] and they claim to have hit the nail on the head when they only cite Romans 4[:3], how Abraham received God's grace freely. But they fail to take account of Genesis 15 and Psalm 32: "Blessed is he whose transgression is forgiven." In Romans 4, Paul describes how a person is driven by God, through many pricks of his conscience, to the recognition of grace, which already resided beforehand in his heart.

As highly as St. Paul elevates faith without meritorious works, I elevate suffering the action of God just as highly, Isaiah 5[:11ff.?], John 6[:28]. I agree with St. Paul and not with our scribes, who have stolen their doctrine piecemeal out of his writings, like beasts of the belly; Philippians 3[:19], which asserts that the damned do not suffer the action of God.

Therefore, the scribes imagine Christ to be the fulfiller of the law, so that they do not have to suffer the action of God by pointing out his cross. So the rotten, worm-eaten theology of these old fools is to be equated at every point with the master in the thornhedge [see Prov. 26:9].

The justice of God must kill our unbelief until we recognize that every desire is sin and that, by defending desires, we become greatly hardened. Then a person must be eager to be made conscious of how powerfully insidious his hidden desires are. If a person is not revolted by them, he lets himself be ruled by desires and moved by them, and he satisfies them. And then he is neither to be advised nor helped. St. Paul most certainly announced this, 2 Timothy 3[:2–5]. He says, "People will be lustful, lovers of desires, and they will say that one cannot suffer the action of God, and cannot understand it." That is, they will deny the importance of studying and considering the law, through which the action of God is recognized.

Here you have a brief exposition of the Nineteenth Psalm. Send me a transcription or copy of it. In the year 1524, the first Monday after Trinity Sunday [30 May].

#50. The council and community of Allstedt to Duke John of Saxony. Allstedt, 7 June 1524.[52]

To the most illustrious, highly born prince and lord, Lord John, duke of Saxony, count of Doringen, margrave of Meissen, our most merciful lord and territorial prince.

As a greeting, may the true, eternal, righteous fear of God be with your grace. Merciful lord, we humble people, the council and community of Allstedt, have always been submissive and most willingly obedient to your grace's brother, Duke Frederick [the Wise], the praiseworthy elector, and we wish henceforth duly to fulfill these same obligations to the extent that they are due. We have also shown this obedience beyond measure in the affair of the nuns at Naundorf.[53] Although we have been greatly burdened with dues by these nuns, yet we have let his electoral grace instruct us, and we have paid them dues and tithes that lack any fair Christian obligation, so that we could discharge our obligations to them without rebellion. But all this did not help in any way. Rather, the nuns compelled us to pay dues for the chapel at Mallerbach and the other chapel in the town [of Allstedt]. And they did this with every cunning and unjust pretext, so that they could present their godless, unchristian case in an ugly and envious way,[54] and present it to your grace in a favorable light. But, if their petition has now been accepted by your grace, we poor people will be greatly burdened by it. And we cannot be responsible before God for maintaining and defending such a blasphemy of God. For, according to the testimony of holy Scripture, we are surely without guilt. For it is publicly known that poor people, through lack of understanding and at the time unconsciously, formerly honored and prayed to the devil at Mallerbach, under the name of Mary. And since this devil has been destroyed by good-hearted, pious people, how can we then help to arrest these people for the sake of the devil and imprison them? For we know, through the witness of the holy apostle Paul [Rom. 13:3f.] that your grace has been given the sword in order to punish evildoers and the godless and to honor and protect the pious. But since our people caused no particular harm that retarded the common good, and also because we want to maintain our obligations and obedience to the praiseworthy elector, unless his grace has more regard for mankind than for God—which we in no way presume of him or of your grace—we humble people do not seek protection or great defense before our enemies. So we poor people do not in any way wish to burden your grace or the praiseworthy elector. Yet, at every moment, we are in danger of death from the actions of our enemies, who persecute us mightily and with hateful fury on account of the gospel.

Therefore, for God's sake, we bid that your grace, as a Christian, praiseworthy prince, may regard and take to heart what God our creator said through pious Moses, Exodus 23[:1], "You shall not defend the godless." But since the whole world knows that monks and nuns are idolatrous people, how then in fairness can they be defended by pious, Christian princes? We want to do everything for your grace and our praiseworthy elector, with body and goods, that has been fairly imposed on us. But that we should continue to permit the devil at Mallerbach to be prayed to, so that our brothers are delivered up to him as a sacrifice, this we no more want to do than we wish to be subjects of the Turks. If we are dealt with violently in this matter, then the world, and especially the pious elect of God, will know why we suffer and that we are conformed to Jesus Christ. May Christ guard your grace in the true fear of God.

Written at Allstedt in the year of the birth of Christ our savior 1524.

To your princely grace, from the council and the whole community of your subjects at Allstedt.

#52. To Duke John of Saxony. Allstedt, 13 July 1524.[55]

To the dear duke and head of Saxony, my dear father, Lord John the elder.

My dear father and lord, I wish to present the knowledge of God and faith to poor, miserable Christendom just as I have been undeceivably instructed in it through God's witness, and just as Paul did to the Romans in chapter 8. But if I am to be punished, then I offer myself to the whole world, so that all nations should be informed. And then I want to say and write what is valid and what I can take responsibility for in the face of all generations, regardless of all the learned ones, who evidently lack the spirit of Christ. Should I now be retarded or restrained in this, it is to be considered truly what remarkable damage may arise from further delay, since the people have an insatiable hunger for God's justice, more than I can say, Matthew 5[:6]. In sum, it is announced that the mouth of the perverted ones will be gagged, for they fear the light, John 3[:19]. I will not fear the light. I want to be examined about the way that the elect have been unsatisfiably offended. If you want me to be examined alone before him from Wittenberg [Luther], I do not agree to this. I want to have the Romans, the Turks, and the heathen there. For I address and rebuke uncomprehending Christendom to its foundations, and I know how to take responsibility for the source of my faith. If you wish to allow my books to be published, I am pleased; but if you do not, I will commend it to the will of God. I will faithfully give you all my books to read. What God's revelation recalls to your mind, I will preserve with you in Jesus Christ, our savior. May he protect you, most dearly beloved, together with your subjects. Amen.

Written at Allstedt on the day of St. Margaret [13 July], in the year 1524.

Thomas Müntzer, a servant of God.

#53. To the God-fearing at Sangerhausen. Allstedt, 15 July 1524.[56]

I, Thomas Müntzer, wish all the God-fearing people at Sangerhausen peace, to which the untested world is an enemy. Since God's undeceivable mercy has blessed you with true preachers and instructed you,[57] you should not let yourselves be led into error by the manifold blabbering of the godless. You should not lose heart and not completely become children, as Paul described for the elect and warned them from his heart, Ephesians 4[:14]. Pay attention that you are not led around by the nose with empty threats and with the cunning of greedy people. For it is surely true that they are all worried that the time will once come when judgment will be pronounced on them. And they have never once dreamed of this, never once considered it, and also never intend to consider it. Therefore, you should not be frightened by a ghost, Psalm 118.[58] Let the message of God be held before you in the fear of God, as is written, Psalm 119[:38]: "Establish your word unto your servant who is devoted to your fear." Then all the mistrust of your unbelief will fall away. Then you will find that you must preserve God's judgment in this way: by the instruction and the dying of your heart. But if you truly want to fear God, this must occur by endangering the things we fear on earth through the presumptuousness of our unbelieving nature's fleshly understanding. God's goodness must move you to this, which now has such a rich stock that more than thirty groups and organizations of the elect have been made.[59] In all territories, the play is about to go on. In short, we are in a situation that we must see through to the end.

Do not let your hearts sink, as happened to all the tyrants, Numbers

24[:17–19]. It is God's proper judgment that the tyrants are so fully and miserably hardened, for God wants to tear them out by the roots. Joshua 11[:20] has prophesized this for us. Fear only God, your Lord, then the fear is pure, Psalm 19[:10ff.]. Then your faith is tested like gold in the fire, 1 Peter 1[:7]. There you will find so much wisdom that all our opponents cannot withstand it. I have often greatly wondered why Christians have more fear of tyrants than every other nation, and yet they see before their eyes how every attack of the godless at every moment is ruined. This is the product of unbelief and of useless preachers. So do not let courageous preachers be taken away from you, or you will value over God a poor, miserable, wretched sack of gunpowder.[60] And you will not risk your body, goods, and honor for God's sake. And then you will lose everything you have for the sake of the devil. Pay attention to this—God will not abandon you. At first it will be hard for you, before you are able to suffer a little grief for God's sake. But you can be enlightened in no other way than through great grief, John 16[:20f.].

Out of brotherly duty, I have not been able to suppress this message of instruction and consolation. If something happens to you, my pen, preaching, reciting, and speaking will not be far from you. Take heart! The godless rogues are already fainthearted because of God's justice, which will strengthen you in Jesus Christ our Lord. Amen.

Written at Allstedt on the Friday after the feast of St. Margaret [15 July] in the year 1524.

#54. To the authorities of Sangerhausen. Allstedt, 15 July 1524.

As a greeting, may true, pure divine fear and peace, to which the world is an enemy, be with you, dear lords. Jesus Christ, the son of God, said unmistakably, "Whoever is ashamed of my words before mankind, I will be ashamed of him before God my father and before his angels," Luke 9[:26]. Therefore, I want to be aware of that which might fall·upon me and all servants of the right word. And whatever can happen to a righteous servant of God, this I will accept. Because all members [of the elect] are not able to neglect the protection and aid of one who belongs to their fellowship, I declare on my honor: if you harm Reverend Tile Banse,[61] I will write, recite, and preach against you and always do the utmost against you that I can think of, just as David did to his godless persecutors, Psalm 18[:37ff.], "I have said, 'I will persecute my enemies, I will catch them, I will not stop until they are utterly ruined. They shall fall under my feet, even though they may be most mighty ones.'"

It has not been enough that I have had to listen to you this long year—

how you have most blasphemously hereticized my teaching and forbidden people [at Sangerhausen] from coming to [hear] me [preach] and have imprisoned them for it. Now I should look on while you most blasphemously libel your own preachers. And I should overlook it that you are scheming and use your foolishness as a cloak for your crimes, as though one cannot see that you adore men. I know that there are no more superstitious people in the territory than you. Leave off with your rage. Recognize yourselves [for what you are]; nothing else will count in your favor. Be aware of this and stick to it. Take my warning to heart in a friendly way; I will not count much more in your favor. Do you want to forbid the word of God and still be Christians? Oh, how can you reconcile this?[62] I say to you on my honor, if you do not improve yourselves in this respect, I will not restrain any longer the people who want to do something about it. You must choose one of two things: you must accept the gospel, or you must confess yourselves to be heathens, that is, harder than iron. I will complain to the whole world that you want to be the flies that stink up the salve of the holy spirit, Ecclesiastes 10[:1]. Do not strive against the holy spirit, who may enlighten you. Amen.

Written at Allstedt in the year of Christ 1524 on the day of the sermon of the holy messenger of God [15 July].

Thomas Müntzer, a servant of God.

#55. To the persecuted Christians at Sangerhausen. Allstedt, between 15–22 July 1524.

To all of the beloved brothers in Christ who are in the tyrant's prison at Sangerhausen, I send, instead of my greetings, grace and peace with the pure, uncontrived fear of God. Jesus Christ, the gentle son of God, said this with clear words. And he said it first with sorrowful words to his beloved apostles and friends at the holy meal of his Last Supper. He told them at every opportunity how it would take place and how the lustful world, including the wrathful, would act. He did this so that the members of the elect could begin to recognize the crucified Christ and to grasp for true faith. And thus John 16[:1f.] said, "You should not be angry when the godless expel you from the community, and the hour will come when they will imagine that if they kill you, they will have performed a service for God in doing so." You should take these words to heart and lock them into the foundation of your heart. For now the dangerous times have begun, of which St. Paul spoke [1 Tim. 3:11], when everyone who gladly does what is right and who wants to adhere to the holy gospel must be regarded by the godless as a heretic, a rogue, a rascal, or whatever else they can think up.

But now I have been informed by some pious people in what great tribulation you are. And you are in the hands of mad, insane people and tyrants who are putting you in prison again, and, for this reason, you ask my counsel. Out of Christian duty, I cannot refuse you this, but you must stick to this counsel. Since you gladly want to protect your conscience, it is a start in this direction that you put the pure, righteous fear of God before you and learn to fear God alone above all creatures in heaven and on earth. And, from this fear, you will know and learn what you should do and omit doing, so that God is well pleased. For the beginning of wisdom about God is fear of God, as the spirit of God says in Psalm 111[:10] and in Proverbs 1[:7]. Thus you should sob to God with your whole heart, day and night, and cry and bid him to teach you to fear God alone. For if you do not have this pure fear of God, you will not be able to withstand any tribulation. But if you have this same fear, you will gain the victory over all tyrants, and they will be so utterly ruined that it cannot be described. But the fear of God teaches how a pious man must stand calmly for the sake of God and risk[63] his body, property, house and plot, children and wives, father and mother, in fact the whole world. Oh, what a powerful abomination this is to carnal people, who have devoted all their reason their whole life long to acquiring sustinence[64] and have not thought about life further. They have just thought that God will surely save them if they simply believe what someone else believes. The whole world is now this insane and foolish because no one stands calmly for the sake of God, although the Lord nevertheless clearly says in the Gospel of Matthew 10[:37], "Who loves something more than me is not worthy of me." Here Christ, the son of God, expresses most forcefully the true nature of faith. Now, should you want to be Christians and believe in Jesus Christ and that he has saved you, then you must start with the pure fear of God, for this fear is the beginning of faith, as mentioned above. The sum of all teaching is this: next to God, you must fear nothing—just as, next to the living God, no image should be adored. Here there must be no equivocating, rather the straight and narrow way must be followed. If your prince or his official commands you not to go here or there to hear the word of God, or commands you to swear not to go there any more, you should by all means not swear to such a thing. For that would be to set up fear of man as your idol in place of fear of God. Now, if you imagine that you can please both your prince and God, you will not be able to do this. For everything that competes with God, and seeks to be feared instead of God, is certainly, certainly of the devil himself. You should heed this point. But if the wrathful ones want to maintain that you should be obedient to your princes and lords, you should answer as follows: "The prince and territorial lord has been established to rule over temporal goods, and his power extends no further than that." And this is also the view of Sts. Peter and Paul, where they write about the power of man. Therefore you should be bold and say, "Dear lord, dear lord captain, if our lord the prince is not satisfied with the dues and payments that we give him annually, then he may take all our goods, and we will gladly permit him this. But in absolutely no respect may he rule our souls. For in such matters a person must be obedient to God rather than to man. And you can take this any way you want. If you make us suffer on account of this, we will complain about it to the whole world and let everybody know about it. And they will surely see and hear why we are suffering, even though we are willing, when it comes to temporal goods, to do and omit whatever pleases your eye. What more should we do?"

Therefore, dearest brothers, if you are required either to be obedient or to go to prison again, then stick by these words. But if they want to impose a monetary fine on you, go ahead and pay it, and always give the devil want he wants. Keep only your conscience free and independent, and do not let it be fouled by a tyrannical commandment. For Christ our Lord also thought this, Matthew 10[:28]: "Fear not those who kill your body, for once they have done it, there is nothing more that they can do. Rather I will show you whom you should fear: fear him who has the power not only to kill the body, but also has the power to throw the soul into hellfire. Him, him you should fear!" So let the tyrants exercise their will over you for a little while longer. Due to its lack of faith, the world has not deserved other lords and princes. Therefore, let the princes and lords plague you as long as God permits them to do this and until you have recognized your guilt. For all of Christendom has become a whore, since it prays to men. And how people fear their lords and princes is an adoration of men—as is now clearly evident —so that they must deny God's word and his holy name to the greatest extent for the sake of shameful sustinence and for the sake of their bellies. Indeed, St. Paul, in his Epistle to the Philippians [3:19] also calls them beasts of the belly, and he says that their belly is their god. Oh, take heed, most dearly beloved brothers, that you are not or do not become part of this mass of men. The devil is indeed a clever rogue, and he constantly puts sustinence and life before people's eyes, for he knows that carnal men have a body. This they must renounce for God's sake. Is this not a terrible, shameful absence of faith? Indeed, because you do not believe that God is so powerful that he can give you other sustinence, and more than before, if you risk or abandon your property and bodily sustinence, even including your life, for the sake of God, how then will you believe that he can give you eternal life? It is truly a childish belief to trust God when it comes to sustinence, but to trust God to give you eternal life is a supernatural faith, beyond all human reason. If you show lack of faith when it comes to something small, how then can God entrust you with something great?

Therefore, I admonish you, dear brothers, to pay attention to the example of all the elected friends of God and to how they conducted themselves at times of tribulation. If you have regard for the goods of your body, behold the holy friend of God, dear Job, and how calm he was. It is written in the first chapter of his book [Job 1:21] what he happily stated, when God's messengers came and proclaimed to him that all his children had been killed and all his property destroyed; then he responded calmly, "The Lord gave it to me and the Lord has also taken it away from me."

If you fear for your life, then heed the example of the holy martyrs. What little regard they had for their lives! And how they mocked the tyrants to their faces!

Now, almighty God loves you just as much as he loved dear Job and all the holy martyrs, for he has redeemed you at the same cost—with the blood of his gentle son, Jesus Christ. He also wants to share his holy spirit with you, just as charitably as he did with them. Why then are you so fainthearted? For I tell you truly, the time is at hand when blood will be shed over the hardened world on account of its lack of faith. Then the property of everyone, which previously they did not want to risk for the sake of God, will be taken for the sake of the devil, without his thanks. This I know to be true. How much longer are you going to let yourselves be led around by the nose? It is well known and can be proved with the holy Bible that lords and princes, as they now conduct themselves, are not Christians. Equally, your parsons and monks pray to the devil and are even less Christian. Equally, all your preachers are hypocrites and adorers of men. How much longer are you going to keep hoping? There will be little to hope for from the princes. Whoever wants to fight the Turks should not travel far away, for they are in the territory. But do to them that which I pointed out above—namely, make sure that you have the grievance and complaint against them, and not they against you. And tell them straight to their face, "Dear lord! St. Paul [2 Tim. 2:9] teaches that, 'The word of God should be free and unconstrained.' Why do you seek to prevent us from hearing it? Previously you did not prevent anyone from running to St. Jacob's church and to the devil near Heckenbach,[65] making widows and orphans, and carrying property and money out of the territory. And do you now seek to prevent us from traveling the path we have to follow? And will you not allow us to have true preachers, and also prohibit us from listening to others? If you seek to do this, then I will regard you as a Turk and not as a Christian prince and lord." Tell them this openly and without hypocrisy. Then you will be standing where you fear God alone, and you will not be hypocrites. If you have to suffer anything, God will stand by you and revenge you. But if you are hypocrites, God will make you so fearful that you will never attain truth and with it overcome the great harm to your salvation. For God cannot abandon his elect, although at times he seems to. But he also takes revenge at the right time.

Out of Christian duty, I did not want to withhold such things from you, and for the honor and praise of God. May he preserve your hearts in the most persevering faith. May the grace of our Lord, Jesus Christ, be with you all. Amen.

#57. To Hans Zeiss, official of electoral Saxony. Allstedt, 22 July 1524.[66]

To his dear brother in Christ, Hans Zeiss, electoral official at Allstedt.

I offer you the true undeceived fear of God. Today I wanted to anticipate the filth of the widespread revulsion[67] and to let you know about future treachery, in order to avoid any liability for it and to present the territorial princes with your counsel, so that no one is given improper cause [for violence]. I do this since nearly all the tyrants are actively engaged in persecuting the Christian faith.

Hans Reichart[68] gave the poor refugees[69] [from this persecution] an improper answer, one according to the old customary law of the officials of the princes and their attendants.[70] Then the exiles and the refugees asked me what kind of a gospel we have [at Allstedt]? Whether we were going to sacrifice on the butcher's block and in the most miserable way those people who were willing to suffer for the sake of the Christian faith? Then I said that I have not been informed in any way [of their fate]; if I knew about it, I would gladly do as much as I could [for them]. Just then, as I was talking to the refugees, Hans Reichart came to me from the print shop. Then I said, "What kind of a game is this supposed to be? Do you want to console the people who have been driven out on account of the gospel in this way? Can you not see any more clearly what kind of a game will develop?" Then he said that you ordered him to do it. If an official[71] from Sangerhausen or elsewhere visited Allstedt, the people would have to be handed over to him. Then I replied that this would be just only if rulers didn't persecute the Christian faith. But since they were violating not only the faith but also these people's natural rights, they should be strangled like dogs.[72] And if you officials in every district will not openly complain that your colleague at Schönewerda was the first one to break the common peace[73] and become a robber of his own subjects, then you will soon see what will happen to you. Thus I advise you, my dear brother, to consider well what will happen. Refugees will arrive every day. Should we please the tyrants with the cries of poor people? This does not line up well with the gospel, etc. I tell you that the terrible phenomenon of civil war will be unleashed.

You must no longer hold to the custom of obeying other officials. For it is as clear as the light of day that they think absolutely and completely nothing of the Christian faith. Their power has an end, and it will soon be handed over to the common people. So act carefully. Where the gospel is accepted, Christians are not imprisoned at the pleasure of rogues. I will stick sincerely and willingly to what I promised with my own hand to Prince [John].[74] But truthfully, I do not want there to be any tricks. Wherever the spirit of God compels me, in Christian faith, I shall endure the rulers as my judges. But if they have ordered you to arrest people who are refugees on account of the gospel, and if I knew this in fact to be the case, then I would renounce what I have written to him.[75] I advise you to write the princes yourself (however trivial it may well be to them) about the archrobber, Friedrich von Witzleben, and tell them that he violated the common peace, and so he is an archetype of pure tyranny and the source of all revolt. If he is not punished for this by the other lords, then the common peace will also collapse. For from now on, no people will believe in their own lord. And then the people cannot help the lord, nor the lord the people. Here perceptive and modest people can see the cause of all manslaughter made so pitifully evident that their heart justly trembles in fear. The insane world still mocks this; it thinks things are still as they were in the old life. The insane world always goes around in its dreams, until water is dashed over its head. Dear brother, may God protect you from this. Amen.

Written at Allstedt on the day of Mary Magdalene [22 July] in the year of our Lord 1524.

Thomas Müntzer, your brother.

[P.S.] Whoever wants to be a stone of the new church should risk his neck, otherwise the masons will reject him. Consider this, dear brother—whoever, in these dangerous times, is not willing to risk his neck, also will not test his faith. He will disparage everything so that he does not have to suffer. Therefore, he will have to bear much danger for the sake of the devil, be ruined in the eyes of the all the elect, and finally die at the will of the devil. May God protect you from this. Amen.

With this message I wanted to deliver my pamphlet,[76] which perhaps you recently passed on [to the court] at Weimar. I always consider matters more according to God's honor and will [than man's], for it is now the most dangerous thing to act before those who mock the judgment of God.

In answer to your four questions:[77]

1. The will of God is the whole above all its parts. To know the knowl-

edge of God and his judgment is the explanation of this same will (as Paul wrote to the Colossians 1[:9], and as Psalm 119 says). But the action of God flows from the whole and all its parts.

2. Doubt is the water, the motion to good and evil. Whoever swims in the water without a savior is between life and death, etc. But the hope that is attained after the action of doubt best confirms the person, Romans 4[:18ff.], Genesis 13[:15f.] and 22[:12, 17f.].

3. You have grasped well the judgment about the essential quality of a person, but first the coarse conditions must all be consumed before the person can begin to control his nature. Otherwise a person always goes around with a deceptive appearance, and also deceives himself. Therefore, one must see to it, if he is inclined to unchastity, that he hurts his lust the very first time he sins, by making a determined effort to observe both his lust and the thorns of his conscience. If he keeps his conscience active, then the filth of unchastity consumes itself in horror. In this state of mind, one sees clearly everything that moves a person to filth, to which one becomes an enemy—and first of all an enemy of lust through ennui.[78] When this indifference frustrates him, then he fails again, so that he is again driven by conscience. A person who remains quiet will be easily enlightened.

4. A person cannot come to the first true Christian memory without suffering, for the heart must be torn from clinging to this world through laments and pains, until one is absolutely and completely an enemy to this life. Whoever has attained this is able to generate more good days than bad with a secure conscience, something which is clearly announced in the Gospel of John [Jn. 21:21], and by Elias [2 Kg. 2:11], and by Enoch [Gen. 5:24].

Lastly, in the deplorable, current state of affairs, there remains only this—the refugees are not to be handed over to the power of their lords, so that the lords must capture them where we live. Otherwise the people will become embittered toward us. I say to you that new developments in the present world must be very closely attended to. The old guidelines no longer function at all, for they are vain mire. As the prophet says [Ps. 75:8], "The dregs of the cup of indignation have not yet been drained; all the wicked of the earth shall drink them. Whoever was thirsty for blood shall drink blood," etc.

#58. To Hans Zeiss, electoral official. Allstedt, 22 July 1524

To his dearest brother, Johann Zeiss, official at Allstedt.

Salvation! The affair with the poor people[79] took place as follows: when Hans Reichart came back from your castle, he pretended to be sad beyond measure, and he expressed an attitude of warning. But [the refugees] perceived only that they were to be handed over [to their persecutors]. And so they came to me and asked if this was our gospel—to sacrifice people on the butcher's block. This made me wonder a great deal where such talk came from. Then they told me where. At this I told them that I would write the electoral official [i.e., Zeiss himself], and that I did not know whether he had an order to this effect from his prince. Then, soon afterward, I met Hans Reichart as he was leaving the printer's. And I asked him, "What kind of game is going on here, that the people are going to be handed over?" Then he said that you commanded him to do it. So I said that if officials of Sangerhausen, or other tyrants, came here, they should not assume that their old stupidities are going to be accepted, after they have tried openly to exterminate the Christian faith. Rather, they should be strangled like mad dogs. I cannot speak otherwise about the enemies of the Christian faith, because I will prove it before the whole world that they are plain, living devils.

But it is also far from my intention to saddle pious officials with the anger of the common folk. In every sermon, I have said that there are still pious servants at the lords's courts, and so on. I do not want to encourage the poor people to live at our cost here and to provoke their enemies. Rather, [my point is that] they should direct their blows with a greater knowledge of their and our possibilities—so that they receive no false consolation from us. I know it to be true that everything the tyrants are doing is done from mere fear and despair. In these times, a very different judgment is to be made about the affair of Witzleben. Duke George knows of the affair; he acts from the same motives of fear and despair. You should expect nothing but the very best from me. If such a thing happens again, I will write you at any time. Think about the transformation of the world that is now imminent, Daniel 2. May God help you, amen.

Allstedt, on the day of Mary Magdalene [22 July] in the year of our Lord 1524.

The messenger that [Johann] Lang[80] sent is called Reverend Lamprecht, formerly a Carmelite of Hettstedt; he wants to come here again. I will restrain the prince [i.e., Duke John]. That is not the problem; the only problem is to consider future damage.

Thomas Müntzer, your brother in God.

#59. To Hans Zeiss, electoral official. Allstedt, 25 July 1524.[81]

To his dear brother in the Lord, Hans Zeiss, official of Allstedt.

May the strength and power of the holy spirit be with you, dear brother. What seems like a short time ago I preached on 2 Chronicles,[82] and.I gave my honest advice about how Christendom should conduct itself as I expounded chapters 22 and 23, about holy Joshua,[83] where the priest Hilkias found the book of the law, which he sent to the elders in Judah and Jerusalem [2 Chr. 23:2f.]. And he went with all the people into the temple and made a covenant with God, to which the whole community agreed, so that each of the elect was able to preserve and study the witness of God with his whole soul and heart.

Before Christendom risks its life against those who rage against true faith, it is even more necessary for it to take to heart with diligent zeal [the problem of] how it can avoid the terrible abomination that masterfully patches itself with the Christian faith, Luke 5[:36]. Therefore, I wished that our territorial princes not show so much pride in this matter. The people see plainly enough that the princes have very dangerously set their name and worldly reputation on an unstable foundation. But the people themselves could be scattered in this danger. And the people could also develop insuperable fear, if the princes do not want to do anything more than peek through their fingers, not insist on the election of true priests in their principalities, protect evildoers, and take absolutely and completely no step toward realizing God's most dear will. It is as plain as day that godless rulers themselves violate the territorial peace, putting people in the stocks on account of their commitment to the gospel—and our princes remain totally silent about this. Perhaps, since our princes have been misled by untrue scribes, they think there is nothing wrong with the situation. Nor do they consider that Christendom is still at this time unready to shed its blood for the sake of the faith. Yes, Christendom clings so firmly to the "creaturely" [i.e., the material dimension of life] that it gets worked up about every dispute and squabble, and everyone consumes all his wits, so that he is like a block of oak when someone talks to him about God. It is a mighty, enormous impudence that people want to rely on the old customary law after the whole world has changed so drastically.

By the love and truth of God, I tell you that it is absolutely necessary that you reproach the territorial princes most seriously about this, and truthfully reveal it to them without any fear. And warn the princes not to spook their own people with their negligence, but instead to consider—as long as the people still trust them—how to prevent every evil. I say with a completely sincere heart that, if they waste time too long, they will be much more despised than the other princes. Then it will be said [of them], "Behold the man whom God himself cannot help." May God prevent that. Then there will be effort and work; then the German country will be more evil than a killing pit, because the greed of people will have now attained its peak momentum. Thus the princes must change the heathen duties and oaths with their own people into a true covenant of the divine will, so that their people plainly see that they are doing something to make the uncountable mass of the godless so very miserably frightened that they will not know where in the whole wide world to hide (as is written in Numbers 14[:6–9] and Joshua 11[:6–23]). If you officials want to keep the peace, then one sword must keep another in its sheath.[84] It is no longer acceptable that you conspire with one another, as you did in the past when people were in flight and you wanted to hand them over to their persecutors with a specious rationale of contrived accusations—and yet [you claimed] for the sake of the faith. Rather, a modest league or covenant [Bund] should be made in such a form that the common man unites with pious officials for the sake of the gospel alone. But if, in addition, there are villains and rogues among the people, who would misuse such a league, they should be handed over to the tyrants or judged by the people themselves, according to the circumstances of the matter. Moreover, this policy must be clearly constituted in the league, especially on account of nonresidents, so that the covenant's members are not able to think that, through it, they are freed from giving their tyrants dues. Rather, they should conduct themselves as did the son of God with Peter, Matthew 17[:26], so that a few evil people are not able to think that we have formed a league or covenant for the sake of material things.

The most essential thing of all is to consider the following with infinite care: no one should put his trust in the league, for the person who puts his trust in man is damned by God, Jeremiah 17[:5]. The league should only be a threat to the godless, so that with their rage, nevertheless, they keep quiet while the elect investigate the knowledge and wisdom of God with all valid testimony about it. If the pious make a league, even though evil people are also among them, nevertheless, the evil ones will not be able to realize their evil will. For the upright freedom of the good people will permit the evil ones much less malice than otherwise, so that the whole band cannot be blamed. The league is nothing but a defense for the individual, which the natural judgment of all reasonable people does not deny anyone.

Here the untempted ones want to say, "Why do we need a league so much? We bound ourselves together in baptism. A Christian should and must suffer." My answer is, first learn what baptism is; first learn and discover whether you have found God's witness in you and whether you are able [spiritually] to stand. Consider that the whole stockpile of the knowledge of God must be known and experienced in its length, width, breadth, and depth, Ephesians 3[:18]. Otherwise, impudent carnal people will be martyrs; and the archseducers will sing a little song or two about their martyrs, so that one would swear to the saints that they too were martyrs.[85] Then our cause will be judged to be much worse and more contemptuous by succeeding generations than the coarseness of the Romans. You pious rulers must pay attention to this. For it is a bad thing to believe and be martyred. If the elect should merely let themselves be martyred by these contrived, "good," "pious," etc. people, then the roguery of the godless could never be completely made known, and the witness of God could not attain its right momentum.

From all this, may you consider taking counsel with God-fearing, faithful people, who have the fear of God, who are enemies of greed, and who love truth with all their heart, Exodus 18[:21]. Then you will find a thousand means to act rather than one—you may rely on that. The Lord is with us like a strong warrior [Jer. 20:11]. He who reflects on this will not be afraid. And the flesh presents a formidable danger for a life without fear of God, whom you serve forever. Amen.

Written at Allstedt on the day of the apostle James [25 July] in the year of our Lord 1524.

#61. To George. Without place or date.[86]

As a greeting, may the grace and peace of Jesus always be with you, dear brother George.

After you came to me to receive instruction, as your letter indicates, I did not give you any. This is not to be wondered at, since pastoral care takes away too much time. You know that on the same day you came, I also had other pious people with whom I had my work. And I was very tired on this day on account of the church services. It is now such work to get along with people—like a mother working with the filth of her children. One gets angry, another improves himself according to the movement of his soul, Psalm 89[:30–34].

Instruction in the faith is not the work of a day. For the holy servant of God, St. Paul, says in 2 Corinthians 4[:16], "The outer man decreases from day to day, but the inner man is renewed." He is renewed to the extent that he puts off the outer man. If he believes he has removed the outer man but has only stolen a patch from a new cloth and sewed it on his old garment, then this is worse than if he were a Turk or a heathen in the form of a Christian person. No one can give another the movement of faith, as John the Baptist shows with his baptism. Indeed, a preacher will point out the slaughtered lamb, who hurries after the lost sheep in the desert. So I have instructed you about contrived faith, which must precede true faith and reveal the desire that the holy spirit has planted in us and which breaks through all despair. For the faith of a mustard seed must throw the mountain of our selfishness into the bottom of the sea of all our movement. For Christ, the true son of God, climbs down to those who are almost completely drowned and who no longer have any consolation. Christ comes to them in the night, when the affliction is at its greatest, and the elect think that he is a devil, that he is a ghost. Then he says, "Oh, you most beloved, do not be afraid. It is I, and I cannot enlighten you differently. I have no other way of pouring my grace into you."

Then St. Peter and all of the elect with him jumped into the sea toward Jesus [Mt. 8:28–34], and they would gladly have borne all such movements of the spirit. But the ones from Gadarene bade the Lord to leave their land. These people are the swine who are drowned in the water, who never want to learn about the source of their faith, who want to conceal nature with nature [2 Pet. 2], and who use holy Scripture like a fleshly thing or like books of the heathen. These people have no patience for the swift writer [God],[87] who does not write with ink or other material but rather with the pen of his spirit in the abyss of the soul, where a person recognizes that he is a son of God and that Christ is the highest among the sons of God. What the elect are on account of grace, Christ is through his divine nature. And unless a person comes so far toward receptivity to the divine will, it is never possible for him to believe truly in either the father, or the son, or the holy spirit. This is clearly and obviously testified about in John 7[:17]. Christ says, "Whoever wants to do the will of my father, will recognize whether I have spoken about me or about God, my father."

Now, if we are to recognize God's unchangeable will, this can only happen if our will is submerged [in the water of suffering] with serious contrition and with great tribulation of heart. We must know how to describe and to imagine how a serious, suffering, eager person feels, one who neither believes in God because the whole world believes this or that, nor who can prove anything about God, who is also revealed through the order which has been established in him and in all creatures. And the person should perceive this order and be certain of it, much more certain than about all natural phenomena. This matter requires a joyous and dedicated person, one who must take care of this awareness from day to day. Such a person does not have knowledge like the crazy scribes, who announce their message according to the preferences of the world. Rather, he is a blemish to all untested people and especially [those who call themselves] Christians. How can I know what God or the devil is, what one's appropriate or alien good is, unless I have lost myself? "I am born reduced to nothing and am created like a beast of burden. And I am always with you" [Ps. 73:22f.].

Oh, where is our poverty of the spirit, if we cannot speak about it on account of our slothful practices? How can we escape spiritual poverty, if only it leads God to action? Much must yet be changed, for there are still people who take offense easily. Being offended comes from an imperfect or a contrived faith, which must be rooted out with all mercilessness, as Christ did to his apostles, when they all suffered offense at his suffering. But if the improvement is compared [with how we should be], childish features are preserved alongside [the new person].

I bid you, dear George, together with the good young man who was with you, that you help push to start a German liturgy—and the sooner the better. As you will see, God will stand with you. Do not be afraid, you humble band, for it pleases the strong God Sabaoth to let his name be seen once before the pompous world. It is high time. Arise from the sleep of heathen rites, for their only function is to harden you further, more and more, from day to day. You must practice the liturgy daily with readings of the law, the prophets, and the evangelists, so that the text [of Scripture] is as familiar to the common man as it is to the preacher, etc. It will begin. Only do not seek money or fame, and do not boast about these things! Oh, under the appearance of good, the custom of swearing to the saints easily sets in. And if one really examines it, this is what happens. Take heed that Christ is your stone, and that, in a wind storm, your will is grounded on the same cliffs. Do not turn either to the imperial mandate or to Duke George,[88] for they are flesh and not steadfast like God, as Isaiah 31[:3] teaches you clearly, where he talks about Egypt. All your opponents are people of this kind. Be cautious. If you do not want to use your temporal freedom, which you have in order to further the gospel, it will be taken from you, as it was from the Midianites [Num. 31].

#64. To Frederick the Wise. Allstedt, 3 August 1524.[89]

To the active father and lord, Frederick, elector of the dear territory of Saxony.

Instead of my greeting, I offer you the pure, true fear of God, together with the unconquerable spirit of divine wisdom.

Since the needs of the times require to the greatest extent that we anticipate and confront all the unbelief, which, up to now, has used the appearance of the Christian church, and which now represents itself in the deceiving form of fleshly and contrived goodness, God has decreed that, as Ezekiel says [Ezek. 13:5], I present myself as a wall for poor Christendom,[90] which is being ruined and which deserves not only to be partially punished, as some think, but pulled out by the roots, completely and totally. God has already done this partially in some places, according to the circumstances. But now Satan is driving the godless, learned ones to their destruction, just as he did monks and parsons previously, for they manifest their roguishness in that they mock the holy spirit of Christ in the most despicable way and denounce his spirit in many of the elect as a devil, which lying Luther has now done in his libelous letter to the dukes of Saxony, which is directed against me.[91] He bursts in here, raging and hateful, like a pompous tyrant, without any brotherly admonition. Therefore, I bid you, for God's sake, to consider seriously what kind of nonsense would emerge from this, if I repay his blasphemous snout in kind, which I nevertheless do not intend to do.[92] But it is difficult to forego a reply on account of the anger of many pious people from foreign territories and cities who have heard my teaching.

Therefore, I ask faithfully that your active goodness not prohibit or forbid me from preaching and writing for the benefit of poor Christendom. This is necessary in order to avoid the other danger, that Christendom set itself completely in opposition to Luther, and afterward could only with difficulty be united again.

This finally is my earnest conviction: I preach a view of the Christian faith with which Luther is not in agreement, but one which is in conformity with that in all the hearts of the elect on earth, Psalm 68. And if a born Turk were in question, even he has the beginnings of this same faith, which is the movement of the holy spirit that is described in the case of Cornelius, Acts 10[:2-4]. Therefore, if I am to be examined before Christendom, all the nations of mankind should be sent for and informed of this hearing, and those who have suffered unconquerable tribulations about faith, discovered the despair of their hearts, and, through this, are constantly reminded of true faith. Such people I could bear to have as my judges. Therefore, I want to avoid a private hearing, toward which the scribes are pushing me. Christ did not seek to justify himself before Annas. Rather he asked, "Why do you ask me? Ask those who have heard my teaching."[93] He directed the godless ruler to the people. Why should I throw pearls before the swine who publicly mock and blaspheme the holy spirit and about whom Christ said that they were born of the devil? Why should I trust them in a private hearing? Why should I let them use my patience to conceal their evil? It would be just as though they now said, "Christians should suffer, and they should let themselves be martyred and not defend themselves." But this would be a great favor to the tyrants in that they could easily conceal and carry out their shameful conduct.

Dear lord, I have promised your brother, Duke John, to submit my books for examination prior to printing. But I will submit them not only to the poisonous and pompous judgment of the scribes, but also to that of those who understand that the birth of faith comes only from a crushed heart. Therefore, if you wish to be my gracious lord and prince, then I will let the Christian faith that I have depicted go forth orally and in writing, in bright daylight, before the whole world, and I will make it public in the most faithful way. But, if your goodness disallows this request, you should consider how the common people will be reluctant and will refuse to obey you and others. For the people have put great hope in you, and God has given you greater prudence than other lords and princes. But if you misuse these things, then it will be said of you, "Behold! This is the person who did not want to have God as his protector; rather he relied on worldly opulence." Therefore, through our official [Hans Zeiss], I have written your brother an exposition of the Gospel of Luke[94] and an instruction concerning how a future insurrection should be dealt with in a way which pleases God.[95] I hope you will abide by this message, because the world still regards you as so honorable that the prophecy of Joshua 11[96] will not be fulfilled in your case, as it was on those who despised the counsel of the needy, whose consolation is God himself. May God protect you and all your people according to his most loving will.

Written at Allstedt on the day of St. Stephen [3 August] in the year of Christ 1524.

Thomas Müntzer, an earnest servant of God.

#67. To former followers at Allstedt. Mühlhausen, 15 August 1524.[97]

May the understanding of the divine will and the whole knowledge of God be with you, dear brothers. In my preaching to you I was unable to refrain from most bitterly upbraiding the tyrants [who seek to rule over] the Christian faith and who, under the cover of legitimate authority, put people in the stocks and force them to deny the gospel. In addition I also found reasons for attacking other rulers—those who dare to defend such godless, damned people. In truth I could not do anything but bark at the ravaging wolves, as befits a true servant of God, John 10[:12–14], Isaiah 56[:9–11], Psalm 77[:20]. In fact, I did nothing except to say, in brief, that one Christian should not miserably sacrifice others on the butcher's block and that, since the mighty ones do not want to stop this, government should be taken from them. When I said this earnestly to Christendom, the people did not or could not bring it about because of their fear. What more can I then do? Should I perhaps remain silent like a dumb dog? If so, why then should I live as a cleric?[98] I previously told you everything about how one should conduct himself in a time of tribulation. Perhaps I should let this happen to me and suffer death, so that the godless tyrants could work their arbitrary will on me through my patience. And, afterwards, they would say that they killed a devil. No, this shall not be! The fear of God in me will not yield to the impudence of another.[99] I saw such fear in you, after you remembered your oath and duty, that I could not be with you to burden you further, for I could not have forbidden my lips from speaking out about God's justice, Psalm 40[:9f.] and Isaiah 58[:1f.]. And if something happened to you, you would not have been able to bear it. Therefore, for God's sake, be content. I gladly wanted to help you with letters of consolation, so that you would not once be left standing in fear, but only with relaxed confidence. You wanted to forestall tribulation, which is impossible in our times for those who want to do what is right. Be of good heart. Such preaching cannot and may not develop without giving the greatest offence, for Christ himself was a rock of offence, Psalm 118[:9], Matthew 22[:41–46], Mark 12[:35–40], Luke 20[:41–44], Romans 9[:33], Isaiah 28, and 1 Peter 2 [:8]. This nonsensical, "clever" Christendom must be more severely offended than at any time since its beginning and by an invincible improvement [that has now begun]. Therefore, do not regard this improvement as the world does, with its concern for comfort, but as Job 28[:28] says. Therefore, I want to use this occasion to take leave of you for the present in a friendly and gracious way and be ready to serve you [again in the future] in the most true fashion and with unstinting diligence.

But on account of the threat that, in a very carnal way, you are experiencing from the castle,[100] you must not worry about anything. Your fear of human authorities had to come to light so that I could grasp how completely and totally you have let a human being make you timid, which hinders you beyond measure in recognizing the divine will. I brought you to know this [distinction between fear of man and fear of God] so powerfully and in a miraculous way and brought it out for your benefit. I want to be most friendly toward you, if you will accept it from me. But if you do not (may God prevent this for eternity!), then I must let him take revenge, for the sake of his name, on evildoers, and for the memory of the good.

I want the Mass and vesper books[101] to be sent to Mühlhausen. With all zeal I want to be effective, for the people here are ready to accept [my teaching]. And you should overcome getting along with one another; other people will also protect me until the whole church is aroused by the fire of the offense [it suffers]. I will write you and the community beneficially in the near future; at present I do not have the time. Be commended to God, my most dearly beloved in Jesus Christ our Lord.

I beg you to give my wife a small sum, one that does not offend you. Do as you like. I did not preach to you for the sake of money, rather to seek the name of God. May he protect all of you for eternity. Amen.

Written at Mühlhausen on the day of the Assumption of the Virgin [15 August] in the year of our Lord 1524.

Thomas Müntzer, a servant of God.

#67a. To the City Council of Nordhausen. Mühlhausen, after 15 August 1524.[102]

May the grace and peace of God our father and our Lord, Jesus Christ, be with you.

Dearest brothers in our Lord, since you are our neighbors and, like us, a free imperial city,[103] it is not unseemly for us to open our hearts to you. We have very sorrowfully heard that the inhuman violence of [the devil] Belial has established itself among you most thirstily and with criminal violence, without any justice, in order to sacrifice the blood of Christians to Belial. This usually emerges from the hate and blindness of hardened hearts and by those who try to turn the people of God from the purity of an uncontrived faith and a knowledge of their creator. From this arises tyranny, which ruins the pure fear of God in the hearts of believers and which is the true skill of the sneaky devil—to kill the best people for the sake of the least, namely those who live for the sake of a wooden idol or image. Now this is also plainly said of you, which is not only an offense and a depravity to Christians. To turn them from the creator to creaturely things is eternal death. Therefore, God says: "You shall make no images; pray to, love, or tolerate no images which are made." And notice that God forbids glorifying the sun, moon, and stars or the powers of the elements, much less the work of human hands. Those that do this shall be subject to the death sentence, as shall the prophet who teaches it.

Dearest brothers, who taught you to arrest people on account of an image? In doing this, you make clear that you defend idolatry and images—and subject yourselves to eternal death. Look, the apostle says, "Not only those who eat but those who speak well of eating are worthy of death." Therefore, your teacher,[104] even if he was an angel, is damned and worthy of death. But it is obviously also Satan himself who directs you from God to the work of human hands and from pure teaching to lies. Therefore, according to the punishment of Mosaic Law, he should be stoned. It is the greatest blasphemy against God to deal with images, be it a cross or a circle, for they are wood and dead things. They cannot help themselves. Are you not ashamed of yourselves for wanting to defend saints' images because they are blessed[?] But your foolishness recognizes well that they are idols and cannot help themselves. Therefore, let your preacher expound Wisdom 13, 14, and 15. There you will find the meaning of blasphemy against God, so that you give the elect the eternal name of God, which is in no way stone or wood, above his name [i.e., the preacher, Süsse].

But when blasphemy occurs, then it is the adultery and whoredom about which Hosea writes [Hos. 4:2 and 4:10f.]. Just as one commits adultery outwardly against the spouse, using the sexual organs of the flesh, so adultery also occurs inwardly in the spirit if man delights in images or created things in order to mock him who is unlike all images or creatures. Thus, listen to us, in order to show the heart, with all its desires, what is right, 1 Corinthians 6[:15ff.], Romans 2[:29], Deuteronomy 10[:16], and Jeremiah 3[:17].

Hence we earnestly bid you not to put in the stocks the members [of Christ's body], redeemed through the blood of our Lord, Jesus Christ, and to release those who have been imprisoned. For it is not appropriate for Christians to kill living creatures on account of a piece of wood or an image. Man can make images, but the whole world is not able to give life to man. He who smashes an idol that blasphemes God does no injustice, for his zeal is the zeal of the Lord, and his action praises God. But you have committed an injustice and slapped God in the face much more cruelly than the heathen, John 18[:38], James 2[:25], Luke 22[:48], Matthew 26[:48ff.], and Deuteronomy 9[:6ff.].

In God's name, release the prisoners. Otherwise, you are guilty for all the blood of the just that has ever been spilled on earth—Matthew 23[:34f.], Luke 26 [see, rather, Lk. 11:49f.], and Matthew 5—if, as you think and as is said, they have been imprisoned on account of wood and images. Release them so that God does not get angry with you. Do not sacrifice innocent blood. You do God no service with it, as you think, but rather you do it to God, Luke 9, Matthew 21. But, if you do shed blood for that reason, then you are a terrible abomination to God and to all his elect, 2 Corinthians 6, Deuteronomy 19.

May the peace of God be with you. May it sharpen your senses so that you perceive truth and justice, which the world has not received. Dear brothers, we too adhered to the abomination and the dregs of evil, but through God's grace we have been taught his truth, and to seek the highest good.

#70. To the church of Mühlhausen. [Mühlhausen,] 22 September 1524.[105]

Thomas Müntzer, a servant of God, to the church of Mühlhausen.

In order that I do not eat my bread in sin,[106] I have been occasioned to counsel and serve you most zealously. For I perceive and understand that on account of fear of human authorities you cannot resolve anything. After almighty God has written for you clearly, with coarse letters, about the crimes, misdeeds, transgressions, and diverse seductions of your authorities, it is fitting that you discover these misdeeds, [those committed] publicly and in secret, and that you admonish the authorities in a brotherly way, so that they patiently tolerate being removed [from office] for the sake of avoiding future evils, for God's sake, and for the benefit of all of you.

But if they want to be selfish with a prideful spirit, and if they prefer their private advantage and honor to the common good, and if they do not resign and give way to you, the word, and your justification, then, out of your obligation to God's word, you should publish an account of all their misdeeds, crimes, damage, and all their evil. And you should complain to the whole world about such obstinate people, exposing and accusing them of their evil, so that they may be found guity. Without a doubt, you will accuse your authorities of a hundred crimes and make them public, so that you will not be blamed and blasphemed in the smallest measure. For their evil has been made known to you most fully in that they abuse the word of God as heresy, intend not to accept it, and sacrifice the servants of the word on a cross.

If this is then made public to the whole world in print, their reputation will be brought before all Christendom, so that people will say, "Look, the pious people have had too much patience. They have kept the divine commandments." And then Christendom will say about you what is said about an elect people, Deuteronomy 4[:5–9]: "Look, this is a wise people, it is an understanding people, and it will become a great people. It is a people that takes risks with God. It wants to act right and does not want to fear the devil with all the schemes, tricks, and pomp of this world."

With this publication, on which I will loyally assist you, you will justify your whole cause before other governments. Then the disloyal band of the godless, who have left [Mühlhausen],[107] will not be able to stay honorably in any other city. For the commoners (may God be praised) are receiving the truth nearly everywhere. And you will make the godless so ineffective that they will not be able to harm a hair on your head, Luke 12[:7].

Pay attention that you do not despise the wisdom of the divine word, Proverbs 1[:24ff.]. Otherwise, on account of the devil and your own hypocrisy, you will suffer the evil that you would suffer close to God as only a small affliction, etc. Therefore, be commended to God, who is surely with you. Amen.

Written on the day of St. Maurice [22 September] in the year of Christ 1524.

#75. To the League at Allstedt. Mühlhausen, 26 or 27 April 1525.[108]

As a greeting, the pure fear of God [be with you], dear brothers. How long are you going to sleep? How long will you fail to acknowledge the will of God because, in your view, he has forsaken you? Oh, how often have I told you how it must be—God cannot reveal himself otherwise. You must stand before him in resignation. If you do not do this, then the sacrifice of your heartfelt tribulation is in vain. Afterward, you have to start suffering again from the beginning. This I tell you—if you do not want to suffer for the sake of God's will, you will have to be the devil's martyrs. Therefore, guard yourselves; do not be so timid and negligent; do not flatter any longer the perverted fantasizers, the godless evildoers.[109] Get going and fight the battle of the Lord! It is high time. Make sure that all your brothers do not mock the divine witness, otherwise they are all lost. All of Germany, France, and Italy is in motion.[110] The master [God] wants to present his play,[111] and now the evildoers are in for it. During Easter week, four churches belonging to religious foundations were destroyed in Fulda, the peasants in Klettgau and Hegau in the area of the Black Forest[112] have risen, three thousand strong, and the band is getting bigger every day. My only worry is that foolish people will allow themselves to be drawn into a false compromise because as yet they do not recognize the harm [the godless have caused].

Even if there are only three of you who are firm in God and who seek only his name and honor, you need not fear a hundred thousand. Now, at them, at them, at them! It is time. The evildoers are obviously as timid as dogs. Stir up the brothers, so that they arrive at peace and give witness to their [soul's] agitation. It is infinitely, infinitely necessary. At them, at them, at them! Do not be merciful, even though Esau offers you good words, Genesis 33[:4]. Pay no heed to the lamentations of the godless. They will bid you in a friendly manner [for mercy], cry, and plead like children. Do not let yourselves be merciful, as God commanded through Moses, Deuteronomy 7[:1–5]. And God has revealed the same thing to us. Stir up the villages and cities, and especially the miners with other good fellows who would be good for our cause. We must sleep no longer.

Look, as I wrote these words, I received a message from Salza[113] informing me how the people wanted to take the official of Duke George from the castle,[114] because he secretly wanted to kill three of them. The peasants of the Eisfeld have taken up arms against their lords, and, shortly, they will show them no mercy. May events of this kind be an example for you. You must go at them, at them! The time is here! Balthasar and Barthel Krump, Valentin, and Bischof[115] advance first to the dance! Pass this letter on to the miners. I have received word that my printer will come in a few days.[116] Right now I can do nothing else. Otherwise I would give the brothers enough instruction for their hearts to become greater than all the castles and armor of the godless evildoers on earth.

At them, at them, while the fire is hot! Do not let your sword get cold, do not let your arms go lame! Strike—cling, clang!—on the anvils of

Nimrod. Throw their towers to the ground! As long as [the godless] live, it is not possible for you to be emptied of human fear. You cannot be told about God as long as they rule over you. At them, at them, while you have daylight! God leads you—follow, follow! The story is already written—Matthew 24, Ezekiel 34, Daniel 74, Ezra 16, Revelation 6—scriptural passages that are all interpreted by Romans 13.[117]

Therefore, do not let yourselves be frightened. God is with you, as it is written in 2 Chronicles 12.[118] God says this: "You shall not be fearful. You shall not fear this great multitude, for it is not your fight, but rather that of the Lord. It is not you who fight there. Act bravely. You will see the hip of the Lord above you." When Jehoshaphat heard these words, he fell down. Do likewise and through God—may he strengthen you—without fear of man and in true faith. Amen.

Dated at Mühlhausen in the year 1525.

> Thomas Müntzer, a servant of God against the godless.

#79. To Count Günther of Schwarzburg. From the field before Duderstadt, 4 May 1525.[119]

To the young Günther, leader of the Christian community in the territory of Schwarzburg, our dear brother in the Lord.

May the eternal, constant grace of God be with you, most dearly beloved brother. Our brothers have received your letter and have accepted into our League your brothers Curt von Tucheroda, Heinrich Hake, Christoph von Aldendorf, and Balthasar von Bendeleben.[120] [Our brothers] have promised them Christian freedom and not to molest them or trouble them in an unseemly way. I promised them security in writing. I have also checked to see that it is true that they did not hinder the justice of God and did not persecute preachers. But, if they have done any of these things, they should in justice have to offer reparations to the community for their misdeeds. And they should affirm that they will not dare to hinder any longer humiliated Christian unity. I have not concealed my view about this from you in this present letter. In this way, I have submitted the whole problem to the recognition of the divine will.

Written from the field before Duderstadt on the Thursday after Walpurgis [4 May] in the year of Christ 1525.

> Thomas Müntzer, a servant of God.

#81. To the Christian brothers of Schmalkalden. Mühlhausen, 7 May 1525.

To the Christian brothers of Schmalkalden, now encamped at Eisenach.

As a greeting, the pure, righteous fear of God [be with you], most dearly beloved. You should know that we want to come to help and protect you with all our resources and strength. But recently our brothers, Ernst von Hohnstein and Günther von Schwarzburg, sought our help, which we promised them and are now disposed to deliver. If you are fearful because of this, we and the whole band from the surrounding area will also come to your encampment. We will come to help you with everything we have at our disposal. You must only be patient with our brothers for a short time. We have an enormous amount to do to muster them, for they are a coarser people than anyone can imagine. But you have become conscious of your grievances in many aspects. With all our efforts, we cannot get our brothers to recognize these grievances. We must accept it that they only act when God compels them with force.

I especially want to bid God to be among you and to advise and help you. And this advice and help are accomplished much better through difficulties than by stupidly thinking that you know everything; however, God wants to choose foolish things and reject clever ones.[121] Therefore, it is a weakness that you are so afraid. For you can indeed plainly grasp how God is standing with you. Have the greatest courage and recite with us, "Before a hundred thousand I will have no fear, even though they have surrounded me" [Ps. 3:7]. May God give you the spirit of strength. This, through Jesus Christ, he will never fail to do. May he preserve all of you, most dearly beloved. Amen.

Written at Mühlhausen on the day of Jubilate [7 May] in the year 1525.

Thomas Müntzer with the whole community of God at Mühlhausen and from many places.

#84. To the people of Eisenach. Mühlhausen, 9 May 1525.

To our dear brothers, the whole community at Eisenach.

As a greeting, the pure righteous fear of God [be with you], dear brothers. God is now moving nearly the whole world to a recognition of divine truth, and this recognition is also proved with the greatest zeal against the tyrants, as Daniel 7[:27] clearly says. There Daniel prophesized that power shall be given to the common people, which is also indicated in Revelation 11[:15]—that Christ shall have jurisdiction over the kingdom of this world. Then the false glosses [on Scripture] of the defenders of godless tyrants will be completely and totally rejected. The tyrants will be ruined not with words, but with deeds. But it is as plain as day that God, in a friendly way, lets his own people punish the adversaries only with respect to their property, through which they have hindered the kingdom and justice of God from the beginning, as Christ himself proves with a fundamental judgment in Matthew 6[:24]. How could it ever be possible that the common man, who has such cares on account of temporal goods, should be able to receive the pure word of God with a good heart, Matthew 13[:3–24], Mark 4[:3–13], and Luke 8[:4–15]?

For this reason, dear brothers, you should not have so unfaithfully robbed our companions, taken away their strongbox, and seized their captain [Hans Sippel]. The good, simpleminded group relied on your pompous façade, after you unceasingly made such a clamour about the justice of faith. In truth, to have done this to our brothers proves your deceitfulness. If you now wish to acknowledge this, we bid you in a friendly manner to make good the damages. In short, what harms them harms us all, just as what benefits them benefits us all. You are to be counseled not to despise the little ones (as you are accustomed to), for the Lord uses the weak in order to knock the mighty from their thrones, and he uses unlearned people in order to bring about the ruination of the untrue, treacherous scribes.

If we attain the release of our brother, the captain, and [our people's] goods through violence, you shall indeed perceive whether the Lord is still alive, who may move and enlighten you to recognize the false light, Matthew 6[:23]. The false light is spread through false servants of the word, to the corruption of the world without end, and it is spread among the common people with blasphemous preaching. Through this, the contradiction has become so great that the true light must be darkness, and the darkness of private interests is supposed to be light. May the Lord avert this for you. Amen.

Written at Mühlhausen on the Tuesday after Jubilate [9 May] in the year of Christ 1525.

Thomas Müntzer with the sword of Gideon.

#88. To Count Ernst of Mansfeld. Frankenhausen, 12 May 1525.

An open letter for the conversion of Brother Ernst at Heldrungen.[122]

May the whole power of God, the mighty fear of him, and the constant basis of his just will be with you, brother Ernst. I, Thomas Müntzer, formerly minister at Allstedt, warn you—as a superfluous encouragement—that, for the sake of the name of the living God, you should give up your tyrannical raging and no longer call down the wrath of God over you. You have begun to torture Christians. You have upbraided the holy Christian faith as a roguery. You have dared to wipe out Christians. Say, you miserable, needy bag of maggots, who made you a prince of people whom God has won with his precious blood? You must and shall prove whether you are a Christian. You shall and must give an accounting of your faith, as 1 Peter 3[:8ff.] commanded. In a fair trial, you shall have a good, secure chance to bring your faith to light. A whole community, meeting in a circle, has promised you this.[123] And you must also apologize for your evident tyranny. And you should also declare who it is that has made you so bloodthirsty that you want to be a heathen evil-doer, one who in the name of being a Christian seeks to harm all Christians. If you reject this challenge and do not settle the matter that has been put to you, then I will cry aloud to the whole world that all the brothers should confidently risk their blood against you, as they did formerly against the Turks. You shall be persecuted and annihilated. For each one who has bought an indulgence from you will become much more zealous [in his anger] than those who formerly bought them from the pope. We know of no other way to reach you. You are shameless; God has hardened you like King Pharoah and like the kings that God wanted to wipe out, Joshua 5 and 11.[124] May it always be complained about to God that the world did not perceive your coarse, bullish, raging tyranny earlier. Since you have caused such manifest and irreparable damage, what else can happen except that God himself take pity on you? In brief, through God's mighty power, you have been delivered up for destruction. If you do not want to humble yourself before the little people, then an eternal shame before all Christendom will fall on your neck, and you will become a martyr for the devil.

So that you also know that we have a strict order about it, I say: The eternal living God has ordered us to push you from your throne with the power that has been given us.[125] For you are of no use to Christendom. To the friends of God you are a harmful scourge. God has spoken of you and your kind, Ezekiel 34[:1f.] and 39[:1], Daniel 7[:11f.], Micah 3[:1–4]. Obadiah the prophet says [Ob. 4] that your lair must be torn apart and smashed to pieces.[126]

We want to have your answer by the end of the day, or, in the name of the God of hosts, we will afflict you. You may depend on this. We will unhesitatingly do what God has ordered us. You do your best as well. I will be there.

Written at Frankenhausen the Friday after Jubilate [12 May] in the year of our Lord 1525.

Thomas Müntzer with the sword of Gideon.

#89. To Count Albrecht of Mansfeld. Frankenhausen, 12 May 1525.[127]

Written to convert Brother Albrecht.[128]

Fear and trembling to everyone who does evil, Romans 2[:9]. I pity the fact that you so evilly misuse the letters of Paul. Through this you want to confirm the evil authorities in all respects, just as the pope made Peter and Paul into jailers. Do you think that the lord God in his wrath cannot arouse his uncomprehending people[129] to set aside tyrants, Hosea 13[:11] and 8[:4]? Did not the mother of Christ, speaking from the holy spirit, prophesize concerning you and your kind? Luke 1[:52]; "He toppled the mighty from their thrones and elevated the lowly" (whom you despise). Have you not been able to find in your Lutheran grits and your Wittenberg soup what Ezekiel 37[:23, 26] prophesizes? And have you not been able to taste in your Martinian manure[130] what the same prophet says later, Ezekiel 39[:17–20], how God commands all the birds of the heavens to devour the flesh of the princes and commands the unreasoning animals to quaff the blood of the mighty ones, as is also described in the secret Revelation 18[:2–6] and 19[:17–21]? Do you think that God does not set more store on his people than on you tyrants? Under the name of Christ, you want to be a heathen, and to cloak yourself with Paul. But your way will be blocked. You may depend on that. If you want to recognize, Daniel 7[:27], that God has given power to the community, and if you want to appear before us and justify your faith, we will gladly give you this opportunity and regard you as a common brother. But if not, then we will pay no respect to your lame, insipid face, and we will fight against you as against an archenemy of the Christian faith. You may depend on that.

Written at Frankenhausen on the Friday after Jubilate [12 May] in the year 1525.

Thomas Müntzer with the sword of Gideon.

#91. To the people of Erfurt. Frankenhausen, 13 May 1525.

To our dear brothers, the whole community at Erfurt.

Strength and consolation in Jesus Christ, most dearly beloved. We have heard about your steadfast love and your joyful conversion to the truth. And therefore, we want to encourage you. You will not be defeated unless the Lutheran pap-eaters have made you soft with their greased mercy, with which we have much experience. Paul says that, in our times, pleasure-seeking people cover themselves with the very best appearance of good or of pious conduct, and yet they strive both physically and verbally against the power of God. Anyone with eyes that see can easily grasp this.

Therefore it is our urgent request of you that you no longer give credence to lackeys[131] [of the princes], and that you do not let yourselves be restrained any longer from helping common Christendom and combating with us the godless, villainous tyrants.

Help us in every way that you can, with manpower and artillery, so that we fulfill what God himself has commanded, Ezekiel 34[:25], where he says, "I will release you from those who have beaten you with their tyranny. I will drive the wild animals from your land." Later God says through the same prophet in Ezekiel 39[:17–20], "Come you birds of the skies and devour the flesh of the princes, and you wild animals drink the blood of the mighty ones." Daniel 7[:27] also says that power shall be given to the common people, Revelation 18[:2–6] and 19[:17–21]. Nearly every judgment of Scripture testifies that creatures must be free if the pure word of God is to dawn.

If you now desire truth, join with us in the circle dance that we want to dance right now, so that we faithfully repay the blasphemers of God for the dirty trick they pulled on poor Christendom. Write us back your opinion, for we are well disposed toward you, most beloved brothers.

Written at Frankenhausen on the Saturday after Jubilate [13 May] in the year of our Lord 1525.

     Thomas Müntzer for the cause of common Christendom.

10

Last Words: Confession, Retraction, and Final Letter

I. Confession

The confession of Reverend Thomas Müntzer, formerly pastor at Allstedt and now found in the rebellious band at Frankenhausen, made on the Tuesday after the feast of Cantate [16 May] in the year 1525.

1. He [Müntzer] does not want the holy, most worthy sacrament [of communion] to be outwardly adored, but only [regarded] in a spiritual way; however he says this is a matter for the judgment of each.[1]

2. He says that he gave the sacrament to the sick, and himself partook, in the afternoon after he ate [at midday], and also that he took the sacrament at night, at every opportunity. He took [ordinary] bread and wine and consecrated them.

3. In the Klettgau and Hegau regions near Basel, he proposed some articles on how one should rule according to the gospel.[2] And he made therefrom further articles.[3] The peasants there gladly would have accepted him [as one of their leaders], but he declined them with thanks. He did not cause the insurrection in those regions [i.e., in the Klettgau, Hegau, and Upper Swabia generally], rather the people were already in revolt [when he arrived]. Oecolampadius and Hugowaldus[4] instructed him to preach to the people there. He also preached there that unbelieving rulers make an unbelieving people and that, because of this, there would be a [divine] judgment. His wife has the letters that Oecolampadius and Hugowaldus wrote him in a bag at Mühlhausen.

4. He says that [lords'] castles are very onerous and overloaded with services and other burdens on the subjects.[5]

5. He says he said that princes should only ride with eight horses, a count with four, and a nobleman with two, and not more.[6]

6. Present in his league or covenant [*Verbundnis*[7]] were firstly the Allstedter Barthel Krump, a tanner, and Balthaser Stübner, a glazer from the same town. They began the insurrection with him. The official [Hans Zeiss] was also in the league, although initially he complained about join-

ing it. The league was directed against those who persecuted the gospel.[8] And the register, in which the league's members were enrolled, was in the possession of the two members Krump and Stübner mentioned above.

7. Reverend Tile Banse,[9] a preacher at Sangerhausen, urged him to write a letter to the congregation there, that they should stand by the gospel and persecute those who are opposed to it. This he did.[10]

8. He says that he spoke to Dr. Strauss at Weimar, where he appeared at the written request of Duke John of Saxony and others.[11] At that time Strauss was engaged in a dispute with the Franciscans, and Müntzer was heard to say to the brothers: "If the Lutherans do not want to achieve anything other than to cause trouble for the clergy, monks, and parsons, they might as well forget about it." Since that time, Müntzer wrote against [Luther] to one Johann Koler of Mühlhausen,[12] saying that if it is not too far for Müntzer to travel, he would indeed like to come to Mühlhausen and drive him out. Perhaps this happened because Müntzer wanted to be there.[13]

9. The reason that he accused and reviled the gracious lord, territorial prince and count, Ernst of Mansfeld, was that Count Ernst's subjects complained that the word of God was not being preached to them, it was forbidden them, and they were not permitted to go hear it [at Allstedt]. Müntzer commanded them all to denounce their superiors. If the word of God was not preached to them, he said that they should then come to him. He wanted to preach it to them himself, and they should not let themselves be prevented [from hearing it] by anyone.

10. The people of Mühlhausen let him into the city,[14] and Johann Rode, a furrier, and the brandy-distiller near the church of Saint Blasius took him in.

11. He was at Mallerbach and saw how the people of Allstedt removed some pictures from the church and afterward burned the church.[15] He preached that the Mallerbach chapel was an evil den and that the business with the waxen images which were brought there was a superstition, not something commanded by God. The hermit of the place[16] was warned to move away, and this happened. Afterward, as already heard, the church was burned down.

12. Apel von Ebeleben's[17] house was wrecked and plundered by the brothers at Mühlhausen because it was an onerous house, according to sundry articles that the brothers discussed, but which were not known to him. The articles in question are partly the "Twelve Articles of the Black Forest Peasants"[18] as well as others.

13. The city council of Mühlhausen did not want to join the league, but instead relegated it to the common man.[19]

14. Nicholas Storch and Marcus [Thomae or] Stübner of Zwickau[20] were with Luther in a drink shop at Wittenberg, a place where Müntzer

has also been. To refute Storch and Stübner, Luther told them that he punched the spirit of Allstedt [Müntzer] in the snout. But Müntzer was not personally present [at Wittenberg] at this time.

15. Reverend Gandolf, the hospital preacher [at Frankenhausen] formed a military unit[21] and the people of Herringen and Greussen were in it.

Confessed Under Torture:[22]

1. Heinrich and Hans Gebhart of Zwickau, residing in the Hundesgasse, and all their dependents[23] are wool weavers, and they joined his association.

2. Reverend Heinrich Pfeiffer[24] stated that one castle in every region was enough. The others should be destroyed.

3. He [Müntzer] pronounced sentence on Matern von Gehofen and the other servants of Count Ernst[25] in the name of the common assembly, and he agreed with the sentence. And he did this out of fear.[26]

4. He fled to Mühlhausen and took refuge there, since it pleased him there so much and it was a secure city. His principal supporters there were Hans Kule, who lives near All Souls church and the two people mentioned above, the furrier and the brandy-distiller near Saint Blasius.

5. He confesses that if he had conquered the castle of Heldrungen, as he and all his followers intended, he would have beheaded Count Ernst, as indeed he often publicly announced.

6. He undertook the rebellion so that the people of Christendom would all be equal[27] and so that the princes and lords who did not want to support the gospel [and who refused to accept the league after being admonished to do so in a friendly way[28]] would be banished or executed.

7. The principal members of the league at Allstedt were:

Barthel Krump
Barthel Zimmerman
Peter Warmuth
Nicholaus Rukker   } all of Allstedt
Andreas Krump
Bischof zu Wolferode

8. It was their article of belief and they wanted to establish this principle, "All property should be held in common" (*Omnia sunt communia*) and should be distributed to each according to his needs, as the occasion required. Any prince, count, or lord who did not want to do this, after first being warned about it, should be beheaded or hanged.

9. Also members of the league were:

Hans Rodeman
Peter Schutze   } in Mansfeld Valley
Peter Bahr
Tile Fischer of Weymelburg

Tile Banse of Sangerhausen

Peter Rodeman of the same place.

The register of those who enrolled in the league was in the possession of Barthel Krump of Allstedt.[29]

10. He also made a league among the youths, when he was an assistant teacher at Aschersleben and Halle. Among the members of this association were Peter Blinde of Aschersleben; Peter Engel, a churchman of Halle; and Hans Buttener and Cuntz Sander of Halle, who lived at Stone Gate.

This league was directed against Bishop Ernst [of Magdeburg],[30] of highly praised memory.

11. If all had gone as he intended and planned—it was his opinion and publicly known by all the commoners of his association—he wanted to occupy the land up to a ten mile radius around Mühlhausen and to occupy the territory of Hesse,[31] and he would have dealt with the princes and lords as indicated above. The majority of the league's members knew this well.

12. The people of Mühlhausen lent him eight artillery pieces.

Count Bodo of Stolberg lent those at Frankenhausen a small field piece.

II. Fragment with Further Testimony of Müntzer

1. At Zwickau, the parishes of both St. Catherine's and Our Lady's selected him [Müntzer] to be a preacher. I was[32] also there a year; there my testimony [concerning faith] was well received.

2. Reverend Heinrich Pfeiffer first took to the field in order to assist those at Salza.

3. Reverend Heinrich Pfeiffer began the first revolt at Mühlhausen; he preached there for a year and a half.[33]

4. Müntzer spoke to the peasants of the Klettgau and Hegau regions near Basel, [asking them] whether they would march with him to Mühlhausen and this region. They said they would do so if they were paid.

III. Müntzer's Retraction. 17 May 1525.

Thomas Müntzer recited the following articles, uncoerced and well considered in his own good conscience, in the presence of the noble, well-born Lord Philip [of Hesse], Count of Solms, etc.; Lord Gebhart, count and lord of Mansfeld, etc.; Lord Ernst von Schonneberg, the lord of Glaucha and Waldenberg; the most strictly honorable and scrupulous Herr Apel von Ebeleben; and the knights Simon von Greussen, Hans von Berleb-schen, and Christoph Law. And he begs them to keep these same articles in mind, lest he forget them, so that before his end he can present them to everyone and declare them personally.[34]

Firstly, concerning authority, to which one should be obedient and perform one's sworn duty, he has preached to the contrary, far too frivolously—and indeed the opposite. The result of this was that his listeners and subordinates also took [the authorities and their duties toward them] too frivolously. And he, who entered into such a wanton and devilish rebellion, insurrection, and disobedience with them, begs them in the name of God not to be offended by the authorities, but to live in obedience to the authorities ordained and set over them by God, and to forgive him that [which he has done].

Secondly, since he preached seditiously and misleadingly many opinions, delusions, and errors concerning the most worthy sacrament of the holy body of Christ, and contrary to the order of the common Christian church, he vows to hold in peace and concord everything that this same holy Christian church has held in all matters and now holds. And in every respect he wants to die as a truly incorporated and once again reconciled member of this same church, bidding it, for God's sake, to bear witness concerning him before God and the world, to intercede with God for him, and fraternally to forgive him.

Finally, he bids that his open letter, recently written, be sent to the people of Mühlhausen[35] and that his wife and child be permitted to have all his possessions.

IV. Final Letter. #94. To the people of Mühlhausen. 17 May 1525.[36]

Firstly, dear brothers, [I wish you] salvation and blessedness through fear, death, and hell. It has pleased God that I end my life here, in true knowledge of the divine name[37] and in restitution for some mistakes by people who did not properly understand me and only regarded their selfish interests,[38] which led to the downfall of divine truth. Because of this, I am also sincerely content that God has arranged matters thusly, as with all the works that he performs, which must be judged not according to external appearances, but according to their true substance, John chapter 7[:24].[39] Therefore, you should not be grieved by my death, which occurs to benefit both good people and those lacking in understanding.[40] Thus it is my friendly request of you that you allow my wife to receive the goods which I had, such as books and clothing and the like, and for the sake of God that she not be made to suffer.[41]

Dear brothers, it is most necessary for you not to accept such reversals as those at Frankenhausen, for that occurred without a doubt because each person sought his own private interests rather than justice for Christendom. So show good discrimination in this, and take care in your affairs, so that you do not cause further harm to yourselves.

I write this so that you may benefit from the events at Frankenhausen, which occurred with great bloodshed, namely more than four thousand [deaths].[42] Abide with the clear steadfastness of divine justice, so that such a thing does not happen to you again. I have often warned you that the punishment of God, brought about through the authorities, cannot be avoided unless the harm [that has befallen Christendom] is recognized. Whoever recognizes the harm at all times can avoid [God's punishment]. Therefore, remain at peace with everyone and no longer embitter the authorities, as many have done through selfish interests. I commend you to the grace of Christ and his spirit.

With this manuscript, [delivered] by Christoph Law, I commend my spirit into the hands of God and wish you the blessing of the father, and of the son, and of the holy spirit. Diligently help counsel my wife and, finally, avoid bloodshed, of which I truly want to warn you now. For I know that the majority of you at Mühlhausen were never adherents of this seditious and selfish rebellion, but always wished to prevent it and guard against it.[43] So that you innocents will not fall into the same affliction that has befallen some at Frankenhausen, do not join the assembly and rebellion now. And you should petition the princes for mercy, whom I hope you will find to have such princely hearts that you will be shown mercy.[44] I wish to express this now, as my last words, with which I want to remove the burden from my soul, so that no further rebellion take place and so that no more innocent blood is shed. Given at Heldrungen in my prison and at the end of my life.

Wednesday after the feast of Cantate [17 May] 1525.

Thomas Müntzer

Notes

The following abbreviations have been used in the notes:

MSB   *Thomas Müntzer. Schriften und Briefe. Kritische Gesamtausgabe*, Günther Franz ed. Quellen und Forschungen zur Reformationsgeschichte, vol. 33 (Gütersloh: Gerd Mohn, 1968).

WA   Martin Luther, D. *Martin Luthers Werke: Kritische Gesamtausgabe*, 58 vols. (Weimar: Hermann Böhlau und Hermann Böhlaus Nachfolger, 1883–).

Introduction

1. Siegfried Bräuer and Wolfgang Ullmann, eds. *Thomas Müntzer, Theologische Schriften aus dem Jahr 1523*, 2d ed. (Berlin: Evangelische Verlagsanstalt, 1982).

2. Carl Hinrichs ed., *Thomas Müntzer. Politische Schriften* (Halle [Saale]: Max Niemeyer, 1950).

3. *Ein Brief an die Fürsten zu Sachsen von dem aufrührischen Geist* (1524), WA 15, pp. 210–221.

4. Ulrich Bubenheimer, *Thomas Müntzer, Herkunft und Bildung* (Leiden: E. J. Brill, 1989), pp. 232–36.

5. Günter Vogler, *Thomas Müntzer* (Berlin: Dietz, 1989), pp. 82–93.

6. Max Steinmetz, *Thomas Müntzers Weg nach Allstedt* (Berlin: Deutscher Verlag der Wissenschaften, 1988), p. 36, pointed out that the family name "Müntzer," variously spelled, was so common around 1500 that it cannot be concluded firmly that those bearing it were the practitioners of the craft. But Ulrich Bubenheimer has discovered a series of contacts that Müntzer had over the course of his life with goldsmiths, long-distance merchants dealing in precious metals, and others linked to the craft of minting coins; Bubenheimer, *Thomas Müntzer*, pp. 29–36, 139–40. Bubenheimer's conclusion (pp. 38–41) is that Müntzer may have come from the same social milieu—the propertied and educated citizenry of Thuringia—as did Luther.

7. It is not known which university or universities conferred these degrees. Müntzer's name does not appear on the degree lists of either Leipzig or Frankfurt-on-the-Oder. While it is not impossible that university records were later altered in order to remove his name, it is more likely that he also studied and received his degrees elsewhere.

8. Bubenheimer, *Thomas Müntzer*, pp. 17–19, notes that the most precise estimates of Müntzer's birth year are made on the basis of the presentation of the Brunswick prebend and on the assumption that, in 1514, he had recently reached the minimal age for ordination according to canon law, completion of the twenty-fourth year. Müntzer may have been older—or, alternatively, he may have re-

ceived a dispensation permitting an early ordination. Bubenheimer has also raised doubts about whether the "Thomas Munczer de Quedlinburg" who matriculated in the arts faculty at Leipzig in 1506 was the same "Thomas Müntczer Stolbergensis" who enrolled at Frankfurt-on-the-Oder in 1512, but this remains to be confirmed.

9. Bubenheimer, *Thomas Müntzer*, p. 235.

10. One observer, evidently confused about just who Müntzer was, reported having heard two sermons in university chapels by "Magister Thomas Lutheranus." Walter Elliger, *Thomas Müntzer, Leben und Werk* (Göttingen: Vandenhoeck & Ruprecht, 1975), p. 184.

11. There is no agreement as to the order in which the various versions were composed. In the older literature, the most common sequence is: (A) Shorter German version, (B) Longer German version, (C) Latin version, and (D) Czech version. See Annemarie Lohmann, *Zur geistige Entwicklung Thomas Müntzers. Beiträge zur Kulturgeschichte des Mittelalters und der Renaissance*, Bd. 47 (Leipzig und Berlin, 1931), pp. 18–19. Lohmann's work was a pioneering effort in comparing different versions of the text, but this order of composition has been challenged recently. Elliger, *Thomas Müntzer*, pp. 205–6, argues that the Latin version probably preceded the two German ones. This is also the sequence advocated by Friedrich de Boor, " Zur Textgeschichte des Prager Manifests," in *Thomas Müntzer. Prager Manifest*, ed. M. Steinmetz et al. (Leipzig: Zentralantiquariat der Deutschen Demokratischen Republik, 1975), p. 13.

12. Although no autograph of this version has survived, the text comes to us from a contemporary transcription, and no scholar has doubted its authenticity. For information about the manuscript and printed editions, see *MSB*, p. 495, and de Boor, "Zur Textgeschichte," p. 7.

13. One of Müntzer's marginal notations to the works of St. Cyprian (d. 248), made at about the same time as his trips to Bohemia (i.e., 1520–21), set forth the principle "Nothing without the consent of the people" (*nihil sine consensu populi*). Siegfried Bräuer and Hans-Jürgen Goertz, "Thomas Müntzer," in Martin Greschat, ed., *Gestalten der Kirchengeschichte*, Bd. 5, Die Reformationszeit I (Stuttgart: W. Hohlhammer, 1981), p. 351, describe Müntzer's ecclesio-social vision as a "democratically conceived theocracy" or "theocratically conceived democracy."

14. Carl Hinrichs, *Luther und Müntzer, Ihre Auseinandersetzung über Obrigkeit und Widerstandsrecht* (Berlin, 1952), p. 1.

15. I have developed this point at greater length in an article, "Theology and Politics in the Thought of Thomas Müntzer: The Case of the Elect, *Archive for Reformation History* 79 (1988): 98–118.

16. Widemar opened his print shop at Eilenburg in the summer of 1523 at the earliest, and Müntzer's *Open Letter to the Brothers at Stolberg* was among his first publications. Widemar acted as the publisher of all Müntzer's works until a press was established at Allstedt in the summer of 1524.

17. For the following background information, see Bräuer and Ullmann, eds., *Theologische Schriften*, pp. 12–13.

18. *MSB*, p. 21.

19. Siegfried Bräuer, "Die Vorgeschichte von Luthers 'Ein Brief an die Fürsten zu Sachsen von dem aufrührerischen Geist'," *Lutherjahrbuch* 47 (1980): p. 48.

20. The inclusion of Haferitz, who inclined toward Luther, was an error, but no doubt the investigators did not want to omit another possible source of trouble in Allstedt. Perhaps they feared that he had fallen under Müntzer's influence.

21. Also printed by Nikolaus Widemar at Eilenburg.

22. *MSB*, pp. 25–206. For the following, see Bräuer and Ullmann, *Theologische Schriften*, pp. 52–54. Siegfried Bräuer has recently edited a facsimile edition of the German Mass, *Thomas Müntzer, Deutsche Evangelische Messe* (Berlin: Evangelische Verlagsanstalt, 1988).

23. There is a valuable discussion of the place of Müntzer's liturgical changes in the larger context of his reform program in Gerhard Brendler, *Thomas Müntzer, Geist und Faust* (Berlin: Deutscher Verlag der Wissenschaften, 1989), pp. 95–106.

24. Bräuer, "Die Vorgeschichte," p. 43, n. 12. Bräuer's view has been accepted by Tom Scott, *Thomas Müntzer, Theology and Revolution in the German Reformation* (New York: St. Martin's Press), p. 84, who revises the argument developed in his "The 'Volksreformation' of Thomas Müntzer in Allstedt and Mühlhausen," *Journal of Ecclesiastical History* 34 (1983): 194–213. Scott's *Thomas Müntzer* is especially strong on Müntzer's political activities and his use of the "league" (*Bund*) as an organizational form at both Allstedt and Mühlhausen.

25. Vogler, *Thomas Müntzer*, p. 155–57. See also letter #50, written by Müntzer to Duke John on behalf of the council and community of Allstedt.

26. Bräuer, "Die Vorgeschichte," p. 62, who sees Luther as increasingly prepared to take action against Müntzer in the spring of 1524.

27. The older view (see, e.g., Hinrichs, *Luther und Müntzer*, pp. 37–38) was that the sermon was preached at the princes' request, as part of their effort to investigate what was afoot at Allstedt. More recently, Siegfried Bräuer has argued that it was Müntzer who made the request to preach the sermon; Bräuer, "Die Vorgeschichte," p. 65. See also Vogler, *Thomas Müntzer*, p. 161.

28. A press was established at Allstedt in early July 1524, and, at the time, Müntzer and town officials agreed not to publish anything without the permission of electoral authorities. Siegfried Bräuer, "Hans Reichart, der angebliche Allstedter Drucker Müntzers," *Zeitschrift für Kirchengeschichte* 85 (1974): 395. Bräuer shows that Hans Reichart was not Müntzer's Allstedt printer, as was long assumed, but an Allstedt councilman; the name of the printer is not presently known, but typeface evidence suggests that he was an associate of Nikolaus Widemar, Müntzer's Eilenburg printer.

29. H. G. Koenigsberger, *Estates and Revolutions* (Ithaca and London: Cornell University Press, 1971), p. 219.

30. See letters #44, to Count Ernst of Mansfeld, 22 September 1523, and #45, to Frederick the Wise, 4 October 1523.

31. The contents of this important sermon have not survived in detail. But see letter #59, written to Zeiss the day after, in which Müntzer summarized its message.

32. Müntzer did not publish the *Witness of the First Chapter of the Gospel of Luke*. On the relation of the two works, see Hinrichs, *Luther und Müntzer*, pp. 81 and 125–26, and Vogler, *Thomas Müntzer*, p. 203.

33. For the following, see Hinrichs, *Luther and Müntzer*, pp. 91–92 and Vogler, *Thomas Müntzer*, pp. 180–83.

34. This position was in keeping with the official Saxon policy of "neutrality" on religious questions on the ground that the electoral government was responsible for temporal, but not spiritual, affairs. Hinrichs also argues, *Luther und Müntzer*, pp. 82–83, that Duke John was caught in a dilemma. He may have wanted to deal more firmly with Müntzer, but was reluctant to admit, as he would by arresting Müntzer, that shortly before he had listened without complaint to a sermon,

now in print, preached by a social revolutionary. This would reveal his uncertainty and incompetence before his fellow princes, the emperor, and the *Reichsregiment*, the regency government exercising power in the emperor's absence.

35. Formerly, it was thought that Müntzer visited Hut after his departure from Allstedt and before his arrival in Mühlhausen (see Hinrichs, *Luther und Müntzer*, pp. 135–36). But in Hut's later confession, he said that Müntzer came to see him when he had been "banished" (*verjagt*), which implies that Müntzer came to Hut after his expulsion from Mühlhausen. See Vogler, *Thomas Müntzer*, p. 202.

36. It is also possible that Hergot was less than forthright in claiming that he had no knowledge of the work's publication. Hergot himself was executed at Leipzig in 1527 for distributing (and probably writing) the radical tract, *On the New Transformation of the Christian Life* (*Von der neuen Wandlung eines Christlichen Lebens*), which shows traces of Müntzer's influence.

37. A common claim; see, e.g., Hans-Jürgen Goertz, "'Lebendiges Wort' und 'totes Ding.' Zum Schriftverständnis Thomas Müntzers im Prager Manifest," *Archive for Reformation History* 67 (1976): 165–66.

38. The parallel is examined in Hans-Jürgen Goertz, *Innere und aüssere Ordnung in der Theologie Thomas Müntzers* (Leiden: E. J. Brill, 1967), although the discussion of the social dimension, pp. 133–49, is brief.

39. Hinrichs, *Luther und Müntzer*, pp. 185–86.

40. Georg Baring, "Hans Denck und Thomas Müntzer in Nürnberg 1524," *Archive for Reformation History* 50 (1959): 145–80.

41. Max Weber, *The Sociology of Religion* (Boston: Beacon Press, 1964; first German ed. 1922), pp. 166–68.

42. On this, see the work of Andrew Drummond, "The Divine and Mortal Worlds of Thomas Müntzer," *Archive for Reformation History* 71 (1980): 99–112; and "Thomas Müntzer and the Fear of Man," *Sixteenth-Century Journal* 10 (1979): 63–71.

43. Friedrich Engels, *The German Revolutions, "The Peasant War in Germany" and "Germany: Revolution and Counter-Revolution"*, ed. L. Krieger (Chicago: University of Chicago Press, 1967), p. 19.

44. Eike Wolgast, "Beobachtungen und Fragen zu Thomas Müntzers Gefangenschaftsaussagen 1525," *Lutherjahrbuch*, 56 (1989): 26–50.

45. Manfred Bensing, *Thomas Müntzer und der Thüringer Aufstand 1525* (Berlin: Deutscher Verlag der Wissenschaften, 1966), p. 231.

46. Ulrich Bubenheimer, "Thomas Müntzer, Prediger—Prophet—Heerführer," in *Thomas Müntzer* (*vor 1491–1525*), G. Scholz, ed., Böblinger Museumsschriften, 4 (Böblingen: Böblinger Bauernkriegsmuseum, 1990), pp. 47–49. By contrast, Wolgast, "Beobachtungen und Fragen," pp. 36 and 40, accepts 17 May as the date when the letter was written.

47. For the following, see Ulrich Bubenheimer, "Thomas Müntzer," in *Protestantische Profile, Lebensbilder aus 5 Jahrhunderten*, K. Schoeller and D. Kleinman, eds. (Königstein /Ts.: Athenäum, 1983), pp. 45–46.

Chapter 1. The Prague Protest

This work was not published by Müntzer, but survived in several different manuscript versions; the longer German version, the most radical variant and dated 25 November 1521, is presented here.

1. Jan Hus or John Huss (ca. 1369–1415) was the Czech leader of a reform movement in the Bohemian church. As a theologian he was influenced by Wyclif, and Hus came to assert the ultimate authority of Scripture and the right and duty of the state to supervise the church. He was excommunicated and burned at the stake by the Council of Constance. In Bohemia, he was viewed as a martyr, and, after his death, a massive rebellion occurred that was simultaneously a religious struggle against the Roman Catholic church, a Czech national conflict against the Holy Roman Empire, and a social upheaval directed against the power of the landed magnates. The rebellion led to a series of Hussite Wars in the first half of the fifteenth century. In traveling to Prague, Müntzer undoubtedly hoped to make contact with or to rekindle the radicalism that Hus had initially inspired.

2. A reference to the sacrament of ordination.

3. *dye heilsamen anfechtunge und nutzbarlichen abegrundt des fursehen gemutes in seiner lehrmachung.* Here, and occasionally elsewhere in his writings, Müntzer used the spiritual language of the German mystics to describe a process of purgation through suffering that the soul must undergo before it is prepared to receive divine revelations.

4. In addition to the traditional theological notion of the seven gifts of the holy spirit that are conferred by sanctifying grace, Müntzer was also drawing on the mystical ideas of Johann Tauler (d. 1361).

5. Müntzer's notion of "order" (*ordennünge, ordo rerum*) was central to his thought. In addition to being a metaphysical or ontological notion, it also included rhetorical as well as soteriological dimensions.

6. *das gantze adder unvolkomene*; literally "the whole or imperfect." The text appears to be defective at this point. *MSB*, p.496, n. 23, suggests that the word *unvolkomene* (imperfect) may have resulted from an unintended contraction and that what Müntzer intended to write was *ungetheylt vokomene* (undivided perfection). This view is supported by the following description of the order as "a uniform measure superior to all parts."

7. Evidently an error; perhaps Müntzer intended Ps. 89:7.

8. *vom hunrotussem babst.* The text here is mutilated; the Czech version contains the description of the papacy as Nimrodian. Nimrod in the Old Testament is described as a "man of might" on earth, but Müntzer saw him as a figure of tyranny and depredation: see Gen. 10:8 and 1 Chr. 1:10.

9. The reference to Zechariah seems clearly wrong; Jeremiah 10:5 speaks of heathen idols, evidently equated by Müntzer with the clergy, being like scarecrows in a cucumber field.

10. *Ezechiel hat vorflossen auffgegessen* (evidently a mistake for *aufgeschlossen*).

11. See Lk. 19:12–27 for the parable of the man who gave each of his servants a talent, which they were to increase in his absence. Müntzer commonly referred to this parable as a way of talking about spiritual growth or sanctification.

12. I.e., hell; see Lk. 8:33 and Rev. 21:10.

13. *volk*; but as *MSB*, p. 500, n. 97, points out, in the Czech version it was "common people."

14. Mt. 23:37, Lk. 13:34.

15. In describing the clergy as Jews, Müntzer intended to call attention to their scriptural literalism and legalism, which he equated with the practices of Jewish scribes. Since this literalism rejected personal revelatory experiences, which Müntzer saw as central to Christian faith, he also described the clergy as heretics.

16. Asmodeus, according to Tobit 3:5, was a lascivious prince of demons.

17. A reference to the traditional scholastic theological doctrine of the *synteresis*, which asserted that even after the Fall there remained an uncorrupted "spark" within the human soul that inclined it toward the good.

18. A Latin translation of Eusebius of Caesarea's (ca. 263–339) *Ecclesiastical History*, which included fragments of the writings of the second-century Christian author Hegesippus, was published in Paris in 1518.

19. Müntzer's condemnation of ecumenical councils, except those of the apostolic church, would have had special meaning for the Bohemian Hussites because of Hus's condemnation and execution at the Council of Constance. But Müntzer was not engaged in political pandering, since he went on to include the issue of the chalice in his list of childish externals that recent councils had dealt with. More significant was Müntzer's stress on the loss of elective government in the postapostolic church as the principal cause of its corruption.

20. Müntzer closed the work by developing the theme of the Apocalypse, only hinted at earlier. One sign of the imminence of apocalyptic upheaval, in Müntzer's view, is that true character of the actions of both the elect and the damned have become fully evident—a development has reached its point of culmination.

21. In 1521, Müntzer envisioned an imminent invasion of the Turks as part of the scheme of apocalyptical events. Later he made no further mention of this, just as—except in his liturgical works—he no longer referred to the Bohemians in his later writings.

Chapter 2. Open Letter to the Brothers at Stolberg

Ein ernster [= *aufrichtiger*] *sendebrieff an seine lieben bruder zu Stolberg unfuglichen auffrur zu meiden.* The published circular or open letter (*Sendbrief*) was a standard sixteenth-century form of communicating with a specific group. This brief communication with associates at his hometown, dated 18 July 1523, was Müntzer's first published work; it was printed at Eilenburg by Nikolaus Widemar in the late summer or fall 1523. In urging his associates to avoid inappropriate rebellion (*unfüglichen Aufruhr*), it is noteworthy that Müntzer did not claim what Luther did in his pamphlet *A True Warning from Martin Luther to All Christians to Guard Themselves Against Insurrection and Rebellion* (*Eine treue Vermahnung Martin Luther zu allen Christen, sich zu verhüten vor Aufruhr und Empörung*), *WA* 8, pp. 676–87, written in 1522—that no revolt is justified, no matter how legitimate the cause. Instead, Müntzer suggested that the proper conditions do not yet prevail.

1. Müntzer often referred to the elect as "the friends of God," in contrast to God's enemies, the godless.

2. *alles trostes aller creaturn*; literally, all consolation of all creatures. Genuine poverty of the spirit is a psychological condition in which any trust in or reliance on the material aspects of life has been abandoned.

3. Müntzer described, as "the raging of tyrants," the persecution of the evangelical movement by secular political authorities and, more generally, any governmental injustice or oppression. The charge of tyranny against a government implied that revolt against it was legitimate.

4. *der faulen ausserwelten*. Müntzer thus divided the elect, or those who appear to be among the elect, into two groups and the criterion for separating the false

from the true elect is the lack of action, including political action, of which some are guilty.

5. There is an odd shift from believing against belief and hoping against hope to hating against love.

6. *die Rassa*, an obscure term of abuse. See Mt. 5:22, whoever "says Raka" to his brother. . .

7. Because of their coercive power, Müntzer sometimes referred to secular authorities, especially unjust princes, as "sacks of gunpowder." Many in the early sixteenth century regarded gunpowder as diabolic; the metaphor also suggested corpulence as a common feature of worldly rulers.

8. *in der lenge der wage* (evidently a misprint for *tage*); literally, in the length of our days.

Chapter 3. Protest or Offering

Protestation oder Erbietung. Walter Elliger, *Thomas Müntzer* (Göttingen: Vandenhoeck & Ruprecht, 1975), p. 395, n. 137 suggests that *Erbietung = erklärende Nachweisung*, i.e., an explanatory demonstration. But the more literal "offering" is perhaps better in that, in addition to protesting two notions of the Christian faith that he finds dominant in society, Müntzer in this work also offered a brief account of his understanding of the faith and baptism. Elliger's suggestion that *Protestation = Bezeugung, Darlegung*, i.e., a declaration or account, is likewise unnecessarily complicated in that the *protestatio*, originally a formal intervention in a legal proceeding, was an acknowledged rhetorical form in the sixteenth century. Müntzer used the same term in the title of his *The Prague Protest*. The *Protest or Offering* was printed at Eilenburg by Nikolaus Widemar in early 1524. As the material following the title indicates, Müntzer saw it's publication as a proclamation to the world for the new year; it was undoubtedly written earlier, toward the end of 1523.

1. The material contained in this paragraph appeared at the bottom of the title page, beneath the Allstedt coat of arms that decorated the cover of the tract.

2. Müntzer's symbolism here is that of society as a wheat field in which tares (the godless, the enemies of Christ) have become intermixed with the wheat (the elect). The tares have grown above the wheat and present an appearance that is superficially more beautiful, although they are actually dangerous and harmful. In the following passage, Müntzer lists various forms of tares that present beautiful blossoms and dangerous thorns. When he returns to this symbolism in the twelfth section below, the wheatfield is a symbol for the human heart from which God must purge the tares, or false notions about the meaning of salvation, before an authentic faith can be experienced.

3. In the opening section of the work Müntzer argued that, although Christendom is so corrupted by the intermixture of the godless and elect that even its lamentations to God ring false, insofar as these lamentations do express genuine distress, they can serve as the point of departure for the search for an authentic faith.

4. *klicken* (= *klecksen*). In *The Prague Protest*, Müntzer used this term in connection with a chicken coop; hence he means droppings, filth, as well as ink smears.

5. *Du tochter Sion, erkenne dich doch*; i.e., the Christian church, the community of Christians, must possess self-knowledge.

6. *er*. The pronoun antecedent would seem to be God, whose will about true baptism, according to Müntzer, has not been expressed in the traditional teachings of the church.

7. I.e., a conception of Christ as redeemer that denied the necessity of personal hardship and suffering by holding that Christ's sacrifical atonement has obviated the need for his followers to imitate his suffering.

8. In his *Highly Provoked Defense*, Müntzer also used Malvasian wine as a symbol of luxurious living and accused Luther of drinking it.

9. I.e., Müntzer's interpretation of Jn. 7 concerning baptism agrees with his interpretation of Jn. 3, in which water is a symbol of the movement of the human spirit in the divine spirit.

10. In the ceremony of baptism, the godfather speaks for the infant and makes promises in the infant's name.

11. As Müntzer moves from dogs in general to the hellhound in particular, he switches from sausages to soup.

12. I.e., the whore of Babylon of Rev. 17:4 and 18:6; in *The Prague Protest*, Müntzer also identified the Roman church as the whore of Babylon.

13. *Gantz Asia*, evidently a reference to the Greek Orthodox Church.

14. I.e., the biblical scribes accepted past revelations contained in the Old Testament while denying the revelations they themselves witnessed. Müntzer's use of Jn. 9 here may have led to Luther's subsequent argument that, if Müntzer was indeed a prophet who had received divine revelations, he should prove it through miracles.

15. *MSB* p. 232, n. 95, suggests that *expiravit* is a reference to Ovid rather than an ecclesiastical hymn. But more concretely, Müntzer is dealing with inheritance law and the selfish conflicts that begin as soon as there is a death in the family. There may have been a personal aspect to this point; following the death of his mother, Müntzer became involved with his father in a dispute over his inheritance (see letter #14).

16. *zarten kreuter*; literally, tender herbs, i.e., those immature in their faith and reluctant to accept suffering. Elsewhere Müntzer also described those accustomed to a life of ease and plenty as "tender" in the sense of pampered.

17. As a precondition for the scribes being taught by God, they would have to admit their failure to understand Scripture.

18. *wolgefellig der morderischen unser natur*; literally, well pleasing to what is murderous in our nature, i.e., unredeemed humanity enjoys hearing that it does not have to suffer with Christ in order to be saved.

19. I.e., Peter recognized that his initial confidence and boldness were based on a contrived faith.

20. Although Luther was not mentioned by name in the work, this accusation—in fact, Müntzer's whole notion of "contrived faith"—is directed clearly against Luther's theology of justification by faith alone.

21. Müntzer used the term "abyss of the heart" (*Abgrund des Hertzens*), derived from the medieval mystics, to refer to the deepest, most fundamental part of the human soul.

22. *seine inwendige augen*; i.e., one's self-reflective capacity or conscience.

23. *unter den seugelingen*; literally, among the sucklings; i.e., lay commoners who have begun to seek the true meaning of the faith and who require spiritual nourishment.

24. Müntzer rejected a closed hearing before a small group of professional theologians as an acceptable forum for determining the validity of his religious ideas; instead he insisted upon a public debate.

25. At the close of *The Prague Protest*, Müntzer similarly pledged his willingness to die for his understanding of the faith. At the end of the series of conclusions that bring his *Protest or Offering* to a close, Müntzer requested not simply a public examination but one conducted before representatives of all the religions of the world.

Chapter 4. On Contrived Faith

Auff nechst Protestation aussgangen, a reference to the preceding work, *Protest or Offering*. *On Contrived Faith* was written at about the same time as the *Protest or Offering*, in late 1523, but *On Contrived Faith* was evidently published, at Eilenburg by Nikolaus Widemar, somewhat later than the *Protest or Offering*. The two works are incorrectly ordered in *MSB*. According to the letter to Hans Zeiss, the electoral official at Allstedt, which Müntzer appended to *On Contrived Faith*, he must have finished writing the work by 2 December 1523.

1. *yrs glaubens ankunfft und rechenschafft geben*; i.e., can justify their claim that they possess an authentic faith by presenting a convincing account to others of their faith and how they came to it. Just before the Battle of Frankenhausen, Müntzer challenged his enemies among the secular rulers, the counts of Mansfeld, to do this (see letters #88 and #89).

2. I.e., God told Abraham to leave Mesopotamia and made him wander for a long period before God promised Israel, not to Abraham, but to his descendents.

3. Moses's proclamation of a divinely revealed law implied that natural reason is insufficient to grasp God's will for man.

4. *Yme keinen hund vorm lerben schlüg*; literally, that the devil has not put a dog before him as a ghost.

5. See Mt. 7:6 and 7:27. Müntzer commonly used *wollüstig*, "lustful" or "pleasure-seeking" to refer to greed for material things—wealth, prestige, power—rather than to sexual desire.

6. I.e., a covenant that is presumed to exist on the basis of natural reason.

7. I.e., in a mental condition based not on fasting or other ascetic deprivations, but on "poverty of the spirit," the emptying from the soul of all earthly attachments and values.

8. *mutzet* (evidently a misprint for *nutzet*) *und putzet sich*.

9. Two animals that are spotted or mottled in color.

10. *ein meytlin*; i.e., a *Meit*, a copper coin of the smallest denomination.

11. I.e., both the elect and the damned realize that they will die, but the elect perceive a higher purpose in their death while the damned do not.

12. See Mt. 16:6 for Christ's warning against the leaven of the Pharisees and Sadducees.

13. I.e., the negative purpose of killing—of revealing unbelief—rather than vivifying or bringing faith.

14. See Mt. 17:20, not Mt. 7, which Müntzer cites in a marginal reference, for the parable of the mustard seed.

15. Inverted or reversed in the sense that it attempts to know spiritual things by means of material evidence, rather than as a result of direct illumination.

16. The printed version of *On Contrived Faith* contained the following open letter addressed to the electoral official Hans Zeiss as an appendix. *MSB*, p. 224, n. 85 calls attention to this, but includes the letter as part of Müntzer's correspondence (letter #46, pp. 397–98). The letter contains material clarifying the meaning of the text and pertaining to Müntzer's presumed millenarianism; it merits presentation with the work.

17. *Adam ist ein muster Christi im schaden* (= *Schatten*), *Cristus aber das kegenteil.* Müntzer's contrast turns on the opposition of shadow and sunlight. Adam is Christ standing in the shadows, Christ is Adam transformed by the sun.

18. In short, Müntzer condemned both what he views as the traditional Roman Catholic teaching that righteousness is attained partly through works, as well as Luther's theory of justification by faith alone, which Müntzer here equated with the "contrived faith" (*getichte glaube*) of the work's title.

19. *das sie dise lere dem apt Joachim zuschreiben.* The Calabrian abbot Joachim of Fiore (d. 1202) acquired fame as a prophet in the thirteenth and fourteenth centuries, especially among Franciscan radicals, who credited him with predicting the dawn of a new "Age of the Spirit" that would be characterized by direct revelations. Most interpretations of Müntzer as a millenarian stress the influence of Joachim's ideas on him, yet here Müntzer disavowed any major dependence on Joachimite thought.

20. Müntzer is probably referring to the *Scriptum super Hierimiam*, a commentary on Jeremiah, published at Venice in 1516, which was commonly—but erroneously—regarded as an authentic work of Joachim.

Chapter 5. Selected Liturgical Writings

1. Two headings are presented for this work. The first was contained on the title page of the printed edition, and the second on the first page of the text. The two dates on the title page are the result of the delay between the work's composition in late 1523 and its publication in early 1524.

2. *der gantzen gemein* (= *Gemeinde*); the term *Gemeinde*, community or congregation, has both ecclesiastical and socio-political dimensions.

3. I.e., Müntzer's German Mass is designed to make clear to the laity, and in this sense to edify and elevate it, the basic message of the scriptural word—that God's elect receive direct, personal revelations. Teaching this point is the essential function of his liturgy.

4. The traditional organizational divisions of the Mass were presented in the marginal notes of the printed edition.

5. Immediately after the community's confession of sin comes a reminder of God's mercy.

6. Here Müntzer used the term "wheat" (used above to speak of God's word) to refer to the elect, whom he also described as "sons of God," which equated them with Christ.

7. Psalm 51 is chanted in Müntzer's favorite eighth psalmtone.

8. The gradualism was intended to avoid giving offense to those who remained attached to the traditional liturgy.

9. *die getichten christen*; literally, contrived Christians, i.e., those who rely on a counterfeit or contrived faith; see chapter 4.

10. Müntzer envisioned an audience for his liturgical ideas that extended beyond Christendom.

11. *kein opffer in der geheim Gotis*; i.e., Müntzer wanted to make clear his opposition to the traditional conception of the Mass as a sacrifice.

12. *durch etliche hirtten auff dem felde.* Müntzer disputed the justification that was commonly given by Catholic authorities for retaining the words of the consecration as a formula spoken privately by the priest, namely, that in the past, their public pronouncement had led to the abuse of the sacrament by young people who repeated thoughtlessly or in jest what the priest had said.

13. I.e., the validity of the sacrament is guaranteed by the presence in the community of at least some members of the elect.

14. Liturgical theologians are described as competitive petty shopkeepers who bring their wares to market.

15. *vor yedermann*; literally, for everyone, but cf. Eph. 5:20.

16. I.e., any baptismal name.

17. I.e., the antiphon *Media vita in morte*, which was translated into German in the fifteenth century. *MSB*, p. 215, n. 85.

18. As noted in the Introduction, the prefatory material to the *German Evangelical Mass* included two separate statements in which Müntzer responded to both his Roman Catholic and his evangelical critics.

19. *uber die masse ganz und gar yns wessn gefurth seint*; literally, be led into their essence absolutely and totally beyond measure. *MSB*, p. 161, n. 8 suggests *gefurth = Getue, Unwesen, zum Bösen*; but *geführt* seems better since Müntzer is discussing the full realization of the prophecies of future damage that the church will suffer.

20. *buch der erklerunge*; a reference to Josephus' *History of the Jewish Wars*; Müntzer's claim that Josephus was a pupil of the apostles is not accurate.

21. See Eusebius IV, 22, 4–6. Müntzer also cited Eusebius in his *The Prague Protest* to support the view that the postapostolic church rapidly became corrupt (cf. chapter 1, n. 18).

22. I.e., since the conversion of the Germanic tribes.

23. Müntzer ascribed the schism between Greek Orthodox and Roman Catholic churches to a disagreement about the sacrament of communion.

24. *Es ist ein unfletige sache, menlein kegen menlein zu mahlen*; literally, It is an unclean thing to paint one doll or puppet against another. Müntzer used the term doll or puppet (*menlein*) to refer to what he saw as the idolatry of traditional Christianity; hence a literal translation of the Latin liturgy into German would be to use one form of idolatry as the model for generating another.

25. *funf ampt*; the term *ampt*, services, as well as offices, here refers to divisions of the liturgical year. Müntzer proposes a sequence of five divisions based upon the life of Christ, beginning with Old Testament prophecies of his birth and ending with the spread of his spirit. While centered on Christ, the unifying theme of this organization of the liturgy is the action of the divine spirit.

26. *etliche gelerten*; apparently a reference to Luther and his associates at Wittenberg.

27. In what follows, Müntzer sketched out an alternative way of organizing the liturgical year. Here, as at other places in his liturgical works, Müntzer made it evident that his notions about the proper form and organization of a new liturgy were flexible and tentative.

28. I.e., while the clergy claims that it puts its obligation to nourish people first, Müntzer charges them with spiritually poisoning the people.

Chapter 6. Sermon to the Princes (or An Exposition of the Second Chapter of Daniel)

The sermon was preached on 13 July 1524 at the Allstedt castle before an audience that included Duke John, Crown Prince John Frederick, and several officials of the government of electoral Saxony as well as local authorities. Shortly after being delivered orally, an extended version of the sermon was printed at Allstedt.

1. Dan. 2:35, "The stone that smote the image became a great mountain and filled the whole earth."

2. I.e., the present epoch of world history (see Dan. 2:33–41), which is characterized for Müntzer by a division in power between lay and clerical rulers.

3. Müntzer cited Hegesippus and Eusebius in *The Prague Protest* as authorities for his view that the postapostolic church rapidly became corrupt (see above, chapter. 1, n. 18). In the preface to his *German Evangelical Mass*, Müntzer also cited Josephus and Eusebius to the same end (chapter. 5, n. 20, 21).

4. Müntzer equated the Jewish scribes who rejected Jesus with the learned clergy of his time, including Luther, who accept the authority of Scripture, base their faith on their interpretation of a written text, and deny continuing revelations from God.

5. Fear of God, for Müntzer, is an essential component of an authentic, experienced faith; he also contrasted it with fear of men—specifically, fear of those holding political power.

6. The polemic evidently derived from Müntzer's desire to distance the kind of revelations he meant from visions that stem from monastic asceticism.

7. Müntzer specified three possible sources for phenomena that present themselves as divine revelations; it was obviously crucial for him to be able to distinguish true from false revelations, and, in the work's fourth section, he set forth several criteria for doing this.

8. Dan. 10:1–12; Müntzer offered a paraphrase of what he took to be the meaning rather than a direct quotation.

9. At this point, Müntzer began to present his interpretation of the apocalyptic culmination of history, according to which the existing social and political order will be overthrown by the elect, who will then establish a truly Christian society.

10. I.e., the Holy Roman Empire, like the Roman empire before it, is essentially a coercive apparatus of iron, but now the coercion is blunted and disguised by the intermixture of supposedly Christian elements. The combination of the two is symbolized for Müntzer by the feet of the statue in Nebuchadnezzar's dream (Dan. 2:41), which were of iron and clay. The clay is intensified by Müntzer to "filth" (*kothe* = *Kot*).

11. The true nature of the existing political structure has been concealed behind a cosmetic façade of Christianity.

12. Müntzer was obviously thinking of himself as the best candidate for this position.

13. A reference to Luther's doctrine of two "kingdoms" or "realms," the spiritual and the secular, according to which there is nothing specifically Christian about secular political authority.

14. I.e., unless it has been tested in the fire of spiritual anguish and confirmed, faith is nothing more than the expectation of a reward which is arbitrarily bestowed.

15. Müntzer's interpretation of this passage reversed the usual exposition, including that advanced by Luther, in which the sense of the passage was presented as an injunction for Christians to be obedient to secular authority since it is ordained by God in order to protect good people and to punish evildoers. Müntzer, however, used the passage to enjoin positive action by rulers to promote a Christian society and to legitimize rebellion in the event that rulers failed to fulfill the purpose for which they had been established.

16. Müntzer was, perhaps, justifying the destruction of the Mallerbach chapel near Allstedt by his followers as a deed undertaken with the same righteous anger as Christ's expulsion of the money changers from the temple.

17. Implicit in Müntzer's argument here was a theory of popular sovereignty: as long as the existing rulers perform their proper function of destroying the godless and promoting the well-being of the elect, whom Müntzer associated with the commoners, the rulers may remain in office. But if they fail to do this, the people have the right to take temporal power ("the sword") from them and exercise it themselves.

18. *Wo sie aber das widderspiel treiben, das man sie erwürge on alle gnade.* Müntzer here lays down an exceedingly bold ultimatum to his princely listeners—either they join his cause and that of the commoners, or they will be subject to the death penalty.

Chapter 7. Special Exposure of False Faith

As noted in the Introduction, Müntzer must have already begun this work while he was still in Allstedt, and, despite the information on the title page, it was not printed at Mühlhausen, but at Nuremberg at the end of October 1524.

1. A reference especially to Luther's pamphlet denouncing Müntzer, *Letter to the Princes of Saxony Concerning the Rebellious Spirit*, WA 15, pp. 210–21. The following chapter, Müntzer's *Highly Provoked Defense*, was his detailed reply to Luther's letter.

2. See Ezek. 8:7. In order to expose the false faith of his own age, Müntzer seeks to make "the breach in the wall" even wider than Ezekiel, who saw through it the abomination of the Israelites. Hence the citation from Ezekiel on the title page immediately following the work's title.

3. The "dangerous corner" was an examination at the University of Wittenberg at which Müntzer would be questioned in private by a select group of professional theologians, led by Luther, and from which the public would be excluded. Müntzer rejected this, as he had insisted earlier, in the conclusion of his *Protest or Offering*.

4. The purveyors of a so-called "butter letter" (*Butterbrief*), an ecclesiastical dispensation that permitted the consumption of butter during fast periods.

5. The reference to Rom. 10:14—and to one of Luther's central theological tenants (*fides ex auditu*)—leaves no doubt as to whom Müntzer attributed this reply.

6. I.e., even though evangelical ministers may replace Roman Catholic priests and monks, a corrupt, clerical ruling strata will remain in society.

7. In his *Letter to the Princes of Saxony Concerning the Rebellious Spirit*, Luther asserted that Müntzer should authenticate his faith by performing miracles. *WA* 15, p. 220.

8. I.e., the true nature of politics, conceived as the art of exercising power in the pursuit of selfish interests.

9. A symbol for secular rulers; see chapter 2, n. 7.

10. The Philistine city on the southern border of Canaan where Abraham and Isaac stayed; see Gen. 26.

11. The perverted government referred to, as Müntzer made clear in his *Sermon to the Princes*, is the feudal intermixture of temporal and ecclesiastical authority that characterizes the fifth empire of world history and that, rather than embodying truly Christian principles, claims to serve two masters simultaneously.

12. *spill* (= *Spiel*). Müntzer envisioned the revolutionary transformation of society as a kind of grand play, a theatrical production or game.

13. *mit Juda in der marterwochen ein galgenrew hat*; i.e., a perfunctory repentance to comply with the performance of one's Easter duty.

14. A reference is to the well-off and powerful in general, but also to Luther in particular, whom Müntzer mocked for his chubby cheeks.

15. *heller*, a coin of small denomination named after the city where it was minted, Schwäbisch-Hall.

16. *die langweyl*; also boredom or tedium. The term, derived from the German mystical tradition, refers to a condition of the soul in which worldly values have been purged and worldly pleasures have lost their appeal, but nothing new has yet appeared to replace them. The notion is closely related to the mystical notion of *Gelassenheit*, "resignation," or "tranquility."

17. *der allergelassenste mensch*; a person in a condition of utter resignation and abandonment.

18. Luther's *Letter to the Princes of Saxony Concerning the Rebellious Spirit*.

19. The seventh and eighth organizational divisions have been taken from the shorter version of this work, *Testimony of the First Chapter of the Gospel of Luke*. The original printed version of the *Special Exposure of False Faith* did not contain them as separate sections, but they contribute to organizational clarity.

20. This charge is apparently directed against Luther's follower at Erfurt, Johann Lang, who married a wealthy woman.

Chapter 8. Highly Provoked Defense

Müntzer probably began the composition of his last major tract while he was still in Allstedt, but it was not completed until at least late September 1524, after he was expelled from Mühlhausen. The work is a direct reply to Luther's *Letter to the Princes of Saxony Concerning the Rebellious Spirit (Eyn brieff an die Fürsten zu Sachsen von dem auffrurischen geyst)* published in June 1524; *WA* 15, pp. 210–21. Müntzer's rebuttal was surreptitiously printed in Nuremberg in late November or early December 1524 by the radical printer Hieronymus Hölzel. Nuremberg officials searching for tracts by Karlstadt discovered Müntzer's *Highly Provoked Defense* and the entire pressrun was confiscated.

1. I.e., a member of the community at Allstedt.

2. The source of this Latin quotation is not known; the first line is reminiscent of Ps. 119:134.

3. The salutation is a deliberate parody of Luther's *Letter to the Princes of Saxony*, which opened with a recitation of their titles and traditional attributes; Müntzer countered by declaring his allegiance to Christ and ascribing to him the titles of secular power. The implication was that, while Müntzer served Christ and the cause of Christian government, Luther served the princes.

4. *doctor lügner*, a word play on "Doctor Luther."

5. *doctor ludibrii*, again a play on Luther's name; *ludibrii* is ambiguous, meaning both idle play and mockery.

6. I.e., Luther enjoys an opaque "pap" (*prey = Brei*) derived from mixing together scriptural texts and confusing profound and trivial truths, but he finds distasteful a clear broth (*suppe*) composed of passages of Scripture whose meaning is plain.

7. Müntzer protested what he regarded as Luther's one-sided elevation of the New Testament, which had resulted in an understanding of justification that set aside the law.

8. See Müntzer's *Sermon to the Princes*, the central point of which he summarizes here.

9. This writing has not survived.

10. I.e., Müntzer asserted that secular political power, the power of the sword or of coercion, rests with the community as a whole (*ein gantze gemayn*). It is to this same social source that, in what immediately follows, he also gives the traditional spiritual power of the keys (*den schlüssel der auflösung*). The result, in effect, is to formulate a view of authority in which the community or congregation (*Gemeinde*) emerges as sovereign in both temporal and ecclesiastical matters.

11. I.e., Luther's work *On Commerce and Usury* (*Von Kaufshandlung und Wucher*), *WA* 15, pp. 293–322.

12. I.e., to destroy the false confidence and pride of those who imagine themselves to be spiritually healthy.

13. I.e., after defeating the papists and setting himself up in place of the pope, Luther now fears an unwanted revolution; therefore he seeks to blame Müntzer for the mounting social upheaval. His "fiery" attack on Müntzer also purifies Luther with respect to the princes, whose favor he is attempting to curry.

14. Evidently a reference to Luther's *Formula Missae et Communionis pro Ecclesia Vuittembergensi* (1523), *WA* 12, pp. 205–26. Luther's own German Mass was first published in 1526 after Müntzer's death.

15. In Luther's interpretation of the Tenth Psalm, which he translated and published in 1524, *WA* 31/1, p. 294, he referred to the papacy as Antichrist.

16. I.e., Luther's work of 1523, *Against the Perverted and False Imperial Mandate* (*Wider die Verkehrer und Fälscher Kaiserlichs Mandats*), *WA* 12, pp. 62–67, which Müntzer referred to as the first explanation, in contradistinction to Luther's work of 1524, *Two Contradictory and Opposed Imperial Commands concerning Luther* (*Zwei kaiserliche uneinige und widerwärtige Gebot den Luther betreffend*), *WA* 15, pp. 254–78. The Nuremberg mandate, issued by the imperial governing council in January 1522, forbade ecclesiastical innovations.

17. The fourth article of the imperial mandate specified that members of the clergy who married should be tried and punished according to canon law and that secular authorities should not hinder this. Luther expressed a reluctant willingness to accept this article if all the others were enforced, asserting that those affected, while innocent, should suffer for the sake of the gospel.

18. A reference to Luther's hymn *About Two Martyrs of Christ at Brussels, Burned by the Sophists of Louvain* (*Von den zwei Märterern Christi zu Brüssel von den sophisten zu Löwen verbrannt*), *WA* 35, pp. 411–15. This hymn was composed to commemorate two members of the Augustinian order and followers of Luther who were burned for heresy in Brussels in July 1523. In Luther's view, their execution was a manifestation that the reform movement had finally begun to bear fruit.

19. In 1524, Luther conducted a visitation trip to the town of Orlamünde, where his former colleague Karlstadt had established himself after breaking with Luther in 1521. The radicalized evangelicalism of Karlstadt and his followers rejected traditional titles and honors; Luther protested against this and complained to the elector that "fanatics" (*Rottengeister*) at Orlamünde had refused him his title of doctor of theology. See his *The Treatment of Doctor Martin Luther by the Council and Community of the Town of Orlamünde* (*Die Handlung Doctor Martini Luthers mit dem Rat und Gemeinde der Stadt Orlamünde*), *WA* 15, p. 345.

20. Paul gave Festus no title.

21. Müntzer was referring to Luther's 1524 commentary on the imperial mandate (see above, n. 16), in which Luther warned the princes that the text of Lk.

1:52 could apply to them too; *WA* 15, p. 255. Müntzer dismissed this upbraiding remark as insignificant within the larger context of Luther's social and political views.

22. In his *Letter to the Princes*, Luther had written that Müntzer was using "our peace and protection" (*unserm fride, schirm und schutz*), *WA* 15, p. 211. By this Luther did not mean his personal protection, but that of the elector of Saxony. It is this discrepancy that Müntzer seized on in what follows.

23. As noted in the Introduction, on 24 March 1524, a small group from All-stedt burned the Mallerbach chapel to the ground. According to Müntzer's *Confession*, he was personally present during the action.

24. I.e., the opposite type of St. Lawrence, who was martyred by being roasted alive. The reference is apparently to Lawrence Süsse, a follower of Luther and the first Protestant preacher at Nordhausen. The basis, if any, of Müntzer's accusation that Luther and Lawrence of Nordhausen knew of a plot to kill him with paid assassins remains unclarified.

25. Duke George, the ruler of ducal or Albertine Saxony, was a cousin of Frederick the Wise, ruler of electoral or Ernestine Saxony. Again, the basis of this charge remains unclear.

26. The bagpipe was a traditional instrument of folk music in the Harz region.

27. The papal bull excommunicating Luther, *Exsurge Domine*, of June 1520, accused him of a heretical denial of the freedom of the will. Luther responded, setting forth his position on the bondage of the will, in his *Assertio omnium articulorum. . .* , *WA* 7, pp. 94–151.

28. Luther is compared to a fox that is used by the nobility to deceive inexperienced hunters, the commoners who are searching for the truth.

29. A reference to Luther's and Karlstadt's debate with Dr. Johann Eck of Ingolstadt before the ducal court at Leipzig in June and July 1519. In all likelihood, Müntzer, who was at Wittenberg in the period 1517–19, attended this debate. Here Müntzer refers to a passage in Luther's *Letter to the Princes*, *WA* 15, p. 214, in which he speaks of the danger of his appearance at the Leipzig disputation.

30. Johannes von Staupitz, Vicar-General of the Saxon Province of the Augustinian order, and Luther's friend and adviser.

31. Luther's pamphlet of 1522, *A True Warning from Martin Luther to All Christians to Guard Themselves against Insurrection and Rebellion* (*Eine treue Vermahnung Martin Luther zu allen Christen, sich zu verhüten vor Aufruhr und Empörun*), *WA* 8, pp. 676–87, especially p. 683, where Luther speaks of diabolically inspired rumors and prophecies of his downfall and death.

32. In 1523, Luther published *An Explanation of Two Horrible Figures Found in Meissen, the Pope-ass of Rome and the Monk-calf of Freiberg* (*Deutung der zwo geulichen Figuren, Papstesels zu Rom und Mönchkalbs zu Freiberg in Meissen gefunden*), *WA* 11, pp. 369–85. In this work, which dealt with the birth of two animals of strange appearance, widely regarded as prodigies, Luther declined to offer a prophetic interpretation of the figure of the monk-calf because, he asserted, "I am not a prophet"; *WA* 11, p. 380.

33. Perhaps Nicholas Storch and Marcus Thomae (or, as he was also known, Stübner), two radical associates of Müntzer from Zwickau, who visited Luther at Wittenberg.

34. In Luther's *Letter to the Princes*, he also described his appearance before the imperial diet at Worms in April 1521 as a time of danger, *WA* 15, p. 214.

35. Ecclesiastical property that has been secularized, on the pattern of the Hussite movement in Bohemia.

36. A reference to Luther's sudden disappearance after the Diet of Worms,

where he was declared an imperial outlaw and a heretic. After leaving Worms, a fake kidnapping was arranged, so that Luther could surreptitiously be brought into the Elector of Saxony's protective custody.

37. On 1 August 1524, Müntzer and several officials of Allstedt were interrogated before chancellery officers of Duke John of Saxony at Weimar. Müntzer saw this interrogation as the fruit of Luther's pressure on the Saxon court.

38. After the Weimar hearing, the electoral official at Allstedt, Hans Zeiss, ordered the disbanding of the organization that Müntzer had created at Allstedt, the League of the Elect, as well as the closing of Müntzer's press at Allstedt; he also forbade Müntzer to preach politically inflammatory sermons or to block the prosecution of those who had burned the chapel at Mallerbach. Müntzer had justified the existence of the League on the grounds that its purpose was to defend followers of the gospel from persecution by nearby Roman Catholic lords, especially Count Ernst of Mansfeld, who had prevented their subjects from coming to Allstedt for Müntzer's services. Thus Müntzer saw the prohibition of the League by Duke John as an instance of one tyrant helping others; he was clearly being ironical in saying that the other lords let Duke John have competence in the matter "for the sake of the gospel."

39. A reference to members of the Allstedt council who conveyed to Müntzer the outcome of the Weimar hearing and who then distanced themselves from his cause.

40. During the night of 7–8 August 1524, Müntzer fled Allstedt.

41. The tract closes by citing Ezek. 13:22f. from the Vulgate and then offering a vernacular translation.

Chapter 9. Selected Letters

1. This is Müntzer's only surviving letter to a family member. The numbering of the letters in this chapter follows *MSB*, but I have made three changes in the arrangement of the letters as presented in *MSB*: letter #46 (*MSB*, pp. 397–98) is appended to chapter 4, letter #67a (*MSB*, pp. 573–75) is put in proper chronological sequence, and letter #94 (*MSB*, pp. 473–74) is presented in chapter 10.

2. *zu Stolberk und Quedelingeburgk*. Müntzer was born in Stolberg, and his mother may have come from Quedlingburg. Since university matriculation records at Leipzig show that a "Thomas Munczer de Quedilburck" registered in the arts faculty for the winter semester 1506, it is commonly suggested that during Müntzer's youth the family moved from Stolberg to Quedlinburg.

3. The text breaks off at this point. The paper on which the letter was drafted was later used for a book list, and it is unclear whether the letter was sent.

4. In *The Prague Protest*, Müntzer described personal revelations as the authentic Scripture that the living finger of God writes in the human heart.

5. Since September 1521, while Luther was concealed at Wartburg castle, there were changes in the Mass at Wittenberg and discussions about it. Luther expressed his views on the issue in his work *De abroganda Missa privata sententia*, translated into the vernacular as *On the Misuse of the Mass* (*Vom Missbrauch der Messe*), *WA* 8, pp. 482–563.

6. Müntzer used a similar expression in *The Prague Protest*; see also his *Highly Provoked Defense*.

7. Müntzer apparently came into contact with Luther's follower, Johann Lang, at Erfurt in early 1522, when Müntzer stayed for a time at the cloister of St.

Peter following his return from Bohemia. The exact time and reason for the conflict between Müntzer and Lang is unknown; the emnity between them remained. See above, chapter 7, n. 20.

8. The letter was written just before Müntzer's arrival at Allstedt and refers to events at Halle, from which he was expelled in the winter of 1522 or early spring 1523.

9. Little is known concerning the details of Müntzer's expulsion from Halle.

10. See *MSB*, p. 388, n. 1 for information about two possible abbesses who gave Müntzer this sum, either the abbess of the Marienkammer at Glaucha near Halle, or the abbess Anna von Stolberg at Quedlinburg.

11. Ambrosius Emmen was Müntzer's servant lad or *famulus*.

12. *MSB*, p. 388, n. 7, suggests that the debt was owed to Wolfgang Juche, a bookseller of Halle with whom Müntzer did business.

13. Johannes Sylvius Egranus was the preacher with whom Müntzer came into bitter conflict at Zwickau in late 1520 and early 1521.

14. Gen. 8:7, 2 Pet. 2:5. Later, in his *Highy Provoked Defense*, Müntzer used the same metaphor of the raven released from Noah's ark to describe Luther.

15. Egranus's *Sermon on Confession. . .* (Leipzig, 1523).

16. Disturbances at Zwickau in early 1521 culminated in Müntzer's dismissal from his position on 16 April. When his supporters learned of this, they assembled; fearing an insurrection, the city council arrested more than fifty people.

17. A reference to Müntzer's stay at Wittenberg in the period 1517–19.

18. A reference to two of the so-called "Zwickau prophets," Marcus Thomae (or Stübner, as he was also known) and Nicholas Storch, who visited Wittenberg in the spring of 1522 and met with Luther.

19. A portion of the letter was torn away at this place.

20. Perhaps Müntzer raised the subject of marriage at the close of the letter because he had begun to reevaluate his own position on it. But his letter to Karlstadt (#43 below) indicates that, at the end of July 1523, Müntzer was still unmarried.

21. Attempts to trace the source of this reference to Origen have not been successful. See Dieter Fauth, "Das Menschenbild bei Thomas Müntzer," in *Der Theologe Thomas Müntzer*, eds. S. Bräuer and H. Junghans (Göttingen: Vandenhoeck & Ruprecht, 1989), p. 57, n. 101.

22. At this time, Karlstadt had renounced his university degrees, resigned from his position on the theology faculty at Wittenberg, and was living as a peasant in the Saxon village of Wörlitz.

23. The most likely identification is Nicholaus Rukker, a magistrate at Allstedt.

24. Karlstadt had played an important role in establishing a new community chest at Wittenberg; hence, in Müntzer's view, he was one well qualified to assist the people of Allstedt. The nuns to whom the Allstedters were refusing to pay dues were those at the cloister at Naundorf.

25. I.e., unlike Karlstadt, Müntzer was unmarried and still adhering to his vow of chastity.

26. The letter is Müntzer's response to Count Ernst of Mansfeld who initiated Müntzer's conflict with secular authorities in the summer of 1523 when the count forbade his subjects from attending Müntzer's services at Allstedt.

27. *euer schreyben*, literally, your writing. I.e., a letter from Count Ernst to authorities at Allstedt complaining about Müntzer's liturgy and his attacks on Count Ernst from the pulpit.

28. Müntzer developed this point at greater length in his *Special Exposure of*

False Faith, in which he argued that Christians must fear only God and not human authorities and that secular rulers who seek to be feared more than God are tyrants. It is noteworthy that here—nearly a year before the *Sermon to the Princes* and the *Special Exposure*—Müntzer cited Rom. 13 as a scriptural foundation for this potentially revolutionary political theory.

29. I.e., coercively restraining his subjects from visiting Allstedt.

30. *des zukunftigen zanks one ende.*

31. *der alde rogk reyst anderst*, i.e., the established socio-political order will be shredded.

32. *eyn verstorer der unglaubigen.*

33. Shortly after the preceding letter to Count Ernst of Mansfeld, Müntzer wrote the ruler of electoral Saxony, setting forth his interpretation of the conflict with Count Ernst and seeking to explain his work at Allstedt to his prince. The letter is an important statement of Müntzer's political views in the fall of 1523.

34. *dye lautbaren beweglichen pasaunen.* The opening of *The Prague Protest* used the same expression.

35. *zur eysernen mauren.* The opening citations of Müntzer's *Special Exposure of False Faith* also used Jer. 1:18f.; he saw himself as a "iron wall" between godless rulers and the needy people.

36. I.e., the mandate of the imperial regency government, headed by Charles V's brother, Archduke Ferdinand, which was issued on 6 March 1523, and which prohibited introducing innovations in religious matters. Frederick the Wise published the mandate for his electorate at the end of May. The evangelical reformers took the view that the mandate's specifications were unclear and required interpretation, in effect arguing that some changes were permissible.

37. Müntzer is evidently referring to a clause in the imperial mandate which specified that the mandate was not intended to hinder the truth of the gospel; *MSB*, p. 396, n. 24.

38. Rom. 13:3–4. This scriptural citation was later used in the *Sermon to the Princes*, in which Müntzer also argued that the injunction to obey authorities contained in Rom. 13:1–2 was conditional on their being rulers who protected pious people. The upshot was a political theory that legitimized rebellion when made against rulers who struck fear into the hearts of good people.

39. Christoph Meinard was the cousin and godfather of Hans Zeiss, the electoral official at Allstedt. This and the following letter to him offer spiritual counsel.

40. *das Got dye gantze scrift yn yhm warmache*; literally, that God makes the whole Scripture true in him.

41. *ampt*, office; in this case, that of instruction.

42. I.e., the person who refuses to accept suffering has nothing to do with the Christian life.

43. *in eyne starke vorgleychung*; i.e., the way to understand the Bible is by grasping the unity of its message through comparing its various components, so that the interpretation of a given passage is determined by its context within the whole.

44. This apparently refers to an earlier letter to Meinhard which has not survived.

45. *den unerfarnen toten*; "inexperienced" in the sense of never having had their faith tested—hence, never having come to true faith.

46. *sonderlich das unser name den gottlosen hesslich stinke*; i.e., Müntzer

stresses that the Christian life, one based upon the purgation of worldly ambitions and pleasures, must also be one that arouses hatred among the godless.

47. *exurage, quare obdormis*. Ps. 44:24.

48. *die langweyl*, a term used by late medieval German mystics to describe a psychological condition of stasis, the absence of desire for worldly things. See above, chapt. 7, n. 16.

49. *solten sie auch zuprasten* (= *zerbersten*). Müntzer was referring to Luther's theology.

50. *Das Paulum keyn mal getreumet hat*; i.e., Müntzer held that Paul experienced revelations in dreams and that it is false to allege that he did not.

51. *unser freche bachanten*; evidently a reference to the Wittenberg theologians.

52. Although the letter was written in the name of the Allstedt council, there is little doubt that Müntzer was the actual author; *MSB*, p. 404, n. 1. The letter is evidence of the influence that Müntzer had gained over the authorities at Allstedt, since they permitted him to write to Duke John in their name, defending the iconoclasts who destroyed the Mallerbach chapel.

53. The chapel at Mallerbach was the property of a cloister of Cistercian nuns at Naundorf. See above, n. 24.

54. I.e., the cloister's request to the electoral government that those guilty of the arson at Mallerbach be brought to justice.

55. This letter was written at the time that Müntzer delivered his *Sermon to the Princes* and concerns issues that arose then—permission to have a printing press at Allstedt, prepublication censorship, and an examination of Müntzer's teaching by Wittenberg theologians.

56. In the summer of 1524, followers of Müntzer at Sangerhausen began to suffer persecution. This letter, as well as the following two, deal with the situation.

57. A reference to the Sangerhausen preacher Tile Banse; see also letter #54. In his *Confession*, Müntzer identified Banse as a member of his league.

58. *MSB*, p. 408, n. 4, points out that there is no appropriate passage for this.

59. This remark suggests that the league at Allstedt was part of a network of revolutionary organizations.

60. I.e., a secular ruler.

61. According to *MSB*, p. 410, n. 4, the Sangerhausen preacher Tile Banse (or Tilo Banz) was an Augustinian monk from Quedlinburg who came to Sangerhausen to preach after an uprising at Quedlinburg in 1523.

62. *Ey wye feyn wyl sich das reymen*; literally, oh, how finely can this rhyme.

63. *sich erwegen*, for which *MSB*, p. 411, n. 3 suggests "renounce" (*verzichten*), but Manfred Bensing and Bernd Rüdiger, eds. *Thomas Müntzer. Politische Schriften, Manifeste, Briefe 1524/25* (Leipzig: Bibliographisches Institut, 1973), p. 266, n. 7, argue on the basis of Müntzer's usage that "risk" (*wagen*) is better.

64. *narung*, "nourishment" or "sustinence," is used here in the sense of worldly goods.

65. The location is not presently traceable, but it must have been a village pilgrimage site lying outside the borders of the principality.

66. This and the following letter, written on the same day, were directed to the local electoral official (*Schösser*), Hans Zeiss. Both letters deal with the issue of protecting refugees from persecution, including some from Sangerhausen, who had arrived at Allstedt seeking help.

67. *dem unflat der umligden* (= *umliegenden*) *emporung*; the meaning of this phrase is not clear.

68. Hans Reichart was a member of the Allstedt town council.

69. I.e., those who fled persecution at Sangerhausen and in the territory of the knight, Friedrich von Witzleben.

70. The customary laws were those pertaining to and enjoining the return of refugees to their lords.

71. *amptman*; a low-level law enforcement official such as a sheriff or bailiff.

72. I.e., since the rulers who should enforce the natural law themselves violate it, they should suffer a disgraceful execution.

73. A reference to Friedrich von Witzleben, a knight to whose family the manor of Schönewerda, in the district of Sangerhausen, was attached as a fief; *MSB*, p. 417, n. 5. Witzleben attacked and destroyed part of the village of Schönewerda in July 1524. He arrested some of Müntzer's followers and expelled the remainder. Müntzer charged that he was the first to upset the common peace of the territory. Later, during the Peasants' War, Witzleben performed military service for Count Ernst of Mansfeld in suppressing the commoners.

74. Müntzer was referring to the letter that he wrote to Duke John on 13 July 1524; letter #52 above.

75. I.e., renounce the promise made to Duke John to accept the rule of the princes.

76. I.e., the tract *On Contrived Faith*.

77. The following part of the letter is evidently a reply to four theological questions that Zeiss put to Müntzer.

78. *zum ersten der lust mit langweyle*; i.e., the Christian strives for psychological ennui or stasis to combat sinful desires.

79. I.e., those who had taken refuge in Allstedt.

80. Lang, an ally of Luther, was the theologian who visited Allstedt to investigate Müntzer's views in November 1523. See above n. 7 and chapter 7, n. 20.

81. This letter is apparently the "instruction on how one should meet future rebellion in a godly way," which Müntzer mentioned in his later letter to Frederick the Wise on 3 August 1524; see below, letter #64.

82. I.e., the sermon Müntzer preached on 24 July 1524, in which he advocated that the Allstedt league resist tyrannical rulers. It was a report of the contents of this sermon that precipitated his being called to Weimar for a hearing.

83. In the passage to which Müntzer referred, the priest Jehoiada overthrows the rule of the godless tyrant Athaliah by making a covenant with the people and staging a military insurrection.

84. I.e., secular rulers who want to act in a Christian manner must restrain those who are enemies of the gospel.

85. The "archseducer" here was Luther. See Müntzer's *Highly Provoked Defense*, in which he accuses Luther of producing martyrs and then singing hymns about them.

86. The George (*Jeori*), to whom the letter was written, may have been George Amandus, a preacher at Schneeberg. From the letter's contents, at any rate, he was a cleric who came to Müntzer for spiritual advice, including counsel as to whether he should introduce liturgical reforms.

87. *den swynden* (= geschwinden) *screyber*. The following description of the action of God in "writing" the divine word in the heart of the believer is also presented in *The Prague Protest*.

88. I.e., either to imperial law, which had forbidden ecclesiastical innovations, or to the territorial prince, Duke George of Saxony, who remained loyal to the Roman church.

89. Written after his Weimar hearing of 1 August 1524 and just prior to his flight from Allstedt, this letter expressed Müntzer's final appeal to the elector of Saxony.

90. At the opening of his *Special Exposure of False Faith*, Müntzer also cited this passage of Ezekiel.

91. I.e., Luther's *Letter to Princes of Saxony Concerning the Rebellious Spirit*.

92. This seems disingenuous; by this time, Müntzer, having seen Luther's letter, had probably begun work on a reply, his *Highly Provoked Defense*.

93. Jn. 18:19–21. The preface to the *Special Exposure of False Faith* also cited this text in order to justify Müntzer's rejection of a private examination by Luther and the Wittenberg theologians.

94. I.e., Müntzer's *Witness of the First Chapter of the Gospel of Luke*, discussed in the Introduction, which was delivered to Duke John's officials at the time of the Weimar hearing on 1 August 1524 and which Müntzer later published in an extended and much more radical form as *Special Exposure of False Faith*.

95. See, above, Müntzer's letter #59 to Hans Zeiss of 25 July 1524.

96. I.e., the merciless destruction of the Canaanites.

97. This letter was written a week after Müntzer's flight from Allstedt and just after his arrival at Mühlhausen. He wrote several drafts of the letter before this last one; they show that he had difficulty finding the right tone to use in discussing his flight.

98. *vom altar leben*; literally, live from the altar.

99. I.e., Müntzer's fear of God has removed from his mind the deference and awe of human authority that is necessary for him to submit to unjust rulers.

100. I.e., from Hans Zeiss at the castle above Allstedt, but ultimately from the territorial prince, the elector of Saxony.

101. I.e., the printed copies of Müntzer's liturgical works.

102. Müntzer wrote this letter, appended to the correspondence in *MSB*, pp. 573–75, to defend radicals at Nordhausen who had been imprisoned as a result of attacks on images; hence it is an important statement of Müntzer's position on iconoclasm.

103. *mit uns unterworfen dem reiche*; literally, like us, subject to the Empire— a clear indication that the letter was written from Mühlhausen, the other free imperial city of Thuringia in addition to Nordhausen.

104. The pastor Lawrence Süsse, a follower of Luther, whom Müntzer also criticized in his *Highly Provoked Defense*. See above, chapt. 8, n. 24.

105. This public letter was written during the political turmoil that developed at Mühlhausen shortly after Müntzer's arrival; in it he expressed his views on the current situation and the need for change. The "Eleven Mühlhausen Articles," the program of the commoners seeking to overturn the city council, was in part influenced by Müntzer's views. His participation in the unrest led to his expulsion from Mühlhausen on 27 September 1524.

106. I.e., receive income from a benefice and neglect to perform its spiritual duties.

107. Two mayors of the city temporarily fled, taking the city keys and seal with them.

108. Also called "The Manifesto to the Miners," this letter is undoubtedly

Müntzer's most emotional appeal for insurrection during the Peasants' War. In it, he wrote to former followers and members of the League of the Elect at Allstedt and urged them immediately to form a new center of rebellion.

109. Müntzer may have been referring especially to Jodocus Kern, whom Luther sent to Allstedt. See Bensing and Rüdiger, *Thomas Müntzer*, p. 269, n. 7.

110. This is greatly exaggerated, yet may have been the natural result of the innumerable reports and rumors of risings that spread during the Peasants' War.

111. *der meyster will spiel machen*; i.e., the upheaval is seen as a divinely staged play. In the *Special Exposure of False Faith* Müntzer employed the same metaphor for revolution.

112. As Müntzer testified in his *Confession*, in the fall of 1524, after being forced out of Mühlhausen, he traveled to southwestern Germany, where he preached to the peasantry of these regions and helped them draft proposals for a new government.

113. Now Bad Langensalza.

114. The official was Sittich von Berlepsch.

115. Here Müntzer addressed specific members of the Allstedt league—Balthasar Stübner, Bartel Krump, Valentin Krump, and Bischof zu Wolferode—whom he called on to act as leaders. See his *Confession*, where they are named again.

116. It is uncertain who this was.

117. There are several errors here. Müntzer undoubtedly intended to cite Dan. 7, rather than 74, and Ezra 10, rather than 16. It is noteworthy that Müntzer viewed the first five citations as clarifying and supporting his interpretation of Rom. 13:1–5, which he saw as justifying the overthrow of evil government.

118. Another erroneous citation. Müntzer may have intended to refer to 2 Chr. 20:15–18.

119. Müntzer wrote this letter to explain his conditions for accepting members of the nobility into the commoners' league. Only a few nobles, and most of these only under pressure, joined the cause of the commoners during the Peasants' War.

120. *MSB*, p. 459, n. 1, identifies these as members of the nobility of Schwarzburg, of whom only Heinrich Hake zu Tilleda is otherwise mentioned in documents concerning the Peasants' War.

121. See 1 Cor. 1:27. Müntzer's point is that, even though God's will is foolishness from the standpoint of worldly cleverness, those in rebellion should not act stupidly and deny their difficulties.

122. This heading is not part of the original letter and was added later. The purpose of the letter—as well as the following one to Ernst of Mansfeld's brother, Albrecht—is not to convert; both are ultimatums demanding that the counts of Mansfeld present explanations of their faith which would justify their remaining in power and dissuade the peasantry from overthrowing them.

123. *das hat dir ein ganz gemein im ringe zugesagt*; literally, a whole community in a circle has promised you this. It was common practice in the military formations of the Peasants' War for the insurgents to convene in a circle or ring to settle matters democratically and collectively. Müntzer wanted to specify that the challenge he is issuing is the decision of the group as a whole.

124. See, rather, Jg. 5:24ff. and 11:21ff.

125. In his *Confession*, Müntzer acknowledged that the peasant army had sworn to overthrow Count Ernst.

126. A reference to Heldrungen, the moat-reinforced castle that was Ernst of Mansfeld's military stronghold.

127. Albrecht of Mansfeld was a pro-Lutheran prince, unlike his brother Ernst, who was a Roman Catholic. The religious differences between the two did not affect Müntzer's position about the illegitimacy of their political power, but his comments on the false faith of each are somewhat different.

128. As in the case of letter #88, this heading was added later.

129. I.e., commoners who have been deceived by false faith.

130. *yn deyem Martinischen baurendreck*, i.e., Luther's teachings.

131. *tellerleckern*; literally, plate-lickers.

Chapter 10. Last Words: Confession, Retraction and Final Letter

1. The Roman Catholic princes among Müntzer's captors may have wanted his confession to show that leaders of the Peasants' War shared with Luther and his followers what Roman Catholic authorities regarded as a general disrespect for the Mass and Eucharist. In saying he viewed such things as a matter for the judgment of each, Müntzer evidently saw such issues as peripheral.

2. *habe er etliche artigkel, wye man herschen soll aus dem evangelio angeben*; i.e., he proposed the shape of a Christian government. It is possible that this document is the so-called "Constitutional Draft" (*Verfassungsentwurf*) found by Habsburg officials among the papers of the radical reformer and later Anabaptist leader, Balthasar Hubmaier. On this, see Gottfried Seebass, *Artikelbrief, Bundesordnung und Verfassungsentwurf* (Heidelberg: Carl Winter, 1988), esp. pp. 160–70.

3. In addition to the "Constitutional Draft," Müntzer may have influenced the composition of the "Document of Articles" (*Artikelbrief*) of the Black Forest peasants' army. As expressed here, it is unclear whether the source from which the "further articles" were made was the original articles on government or the gospel.

4. Two followers of Ulrich Zwingli in the Upper Swabian/Swiss border region.

5. This article is only found in the Latin version of the *Confession*; evidently the authorities did not wish to see it presented in the more accessible vernacular version that was published after Müntzer's death.

6. *MSB*, p. 545, n. 22, points out that such demands by the commoners were part of a tradition attempting to limit public displays of wealth and power by the nobility and clergy.

7. The reference here is to Müntzer's first league at Allstedt, the League of the Elect, in contrast to the Eternal League which he formed at Mühlhausen in the spring of 1525. The German term *Bund* or *Verbundnis* includes the notions of a covenant, a league, a federation, and an alliance. The authorities naturally viewed the league as a criminal conspiracy to promote insurrection.

8. Early evangelical reformers used the term "persecutor of the gospel" to refer especially to authorities who attempted to suppress their activities. The claim that the League had only a defensive purpose is open to question, and the religious motivation need not exclude political aims. At least in their final form the leagues at both Allstedt and Mühlhausen were engaged in the Peasants' War

for positive political and social changes which the radicals saw as entailed by the gospel.

9. *MSB*, p. 545, n. 31, points out that, in July 1524, Duke George of Saxony ordered the arrest of Tile Banse on the grounds that he was a follower of Luther and had married.

10. See Müntzer's letters to "the God-fearing at Sangerhausen" and "the persecuted Christians at Sangerhausen," #53 and #55 above.

11. Jacob Strauss, a preacher at Eisenach, was an early evangelical critic of Luther and held radical views on such social issues as usury. Müntzer evidently came into contact with him in late 1522, and the reference is to a hearing at that time, rather than Müntzer's later hearing at Weimar on 1 August 1524.

12. Johann Koler was a former member of the Franciscan community at Mühlhausen who left the order and joined Luther's cause.

13. Müntzer's threatening letter may have been written between September 1524, when he was expelled from Mühlhausen, and January 1525 when he returned.

14. Evidently at the time of his first arrival in mid-August 1524.

15. On 24 March 1524, the chapel at Mallerbach was burned by some of Müntzer's Allstedt followers. The chapel belonged to the convent of nuns at Naundorf, who also received dues from people at Allstedt. The Mallerbach chapel contained an image of the Virgin Mary which was said to work miracles. Müntzer regarded the image and the pilgrimages to it as encouraging superstitious beliefs and practices.

16. *der klausener*, who was the custodian of the chapel.

17. Ebeleben, evidently among the wealthy elite of Mühlhausen and seen by the people as an exploiter, was present at Müntzer's interrogation. Ebeleben is described in Müntzer's retraction as "most strictly honorable and scrupulous."

18. This was the most influential program of peasant demands formulated during the German Peasants' War.

19. I.e., while refusing to identify the city government with the *Bund*, the Mühlhausen city council conceded to the commoners the right to enroll in it. In fact, Müntzer apparently formed the "Eternal League" at Mühlhausen because he regarded the new council, which came to power in mid-March 1525, the "Eternal Council," as too moderate.

20. Storch and Thomae or Stübner were two of the so-called "Zwickau Prophets" who arrived at Wittenberg in December 1521, radicalized the religious reform movement there, and were eventually driven out after Luther returned from the Wartburg in the spring of 1522 and delivered a series of sermons against them. The reference here is to a later visit to Wittenberg and meeting with Luther in late 1522 or early 1523; see also letter #40, above.

21. *hat eyn fenlyn* (= *Fahnlein*) *angenommen*; i.e., an infantry unit with its own banner or standard.

22. *Peynlich bekant.* According to a Lutheran pamphlet that appeared after Müntzer's execution, only the Roman Catholic princes, Duke George and Count Ernst of Mansfeld, together with a secretary and an executioner, were present during the torture session, *MSB*, p. 547, n. 68. This claim may have been an attempt to disassociate Luther from the torture.

23. *sambt irem anhange*; perhaps including apprentices as well as family members.

24. Pfeiffer, who also used the name Schwertfeger, was Müntzer's most important clerical associate at Mühlhausen. Pfeiffer was a native of Mühlhausen, joined

and later fled a monastery, and then became an active reformer in the city before Müntzer's arrival. Additional aspects of Pfeiffer's role at Mühlhausen are treated below.

25. Just before the Battle of Frankenhausen, three followers of Count Ernst of Mansfeld who were being held prisoner—Matern von Gehofen, Georg Büchner, and the priest Stefan Hartenstein—were tried and executed by their peasant captors.

26. As a motive, this seems inconsistent and unlikely. Müntzer probably saw the court martial by the peasant army as a legitimate case of the elect uprooting and destroying the godless.

27. *das dye christenheyt solt alle gleych werden*; the most likely meaning is that legal privileges defining various estates or orders of society would be abolished. Article eight, below, implies that this civil equality was to have been accompanied by the abolition of private property, but there is scant evidence that Müntzer actually envisioned this.

28. This qualification is found only in the Latin version; the result of its exclusion was to make the published vernacular version of Müntzer's *Confesssion* sound more ruthless and brutal.

29. Under torture, Müntzer was not only required to name names; his interrogators also returned to the question, which he had already answered, of who among his supporters possessed the registration book where they could obtain the names of those enrolled in the league.

30. Since Bishop Ernst died in 1513, Müntzer could not have been older than his mid-twenties at the time of this early political activism. However, there is no evidence about this league beyond that contained in the *Confession*, and its existence is doubtful.

31. Perhaps this charge of "urban imperialism" against the free city of Mühlhausen was designed to justify punishing the city for its involvement in the Peasants' War. See the next article.

32. *Bin*; at this point the document shifts to the first person.

33. I.e., for a year and a half prior to Müntzer's arrival at Mühlhausen. To ascribe the initial radicalization of politics in Mühlhausen to Pfeiffer was undoubtedly accurate and not an attempt to shift the blame to him.

34. In fact, several of the following articles appear to be dictated by Müntzer's captors.

35. It is possible that Müntzer agreed to this recantation in exchange for permission to send the following final letter to the people of Mühlhausen.

36. This letter was first composed on 15 May 1525, but then redated—and its contents possibly altered—so as to make it appear that it was written at the same time as the retraction.

37. *in warhaftiger erkenthnis gottlichs namens*, a phrase Müntzer used to refer to correct religious understanding.

38. *eygen nutz*; i.e., their own advantage or private use, in contrast to *gemeyn nutz*, the collective interests of the community.

39. The implication would seem to be that, despite the obvious defeat of the popular cause at Frankenhausen, there are reasons for holding to the ideas that motivated the rebellion.

40. *welcher zur foderung den guthen und unvorstendigen gescheen ist. MSB*, p. 473, n. 7, suggests a textual deficiency here and that the passage should perhaps read, "has occurred *as a warning* in order to benefit . . . "

41. This request, made repeatedly in Müntzer's final statements, was ignored

by the authorities. His pregnant wife and his son were expelled from Mühlhausen without receiving his property. In August 1525, Ottilie von Gersen, destitute, directed a written appeal for mercy to Duke George of Saxony. This request too was turned down. Her letter is the last trace of Müntzer's family to survive in the written records.

42. More recent estimates suggest casualities of more than 5,000 peasant deaths at the Battle of Frankenhausen.

43. The assertion that most residents of the city were not active participants in the insurrection is undoubtedly correct.

44. This hope too was disappointed; Mühlhausen was punished and lost its political independence as a free imperial city.

Bibliography

Editions and Translations of Müntzer's Writings

Baylor, Michael G., trans. "Thomas Müntzer's First Publication." *Sixteenth Century Journal* 17 (1986): 451–58.

——, trans. "Thomas Müntzer's *Prague Manifesto*." *Mennonite Quarterly Review* 63 (1987): 30–57.

Bensing, Manfred, and Bernd Rüdiger, eds. *Thomas Müntzer. Politische Schriften, Manifeste, Briefe 1524/25*. Leipzig: Bibliographisches Institut, 1973.

Bentzinger, Rudolf, and Siegfried Hoyer, eds. *Thomas Müntzer. Schriften, Liturgische Texte, Briefe*. Berlin: Union, 1990.

Bräuer, Siegfried, ed. *Thomas Müntzer. Deutsche Evangelische Messe 1524*. Berlin: Evangelische Verlagsanstalt, 1988.

Bräuer, Siegfried, and Wolfgang Ullman, eds. *Thomas Müntzer. Theologische Schriften aus dem Jahr 1523*. 2d, rev. ed. Berlin: Evangelische Verlagsanstalt, 1982.

Fowkes, Robert A., trans. "Sermon to the Princes," "Well-warranted Speech in My Own Defense," and "Manifesto to the Miners." In *German Humanism and the Reformation*, edited by Reinhard P. Becker, 257–92. The German Library, vol. 6. New York: Continuum, 1982.

Franz, Günther, ed. *Thomas Müntzer. Schriften und Briefe. Kritische Gesamtausgabe*. Quellen und Forschungen zur Reformationgeschichte, vol. 33. Gütersloh: Gerd Mohn, 1968. (*MSB*).

Hillerbrand, Hans J., trans. "Thomas Muentzer's Last Tract against Martin Luther: A Translation and a Commentary." *Mennonite Quarterly Review* 38 (1964): 20–36.

Hinrichs, Carl, ed. *Thomas Müntzer. Politische Schriften*. Hallische Monographien, Nr. 17. Halle (Saale): Max Niemeyer, 1950.

Matheson, Peter, trans. and ed. *The Collected Works of Thomas Müntzer*. Edinburgh: T. & T. Clark, 1988.

"Sermon before the Princes by Thomas Müntzer (1524)." In *Spiritual and Anabaptist Writers*, edited by George Hunston Williams and Angel Mergal, 47–70. Library of the Christian Classics, vol. 25. Philadelphia: Westminster, 1957.

Stayer, James M., trans. "Thomas Müntzer's *Protestation* and *Imaginary Faith*," *Mennonite Quarterly Review* 55 (1981): 99–131.

Steinmetz, Max, ed. *Die Fürstenpredigt*. Berlin: Union, 1975.

Steinmetz, Max, Friedrich de Boor, Winfried Trillitzsch, and Hans-Joachim Rockar, eds. *Thomas Müntzer. Prager Manifest*. Leipzig: Zentralantiquariat der Deutschen Demokratischen Republik, 1975.

Wehr, Gerhard, ed. *Thomas Müntzer, Schriften und Briefe.* Gütersloh: Gerd Mohn, 1978.

Other Primary Sources

Baylor, Michael G., trans. and ed. *The Radical Reformation.* Cambridge: Cambridge University Press, 1991.

Bräuer, Siegfried, ed. *Historien von Thomas Müntzer.* Leipzig: Zentralantiquariat der DDR, 1989.

Brendler, Gerhard, ed. *Der Lutheraner Müntzer. Erster Bericht über sein Auftreten in Jüterbog, Verfasst von Franziskanern anno 1519.* Berlin: Verlag der Nation, 1989.

Fisher, Ludwig, ed. *Die Lutherischen Pamphlete gegen Thomas Müntzer.* Tübingen: Max Niemeyer, 1976.

Franz, Günther, ed. *Der deutschen Bauernkrieg. Aktenband.* Darmstadt: Wissenschaftliche Buchgesellschaft, 1972.

———, ed. *Quellen zur Geschichte des Bauernkrieges.* Darmstadt: Wissenschaftliche Buchgesellschaft, 1963.

Fuchs, Walter Peter, ed. *Akten zur Geschichte des Bauernkrieges in Mitteldeutschland.* 2 vols. Jena: Frommannsche Buchhandlung Walter Biedermann, 1942.

Gess, Felician, ed. *Akten und Briefe zur Kirchenpolitik Herzog Georgs von Sachsen.* 2 vols. Cologne and Vienna: Böhlau, 1985 (lst ed., 1905, 1917).

Kacerowsky, Klaus, ed. *Flugschriften des Bauernkrieges.* Reinbek bei Hamburg: Rowohlt, 1970.

Kobuch, Manfred, and Ernst Müller, eds. *Der deutschen Bauernkrieg in Dokumenten.* Weimar: Hermann Böhlaus Nachfolger, 1975.

Laube, Adolf, Annerose Schneider, and Sigrid Looss, eds. *Flugschriften der frühen Reformationsbewegung (1518–1524).* 2 vols. Berlin: Akademie-Verlag, 1983.

Laube, Adolf, and Hans Werner Seiffert, eds. *Flugschriften der Bauernkriegszeit,* 2d rev. ed. Cologne and Vienna: Böhlau, 1978.

Luther, Martin. *D. Martin Luthers Werke: Kritische Gesamtausgabe.* 58 vols. Weimar: Hermann Böhlau und Hermann Böhlaus Nachfolger, 1883–. (*WA*).

Scott, Tom, and Bob Scribner, trans. and eds. *The German Peasants' War. A History in Documents.* New Jersey and London: Humanities Press International, 1991.

Wehr, Gerhard. *Thomas Müntzer in Selbstzeugnissen und Bilddokumenten.* Reinbek bei Hamburg: Rowohlt, 1972.

Bibliographies, Reference Works, and Aids

Bosse, Hans-Joachim. *Thomas Müntzer und die deutsche frühbürgerliche Revolution: empfehlende Bibliographie.* Berlin: Zentralinstitut für Bibliothekswesen, 1989.

Claus, Helmut. *Der deutsche Bauernkrieg im Druckschaffen der Jahre 1524–1526*. Gotha: Forschungsbibliotek Gotha, 1975.

Götze, Alfred. *Frühneuhochdeutsches Glossar*. Berlin: Walter de Gruyter, 1967.

Grimm, Jacob and Wilhelm Grimm. *Deutsches Wörterbuch*. 32 vols. Munich: Deutscher Taschenbuch Verlag, 1984 (photomechanical repr. of 1873 ed.).

Hillerbrand, Hans J. *Thomas Müntzer: A Bibliography*. Sixteenth-Century Bibliography, no. 4. St. Louis: Center for Reformation Research, 1976.

Lexer, Matthias. *Mittelhochdeutsches Taschenwörterbuch*. Stuttgart: S. Hirzel, 1983.

Ozment, Steven, ed. *Reformation Europe: A Guide to Research*. St. Louis: Center for Reformation Research, 1982.

Spillmann, Hans Otto. *Untersuchungen zum Wortschatz in Thomas Müntzers deutschen Schriften*. Quellen und Forschungen zur Sprach- u. Kulturgeschichte der germanischen Völker, N. F., vol. 41. Berlin: Walter de Gruyter, 1971.

Thomas, Ulrich. *Bibliographie zum deutschen Bauernkrieg und seiner Zeit*. 2 parts. Stuttgart: Dokumentationstelle der Universität Hohenheim, 1976–77.

Secondary Literature

Ackermann, Irmgard. *Thomas Müntzer. Stätten seines Lebens und Wirkens*. Berlin: Henschel, 1989.

Bailey, Richard. "The Sixteenth Century's Apocalyptic Heritage and Thomas Müntzer." *Mennonite Quarterly Review* 57 (1983): 27–44.

Bainton, Roland. "Thomas Müntzer: Revolutionary Firebrand of the Reformation." *Sixteenth Century Journal* 12 (1982): 3–15.

Baring, Georg. "Hans Denck und Thomas Müntzer in Nürnberg 1524." *Archive for Reformation History* 50 (1959): 145–80.

Baylor, Michael G. "The Harvest and the Rainbow: Crisis and Apocalypse in Thomas Müntzer." In *Krisenbewusstsein und Krisenbewältigung in der Frühen Neuzeit—Crisis in Early Modern Europe*, Festschrift für Hans-Christoph Rublack, edited by Monika Hagenmaier and Sabine Holtz, 293–305. Frankfurt am Main: Peter Lang, 1992.

———. "On the Front between the Cultures: Thomas Müntzer on Popular and Learned Culture." *History of European Ideas* 11 (1989): 523–36.

———. "Theology and Politics in the Thought of Thomas Müntzer: The Case of the Elect." *Archive for Reformation History* 79 (1988): 81–101.

Beck, Friedrich. "Persönliche Schriften im Umfeld der frühbürgerliche Revolution in Deutschland: die Handschriften Luthers, Müntzers, Zwinglis und Melanchthons—eine paläographisches Vergleich," *Jahrbuch für Geschichte des Feudalismus* 13 (1989): 89–131.

Bensing, Manfred. *Thomas Müntzer*. 4th rev. ed. Leipzig: Bibliographisches Institut, 1989.

———. "Grundfragen der Revolution in Müntzers Denken und Handeln." *Mühlhäuser Beiträge zur Geschichte und Kulturgeschichte* 4 (1981): 18–27.

———. *Thomas Müntzer und der Thüringer Aufstand 1525*. Leipziger Übersetzungen und Abhandlungen zum Mittelalter, series B, vol. 3. Berlin: Deutscher Verlag der Wissenschaften, 1966.

———. "Idee und Praxis des 'Christlichen-Verbündnisses' bei Thomas Müntzer." *Wissenschaftliche Zeitschrift der Karl-Marx-Universität Leipzig* 14 (1965): 459–71.

Bensing, Manfred, and W. Trillitzsch. "Bernhard Dappens 'Articuli . . . contra Lutheranos.' Zur Auseinandersetzung der Jüterboger Franziskaner mit Thomas Müntzer und Franz Günther 1519," *Jahrbuch für Regionalgeschichte* 2 (1967): 113–47.

Berbig, Hans-Joachim. "Thomas Müntzer in neuer Sicht." *Archiv für Kulturgeschichte* 59 (1977): 489–95.

Blickle, Peter. "Thomas Müntzer und der Bauernkrieg in Südwestdeutschland." *Zeitschrift für Agrargeschichte und Agrarsoziologie* 24 (1976): 79–80.

Bloch, Ernst. *Thomas Müntzer als Theologe der Revolution.* Bibliothek Suhrkamp, Bd. 77. Frankfurt am Main: Suhrkamp, 1972 (lst ed., 1921).

Brackhahn, Michael. *Thomas Müntzer in Mühlhausen.* Diplom-Arbeit, Soziologie, Universität Hamburg, 1986.

Braüer, Helmut. *Thomas Müntzer und die Zwickauer. Zum Wirken Thomas Müntzers in Zwickau 1520–1521.* Karl-Marx-Stadt: Bezirksleitung des Kulturbundes der DDR und Bezirkskunstzentrum Karl-Marx-Stadt, 1989.

Braüer, Siegfried. "Bauernführer und Theologe: das Müntzerbild seit 1945 in der DDR." *GEP Buch Magazin*, spring/summer 1989, 12–13.

———, "Müntzer war unter uns. Zum Mützerverständnis in der evangelischen Theologie." *Zeichen der Zeit* 43 (1989): 200–206.

———. "Thomas Müntzer und der Allstedter Bund." In *Täufertum und radikale Reformation im 16. Jahrhundert*: Akten des internationalen Kolloquiums für Täufergeschichte des 16. Jahrhunderts gehalten in Verbindung mit dem XI. Mennonitischen Weltkonferenz in Strasbourg, Juli 1984, edited by Jean-Georges Rott and Simon L. Verheus, 85–101. Baden-Baden: Koerner, 1987.

———. "Thomas Müntzers 'Fürstenpredigt' als Buchbindermaterial." *Theologische Literaturzeitung* 112 (1987): col. 415–24.

———. "Thomas Müntzers Beziehungen zur Braunschweiger Frühreformation." *Theologische Literaturzeitung* 109 (1984): 636–38.

———. "Die Vorgeschichte von Luthers 'Ein Brief an die Fürsten zu Sachsen von dem aufrührerischen Geist.'" *Lutherjahrbuch* 47 (1980): 40–70.

———. "Müntzerforschung von 1965 bis 1975." *Lutherjahrbuch* 44 (1977): 127–41; 45 (1978), 102–39.

———. "Hans Reichart, der angebliche Allstedter Drucker Müntzers. *"Zeitschrift für Kirchengeschichte* 85 (1974): 389–98.

Braüer, Siegfried, and Hans-Jürgen Goertz. "Thomas Müntzer." In *Die Reformationszeit I*, edited by M. Greschat, 335–352. Gestalten der Kirchengeschichte, Bd. 5. Stuttgart: W. Kohlhammer, 1981.

Braüer, Siegfried, and Helmar Junghans, eds. *Der Theologe Thomas Müntzer. Untersuchungen zu seiner Entwicklung und Lehre.* Göttingen: Vandenhoeck & Ruprecht, 1989.

Brendler, Gerhard. *Thomas Müntzer, Geist und Faust.* East Berlin: Deutscher Verlag der Wissenschaften, 1989.

————, ed. *Die frühbürgerliche Revolution in Deutschland*. Berlin: Akademie-Verlag, 1961.

Brendler, Gerhard, and Adolf Laube, eds. *Der deutsche Bauernkrieg, 1524/25: Geschichte, Traditionen, Lehren*. Akademie der Wissenschaften der DDR, Schriften des Zentralinstituts für Geschichte, Nr. 57. Berlin: Akademie-Verlag, 1977.

Bubenheimer, Ulrich. *Thomas Müntzer: Herkunft und Bildung*. Studies in Medieval and Reformation Thought, vol. 46. Leiden: E. J. Brill, 1989.

————. "Thomas Müntzers Wittenberger Studienzeit." *Zeitschrift für Kirchengeschichte* 99 (1988): 168–213.

————. "Thomas Müntzers Nachschrift einer Wittenberger Hieronymusvorlesung." *Zeitschrift für Kirchengeschichte* 99 (1988): 214–37.

————. "Luther—Karlstadt—Müntzer: Soziale Herkunft und humanistiche Bildung. Ausgewählte Aspekte vergleichender Biographie." *Amtsblatt der evangelische-Lutherischen Kirche in Thüringen* 40, no. 8 (25 April 1987): 60–68.

————. "Thomas Müntzer und der Anfang der Reformation in Braunschweig." *Nederlands Archief voor Kerkgeschiednis* 65 (1985): 1–30.

————. "Thomas Müntzer in Braunschweig." *Braunschweigisches Jahrbuch* 65 (1984): 37–78 (part 1); 66 (1985): 79–113 (part 2).

————. "Thomas Müntzer." In *Protestantische Profile. Lebensbilder aus 5 Jahrhunderten*, edited by Klaus Schoeller and Dieter Kleinman, 32–46. Königstein/Ts.: Athenäum, 1983.

Cohn, Norman. *The Pursuit of the Millennium*. Revised ed. New York: Oxford University Press, 1970.

Davis, Duane Evans. "Faith and the Spirit: The Theological Methodology of Thomas Müntzer." Ph.D. diss. Emory University, 1973.

Demke, Christoph, ed. *Thomas Müntzer—Anfragen an Theologie und Kirche*. Berlin: Evangelische Verlagsanstalt, 1977.

Dismer, Rolf. "Geschichte, Glaube, Revolution: Zur Schriftauslegung Thomas Müntzers." Diss., Evangelische Theologie, Universität Hamburg, 1974.

Drummond, Andrew W. "The Divine and Mortal Worlds of Thomas Müntzer." *Archive for Reformation History* 71 (1980): 99–112.

————. "Thomas Müntzer and the Fear of Man." *The Sixteenth Century Journal* 10 (1979): 63–71.

Ebert, Klaus. *Thomas Müntzer: Von Eigensinn und Widerspruch*. Frankfurt am Main: Athenäum, 1987.

————. *Theologie und politisches Handeln. Thomas Müntzer als Modell*. Urban-Taschenbücher, vol. 602. Stuttgart: W. Kohlhammer, 1973.

Elliger, Walter. *Thomas Müntzer. Leben und Werk*. 2d edition. Göttingen: Vandenhoeck & Ruprecht, 1975.

————. *Aussenseiter der Reformation: Thomas Müntzer, ein Knecht Gottes*. Göttingen: Vandenhoeck & Ruprecht, 1975.

Endermann, Heinz. "Thomas Müntzer und die Sprachwirklichkeit zur Zeit der frühbürgerlichen Revolution." *Mühlhäuser Beiträge* 12 (1989), 12–18.

————. "Wesenszüge der Sprache Thomas Müntzers." *Zeitschrift für Phonetik, Sprachwissenschaft und Kommunikationsforschung* 28 (1975): 574–81.

Engels, Friedrich. *The German Revolutions, "The Peasant War in Germany" and "Germany: Revolution and Counter-Revolution"*. Edited by Leonard Krieger. Chicago: University of Chicago Press, 1967.

Fast, Heinold. "Hans Denck and Thomas Müntzer." *Mennonite Quarterly Review* 45 (1971): 82–83.

Fauth, Dieter. *Thomas Müntzer in Bildungsgeschichtlicher Sicht*. Ostfildern: Privatdruck, 1990.

Federer, Jakob Gottfried. *Didaktik der Befreiung. Eine Studie am Beispiel Thomas Müntzers*. Studien zur Germanistik, Anglistik und Komparatistik, vol. 45. Bonn: Bouvier, 1976.

Fischer, Joachim. "Luther und Müntzer." *Lutherjahrbuch* 57 (1990): 274–77.

Friesen, Abraham. *Thomas Müntzer, a Destroyer of the Godless*. Berkeley and Los Angeles: University of California Press, 1990.

———. "Acts 10: The Baptism of Cornelius as Interpreted by Thomas Müntzer and Felix Manz." *Mennonite Quarterly Review* 64 (1990): 5–22.

———. "Thomas Müntzer and Martin Luther." *Archive for Reformation History* 79 (1988): 59–80.

———. "Thomas Müntzer and the Anabaptists." *Journal of Mennonite Studies* 4 (1986): 143–61.

———. *Reformation and Utopia*. The Marxist Interpretation of the Reformation and Its Antecedents. Veröffentlichungen des Instituts für Europäische Geschichte Mainz, Bd. 71. Wiesbaden: Franz Steiner, 1974.

———. "Thomas Müntzer and the Old Testament." *Mennonite Quarterly Review* 47 (1973): 5–19.

Friesen, Abraham, and Hans-Jürgen Goertz, eds. *Thomas Müntzer*. Wege der Forschung, vol. 141. Darmstadt: Wissenschaftliche Buchgesellschaft, 1978.

Goertz, Hans-Jürgen. "Thomas Müntzer: Revolutionary between the Middle Ages and Modernity." *Mennonite Quarterly Review* 64 (1990): 23–31.

———. *Thomas Müntzer: Mystiker, Apokalyptiker, Revolutionär*. Munich: Verlag C. H. Beck, 1989.

———. *Das Bild Thomas Müntzers in Ost und West*. Hannover: Niedersächsischen Landeszentrale für politische Bildung, 1988.

———. " 'Lebendiges Wort' und 'totes Ding.' Zum Schriftverständnis Thomas Müntzers im Prager Manifest." *Archive for Reformation History* 67 (1976), 165–66.

———. "The Mystic with the Hammer: Thomas Müntzer's Theological Basis for Revolution." Translated by E. Bender. *Mennonite Quarterly Review* 50 (1976): 83–113.

———. *Innere und äussere Ordnung in der Theologie Thomas Müntzers*. Studies in the History of Christian Thought, vol. 2. Leiden: E. J. Brill, 1967.

Gritsch, Eric W. "Thomas Müntzers Weg in die Apokalyptik." *Lutherjahrbuch* 60 (1989): 53–65.

———. *Thomas Müntzer, Tragedy of Errors*. Minneapolis: Fortress Press, 1989.

Grüning, Thomas. "Müntzer contra Luther: der philosophische Gehalt des theologischen Konflikts." *Deutsche Zeitschrift für Philosophie* 37 (1989): 1093–110.

Günther, Gerhard. "Müntzer-Quellen im Stadtarchiv Mühlhausen." *Archivmitteilungen* 39 (1989): 204–6.

———. "Thomas Müntzer und der Harz," *Nordharzer Jahrbuch* 13 (1988): 37–45.

———. "Bemerkungen zum Thema 'Thomas Müntzer und Heinrich Pfeiffer in Mühlhausen'." In *Der Bauer im Klassenkampf*, edited by G. Heitz, A. Laube, M. Steinmetz, and G. Vogler, 157–82. Berlin: Akademie-Verlag, 1975.

Held, Wieland. "Neue Quellenzeugnisse über den Aufenhalt Thomas Müntzers in Zwickau." *Zeitschrift für Geschichtswissenschaft* 37 (1989): 50–55.

———. "Ein zweiter Bericht über das Verhör Thomas Müntzers in Weimar 1524?" *Zeitschrift für Geschichtswissenschaft* 36 (1988): 515–13.

———. "Der Allstedter Schösser Hans Zeiss und sein Verhältnis zu Thomas Müntzer." *Zeitschrift für Geschichtswissenschaft* 35 (1987): 1073–91.

Hillerbrand, Hans J., ed. *Radical Tendencies in the Reformation: Divergent Perspectives*. Sixteenth-Century Essays and Studies, vol. 9. Kirksville, Mo.: Sixteenth Century Journal Publishers, 1987.

Hinrichs, Carl. *Luther und Müntzer, ihre Auseinandersetzung über Obrigkeit und Widerstandsrecht*. Arbeiten zur Kirchengeschichte, Bd. 29. Berlin: Walter de Gruyter, 1952.

Historische Beiträge zur Kyffhäuserlandschaft. Zur frühbürgerliche Revolution im Gebiet Thüringens und des Kyffhäusers und zum Wirken Thomas Müntzers. Bad Frankenhausen: Kreisheimatmuseum, 1989.

Honemeyer, Karl. *Thomas Müntzer und Martin Luther. Ihre Ringen um die Musik des Gottesdienstes*. Berlin: Merseburger, 1974.

Hoyer, Siegfried. "Forschungen zu Müntzer und zur Müntzerrezeption 1976–1988." *Zeitschrift für Geschichtswissenschaft* 37 (1989): 984–99.

———. "Die Zwickauer Storchianer—Vorläufer der Täufer?" *Jahrbuch für Regionalgeschichte* 13 (1986): 60–78.

———, ed. *Reform, Reformation, Revolution*. Ausgewählte Beiträge einer wissenschaftliche Konferenz in Leipzig am 10. und 11. Oktober, 1977. Leipzig: Karl-Marx-Universität, 1980.

Ich, Thomas Müntzer eyn knecht gottes. Historisch-biographische Ausstellung des Museums für deutsche Geschichte, Berlin, 8. Dezember 1989 bis 28. Februar 1990. Berlin: Henschel, 1989.

Irwin, Joyce. "The Theological and Social Dimension of Thomas Müntzer's Liturgical Reform." Ph.D. diss., Yale University, 1972.

Jørgensen, Ninna. "Hat Luther Müntzers Liturgiereform abgelehnt?" *Archive for Reformation History* 80 (1989): 47–67.

Junghans, Helmar. "Die Theologie Thomas Müntzers: Die Bibel als Spiegel der Zeit." *Archive for Reformation History* 82 (1991): 107–22.

———. "Der Wandel des Müntzerbildes in der DDR von 1951/52 bis 1989." *Luther* 60 (1989): 102–30.

Junghans, Reinhard. *Thomas Müntzer-Rezeption während des "Dritten Reiches."* Frankfurt/M, Bern, New York, Paris: Peter Lang, 1990.

Kobuch, Manfred. "Thomas Müntzer in Aschersleben und Frose." *Zeitschrift für Geschichtswissenschaft* 38 (1990): 312–34.

——. "Thomas Müntzers Nachlass." *Archivmittelungen,* Teil 1: 39 (1989), 200–3; Teil 2: 40 (1990), 9–17.

——. "Der erste Bibliograph der Schriften Thomas Müntzers." *Sächsische Heimatblätter* 35 (1989): 214–15.

Koenigsberger, H.G. *Estates and Revolutions. Essays in Early Modern European History.* Ithaca and London: Cornell University Press, 1971.

Kolesnyk, Alexander. "Zu Problemen der revolutionären Theologie Thomas Müntzers." *Deutsche Zeitschrift für Philosophie* 37 (1989): 1071–81.

——. "Probleme einer philosophiegeschichtlichen Einordnung der Lehre Thomas Müntzers." *Deutsche Zeitschrift für Philosophie* 23/4 (1975): 583–94.

Kuenning, Paul P. "Luther and Müntzer: Contrasting Theologies in Regard to Secular Authority within the Context of the German Peasant Revolt." *Journal of Church and State* 29 (1987): 305–21.

Laube, Adolf. "Thomas Müntzer und die frühbürgerliche Revolution." *Zeitschrift für Geschichtswissenschaft* 38 (1990): 128–41.

Laube, Adolf, Max Steinmetz, and Günther Vogler, eds. *Illustrierte Geschichte der deutschen frühbürgerlichen Revolution.* Berlin: Dietz, 1974.

Lindberg, Carter. "Theology and Politics: Luther the Radical and Müntzer the Reactionary." *Encounter* 37 (1976): 356–71.

Lohmann, Annemarie. *Zur geistligen Entwicklung Thomas Müntzers.* Beiträge zur Kulturgeschichte des Mittelalters und der Renaissance, Bd. 47. Leipzig und Berlin: B. G. Teubner, 1931.

Lösche, Dietrich. "Achtmänner, Ewiger Bund Gottes und Ewiger Rat." *Jahrbuch für Wirtschaftsgeschichte* (1960): 135–62.

Lohse, Bernhard. *Thomas Müntzer in neuer Sicht.* Hamburg: Joachim Jungius-Gesellschaft, 1991.

——. "Thomas Müntzer, der Prophet mit dem Schwert." *Luther* 61 (1990): 1–20.

——. "The Marxist Interpretation of Luther and Muentzer." *Australian Journal of Politics and History* 19 (1973): 343–52.

Looss, Sigrid. "Nachdenken über Müntzer: zu einige Aspekten der 'Thesen' zum 500. Geburtstag." *Mühlhäuser Beiträge* 12 (1989): 5–11.

Maczka, Romwald. "Retheologizing Thomas Müntzer in the German Democratic Republic: 15 Years of Marxist and Non-Marxist Research." *Mennonite Quarterly Review* 63 (1989): 345–65.

Martinson, Steven D. *Between Luther and Müntzer: The Peasant Revolt in German Drama and Thought.* Heidelberg: Carl Winter, 1988.

Matheson, Peter. "Thomas Müntzer's Idea of an Audience." *History* 76 (1991): 185–96.

——. "Thomas Müntzer's *Vindication and Refutation*: A Language for the Common People?" *Sixteenth-Century Journal* 20 (1989): 603–15.

Mau, Rudolf. "Heiliger Geist und heilige Schrift bei Thomas Müntzer." *Die Zeichen der Zeit* 43 (1989): 189–94.

Mitzenheim, Paul. "Der Prediger Thomas Müntzer und die pädagogischen Anschauungen der frühbürgerlichen Revolution." *Veröffentlichungen des Museums der Stadt Gera*, Historische Reihe, Heft 5 (1989): 41–48.

Moeller, Bernd, ed. *Bauernkriegs-Studien.* Schriften des Vereins für Reformationsgeschichte, Nr. 189. Gütersloh: Gerd Mohn, 1975.

Müller, Michael. "Die Gottlosen bei Thomas Müntzer—mit einem Vergleich zu Martin Luther." *Lutherjahrbuch* 46 (1979): 97–119.

———. "Auserwählte und Gottlose in der Theologie Thomas Müntzers." Diss. Theologie, Universität Halle, 1972.

Müntzenberg, Gabriel. *Thomas Müntzer ou l'illuminisme sanglant.* Lausanne: Belle Reviére, 1987.

Nipperdey, Thomas. *Reformation, Revolution, Utopie.* Göttingen: Vandenhoeck & Ruprecht, 1975.

Oberman, Heiko A., ed. *Deutscher Bauernkrieg 1525.* Zeitschrift für Kirchengeschichte, vol. 5 (Vierte Folge XXIII): Heft 2. Stuttgart: W. Kohlhammer, 1974.

Ozment, Steven E. *Mysticism and Dissent: Religious Ideology and Social Protest in the Sixteenth Century.* New Haven: Yale University Press, 1973.

Packull, Werner O. "Thomas Müntzer between Marxist-Christian Diatribe and Dialogue." *Historical Reflections* 4 (1977): 67–90.

Prediger für eine gerechte Welt. Beiträge zu Thomas Müntzer. Berlin: Union, 1989.

Probleme des Müntzerbildes. Sitzungsberichte der Akademie der Wissenschaften der DDR, Gesellschaftswissenschaften, 6G (1988). Berlin: Akademie, 1988.

Rüger, Hans Peter. "Thomas Müntzers Erklärung hebräischer Eigennamen und der *Liber de interpretatione hebraicorum nominum* des Hieronymus." *Zeitschrift für Kirchengeschichte* 94 (1983): 83–88.

Rupp, Gordon. "'True History': Martin Luther and Thomas Müntzer." In *History, Society and the Churches, Essays in Honor of Owen Chadwick,* edited by Derek Beales and Gordon Best, 77–87. Cambridge: Cambridge University Press, 1985.

———. "Thomas Müntzer: The Reformer as Rebel." In his *Patterns of Reformation.* Philadelphia: Fortress Press, 1969.

Schaub, Marianne. *Müntzer contre Luther.* Paris: Collin, 1984.

Schnitter, Helmut. *Aber am Volk zweifle ich nicht. Thomas Müntzer—Theologe und Revolutionär.* Berlin: Militärverlag der Deutschen Demokratischen Republik, 1989.

Scholz, Günter, ed. *Thomas Müntzer (vor 1491–1525), Prediger—Prophet—Bauernkriegsführer.* Böblinger Museumsschriften, 4. Böblingen: Böblinger Bauernkriegsmuseum, 1990.

Schwarz, Reinhard. "Thomas Müntzers hermeneutisches Prinzip der Schriftvergleichung." *Lutherjahrbuch* 56 (1989): 11–25.

———. *Die apokalyptische Theologie Thomas Müntzers und der Taboriten.* Beiträge zur historischen Theologie, 55. Tübingen: J. C. B. Mohr, 1977.

Scott, Tom. *Thomas Müntzer: Theology and Revolution in the German Reformation.* New York: St. Martin's Press, 1989.

———. "From Polemic to Sobriety: Thomas Müntzer in Recent Research." *Journal of Ecclesiastical History* 39 (1988): 557–72.

———. "The 'Volksreformation' of Thomas Müntzer in Allstedt and Mühlhausen." *Journal of Ecclesiastical History* 34 (1983): 194–213.

Seebass, Gottfried. "Reich Gottes und Apokalyptik bei Thomas Müntzer." *Lutherjahrbuch* 58 (1991): 75–99.

———. *Artikelbrief, Bundesordnung und Verfassungsentwurf.* Heidelberg: Carl Winter, 1988.

Smirin, M. M. *Die Volksreformation des Thomas Müntzer und der grosse Bauernkrieg.* Berlin: Dietz, 1956.

Stayer, James M. *The German Persants' War and Anabaptist Community of Goods.* Montreal, Kingston, London, and Buffalo: McGill-Queen's University Press, 1991.

————. "Thomas Müntzer in 1989: A Review Article," *Sixteenth Century Journal* 21 (1990): 655–70.

————. *Anabaptists and the Sword.* 2d ed. Lawrence, Kan: Coronado Press, 1976.

Stayer, James, and Werner Packull, eds. *The Anabaptists and Thomas Müntzer.* Dubuque, Iowa: Kendall/Hunt, 1980.

Steinmetz, Max. *Thomas Müntzers Weg nach Allstedt.* Berlin: Deutscher Verlag der Wissenschaften, 1988.

————. "Müntzer und die Mystik. Quellenkritische Bemerkung." In *Bauer, Reich und Reformation*, edited by Peter Blickle, 148–59. Stuttgart: Eugen Ulmer, 1982.

————. "Thomas Müntzer in der Forschung der Gegenwart." *Zeitschrift für Geschichtswissenschaft* 23 (1975): 666–85.

————. *Das Müntzerbild von Martin Luther bis Friedrich Engels.* Leipziger Übersetzungen und Abhandlungen zum Mittelalter, Reihe B, Bd. 4. Berlin: Deutscher Verlag der Wissenschaften, 1971.

Steinmetz, Max, ed. *Der deutschen Bauernkrieg und Thomas Müntzer.* Leipzig: Karl-Marx-Universität, 1976.

————, and Christiane Griese. "Die Müntzeredition und Editoren im 20. Jahrhundert. Ein Beitrag zur Geschichte der Müntzerforschung." *Zeitschrift für Geschichtswissenschaft* 38 (1990): 608–19.

Sünder, Martin. "Zum Aufenhalt Thomas Müntzers 1524 in Mühlhausen." *Mühlhäuser Beiträge* 12 (1989): 35–39.

"Thesen über Thomas Müntzer." *Zeitschrift für Geschichtswissenschaft* 36 (1988): 99–121.

Thomas Müntzer: ein streitbarer Theologe zwischen Mystik und Revolution. Karlsruhe: Rohrhirsch, 1990.

"Thomas Müntzer und das Erbe der deutschen frühbürgerliche Revolution." *Wissenschaftliche Zeitschrift der Universitat Jena* 38 (1989): 399–688.

Thomas Müntzer. Wirken und Wirkungen. Mühlhausen: Mühlhäuser Druckhaus, 1989.

Ullmann, Wolfgang. "Ordo rerum—Müntzers Randbemerkungen zu Tertullian als Quelle für das Verständnis seiner Theologie." In *Theologische Versuche*, Bd. 7, edited by J. Rogge and G. Schille, 125–40. Berlin: Evangelische Verlagsanstalt, 1976.

Van Dülmen, Richard. *Reformation als Revolution.* München: Deutscher Taschenbuch Verlag, 1977.

Vogler, Günter. "Thomas Müntzers Sicht der Gesellschaft seiner Zeit." *Zeitschrift für Geschichtswissenschaft* 38 (1990): 218–34.

————. *Thomas Müntzer.* Berlin: Dietz, 1989.

————. "Thomas Müntzers Verhältnis zu den fürstlichen Obrigkeiten in seiner Allstedter Zeit." *Jahrbuch für Geschichte des Feudalismus* 13 (1989): 67–88.

————. "Müntzers Biographie als Quellenproblem." *Archivmitteilungen* 39 (1989): 198–200.

————. "Thomas Müntzer und die Städte." In *Reformation and Revolution*, edited by Rainer Postel and Franklin Kopitzsch, 138–54. Stuttgart: Franz Steiner, 1989.

Weber, Max. *The Sociology of Religion*. Boston: Beacon Press, 1964 (first German ed. 1922).

Winterhagen, Friedrich. "Thomas Müntzer als nebenberuflicher Spezialist für Halskrankheiten. Ein Brief aus der Nachlass Thomas Müntzers." *Würzburger medizinhistorische Mitteilungen* 6 (1988): 237–44.

Wolgast, Eike. "Beobachtungen und Fragen zu Thomas Müntzers Gefangenschaftsaussagen 1525." *Lutherjahrbuch* 56 (1989): 26–50.

————. *Thomas Müntzer, Ein Verstörer der Ungläubigen*. Berlin: Evangelische Verlagsanstalt, 1988.

Zitelmann, Arnulf. *"Ich will donnern über sie!"* Basel: Beltz, 1989.

Zur Mühlen, Karl-Heinz. "Heiliger Geist und Heilige Schrift bei Thomas Müntzer." *Luther* 60 (1989): 131–50.

Index of Subjects and Names

Index of Biblical References

251